APPLICATIONS DEVELOPMENT USING CASE TOOLS

APPLICATIONS DEVELOPMENT USING CASE TOOLS

KENMORE S. BRATHWAITE, Ph.D.
AKI GROUP, INC.

ACADEMIC PRESS, INC.
Harcourt Brace Jovanovich, Publishers
San Diego New York Boston
London Sydney Tokyo Toronto

ACADEMIC PRESS, INC.
San Diego, California 92101

United Kingdom Edition published by
ACADEMIC PRESS LIMITED
24-28 Oval Road, London NW1 7DX

LIBRARY OF CONGRESS CATALOG CARD NUMBER 90-81051

ISBN 0-12-125880-7 (alk. paper)

PRINTED IN THE UNITED STATES OF AMERICA
90 91 92 93   9 8 7 6 5 4 3 2 1

To Grantley, Gloria, Noel, and Joyce —
My loving brothers and sisters, God bless you all.

PREFACE

The work reported on here and forming the bulk of this text was done over the last two years. It started originally as a research project on the evaluation and selection of CASE tools.

The main objective of the book is to provide readers with definitive information on topics that are crucial to the understanding of the role that CASE tools are now playing in the development of systems software in all areas of business, scientific and commercial applications. In this volume, I provide readers with information on traditional topics such as data analysis techniques, logical and physical data design, structured design methodologies, prototyping, productivity, and application maintenance.

The book addresses topics of interest to data administrators, database administrators, systems programmers, systems analysts, application programmers, information processing managers, data processing managers, software engineers, and database users. It can be used effectively by practitioners in business as well as in government, and also for an introductory course in business or technical schools. The readers need no preparation beyond the application programmer's level, but would benefit more if some experience were obtained in database environments and structured design methodologies.

Chapter 1 introduces various data analysis techniques and shows how these techniques are used in the development of database systems. Chapter 2 discusses data models and data structures, and the role they play in the design and development of database systems. Chapter 3 outlines concepts of logical and physical data design and the issues that must be addressed when conducting these two major phases of database design.

Chapter 4, on structured methodologies for CASE tools, discusses various methodologies used by system designers to develop databases. The chapter places some emphasis on the entity-relationship (E-R) methodology. This methodology is used by about 90% of all system developers and is fully supported by the majority of CASE tools.

Chapters 5 and 6 deal primarily with software and application development processes. They detail the systems development life cycle and the various modeling techniques used in the development process.

Part Two of the book deals with the CASE tool environment, prototyping, and the productivity question. Software engineers are still struggling to establish productivity standards and metrics. The lack of proper metrics in the CASE industry is still one of the major drawbacks to the use of CASE tools. The book seeks to establish some meaningful metrics and productivity measurements in this section.

The third part of the book deals with the management issues that must be resolved when CASE technology is introduced into the data processing environment. Such issues, as environment architecture and CASE tool interfaces, development of safe systems, resistance to technology transfer, data dictionaries, and application maintenance are discussed.

The book ends with a set of selection criteria that one should consider when evaluating CASE tools and a list of some of the major CASE tool vendors.

Finally, as with any large undertaking, errors may remain in this volume. I have worked diligently to maintain the accuracy of this work. However, if errors remain, I solicit your assistance in bringing them to my attention. I, in turn, will do my utmost to ensure that they are corrected.

ACKNOWLEDGMENTS

I am grateful for the comments and suggestions I received from Vic Howard, Stanley Locke, Francis Chin, and Jay Louise Weldon. The initial draft of this manuscript was ably typed by Andrea Drayton and Arlene Bowman. Their efforts are appreciated.

Ken S. Brathwaite
Brooklyn, New York
January, 1990

CONTENTS

Part II　APPLICATIONS DEVELOPMENT

Part III   CASE TOOLS MANAGEMENT ISSUES

INTRODUCTION

The CASE tool industry has made tremendous strides in the last several years, both in the integration of their tools and in the tools' ability to deal with every phase of the systems development life cycle.

However, the usage of the tools, once they have been installed, has not kept pace with the industry wide acceptance. There are several reasons for the non-use of the tools including resistance to change, acceptance of new required methodologies, and overall lack of management planning and support for the tools.

This current work set the stage for the introduction and continued use of CASE tools in the organization. The book is divided into three parts. First, the methodologies, techniques, and models that are supported by the CASE tool are introduced. Secondly, the CASE tool environment, what it is, what it can do, and the benefits are outlined. Thirdly, the management issues of the environment are discussed.

It is the general consensus of CASE consultants that some structured methodology should be in place before a CASE tool is introduced into a data processing department. The data models and data structures that form the bulk of the supported methodologies are discussed in the first part of this text.

The E-R approach to database development has gained almost universal acceptance as the structured methodology best suited for database design and development, enterprise modeling, and, in general, developing corporate data structures. The principles of structured methodology with particular emphasis on the E-R approach are discussed in the first five chapters of the book.

The software development process has been gaining tremendous attention in the literature in the last few years with emphasis on modeling the process, developing the steps with the software development life cycle, creating standards and metrics for the process, and increasing productivity.

The chapters in the application development section place considerable emphasis on the CASE tool environment; what CASE tools are; the classification of the tools; and the capabilities of the tools.

The greatest strength of the CASE tool is its ability to generate rapid prototypes of systems under development. Indeed, for most organizations, this may be the only area where CASE tools may prove effective. The ability to do screen painting, to modify and enhance the screens, and produce hard copy reports from those screens is the most single outstanding benefit to the end user.

IBM has announced two initiatives in the last two years that will greatly increase the marketability of CASE tools. These initiatives are:

- System Application Architecture (SAA)
- Application Development (AD) Cycle

SAA has allowed the data processing industry to develop systems on one platform and run them on a different platform. Cooperative processing is now state-of-the-art. The CASE tool vendors have fully supported SAA. This compliance with SAA will certainly increase the sale of the tools.

As with SAA, the vendors have all jumped on the AD/Cycle bandwagon. Several vendors have announced their compliance and support for AD/Cycle. Indications of this support are shown in Chapter 10.

Finally, the maintenance of old systems consumes about 80% of an organization's budget. Reuse, reverse engineering, and reengineering are words now associated with software maintenance. CASE tools will certainly find a niche in the data processing industry when they have fully addressed the dilemma now existing in software maintenance.

Part I

BUILDING APPLICATION DATABASES

1

DATA ANALYSIS TECHNIQUES

This chapter introduces techniques for conducting data analysis and utilizing these techniques in development of database systems.

Data analysis is defined as the determination of the fundamental data resources of an organization. It deals with the collection of the basic entities and the relationships between those entities.

The chapter begins with definitions for terms that are generally used in data analysis. Such terms as data, data item, entity, attribute, and relationship are defined. It establishes the premise that data is a resource in much the same way as employees, products, natural resources, and finances. It continues by discussing components of data analysis and techniques for performing normalization of data.

1.1 DEFINITIONS AND TERMINOLOGIES

ATTRIBUTE An attribute is a descriptive value or property associated with and individual entity.

DATA The values taken by various data items are called data. For example, the value of the data element Customer Name is data.

DATA ANALYSIS The determination of the fundamental data resources of an organization. It deals with the collection of the basic entities and the relationships between those entities.

DATA ITEM A data item is the smallest unit of named data. A data item is often referred to as a field or data element.

ENTITY An entity is a fundamental thing of interest to an organization. An entity may be a person, place, thing, concept, or event that is real or abstract.

ENTITY MODEL A diagrammatical representation of the relationships between the entity classes. The representation allows us to include only those entities that are required to solve the user's data processing problem.

INFORMATION Data that is processed, accessed, and assimilated or used in the decision-making process. It is the analysis and synthesis of data.

LOGICAL SCHEMA (EXTERNAL STRUCTURE/SCHEMA) The mapping of the entity model into the constructs or constraints of the database management system (DBMS). In general, the logical schema indicates how the model will be stored and accessed.

RELATIONSHIP A relationship is an association between two or more entities.

1.2 DATA AS A RESOURCE

Data must be seen as a resource in much the same way as employees, products, natural resources, finances, and other material products and resources.

Data as a resource must be recognized to have cost and value.

In order to exploit the data resource, it must be understood, conserved, employed, and integrated. It is necessary to learn about its nature and characteristics, how it is used, what it is used for, where it resides and where it comes from.

1.2.1 Information Resource Management

Information Resource Management (IRM) deals with planning for, allocating, maintaining and conserving, prudently exploiting, effectively employing, and integrating the data resource.

To manage data effectively as a resource it is necessary to obtain as much data about the data as is possible. There must be stringent procedures for collecting, maintaining, and using the resource.

1.2.2 Management Control of the Data Resource

Management control of data includes the following:

- Common procedures for access control to the data
- Establishing lines of authority and responsibility for the data.
- Common procedures for collecting, updating, and maintaining the data
- Common formats and procedures for data definition
- Identifying entities that are important to the enterprise
- Evaluating, mediating, and reconciling the conflicting needs and prerogatives of functional departments
- Ensuring the auditability of the data and all transactions against the data

- Controlling the data in order to measure and evaluate the corporation and predict its reaction to changes in its environment and in its own internal organization

1.2.3 Data Ownership Philosophies

The introduction of the database era not only meant a change in traditional data processing, but also in traditional definitions of "data ownership." In traditional data processing, total control over creation, maintenance, and processing of data meant "ownership" of that data. In a database environment, data sharing and data integration have lessened total control and now imply loss of "ownership."

In data analysis, the establishing of data "owners" is important to:

- Control access to the data
- Allow data sharing
- Establish relationships and interfaces between entities
- Establish common definitions for data
- Resolve discrepancies and conflicts over standards and conventions

1.2.4 Different Views of Data

Data about an enterprise is not singularly determined. Different people perceive and describe an enterprise differently, and hence have different starting points concerning what is to be modeled.

It's not merely a matter of scope, of including more or less in the view. People looking at the same thing see it differently.

Examples of different views of data:

- The secretary of a department may be, in someone else's view, the secretary of the *manager* of the department.
- A manufacturing operation might be performed by a certain department, or we might view it as performed by a person *assigned* to that department.
- A social security number is generally considered to identify a person, but it really identifies an *account* which belongs to a person.

1.3 DATA ANALYSIS

The primary purpose of data analysis is to determine the fundamental nature of an organization's data resources and to organize and document all relevant facts concerning this data.

Data analysis has been used to:

- Determine the fundamental data resources of an organization
- Provide a disciplined approach toward cataloging the existing data in terms of the entities and relationships it represents
- Provide an effective means of communicating with non–data processing users as it deals only with things that the users are familiar with and not with such objects as files and records
- Analyze the inherent structure of that data independently from the details of the applications
- Form a basis for data control, security, and auditing systems
- Organize all relevant facts concerning the organization's data
- Produce a point of reference (the Entity Model) against which a logical database structure for each of the database management systems can be designed
- Provide a sound basis for database design

1.3.1   Components of Data Analysis

Data analysis consists of two dependent projects:

1. *Entity analysis*, which provides a means of understanding and documenting a complex environment in terms of its entities and their attributes and relationships
2. *Functional analysis*, which is concerned with understanding and documenting the basic business activities of the organization (Figure 1.1)

1.4   REQUIREMENTS ANALYSIS

Requirements analysis involves:

- Establishment of organizational objectives
- Derivation of specific database requirements from those objectives or directly from management personnel
- Documentation of those requirements in a form that is agreeable to management and database designers (Figure 1.2)

1.4.1   Techniques Used in Requirements Analysis

- Personal interviews with various levels of management and key employees involved in the processing of goods, services, and data in the organization

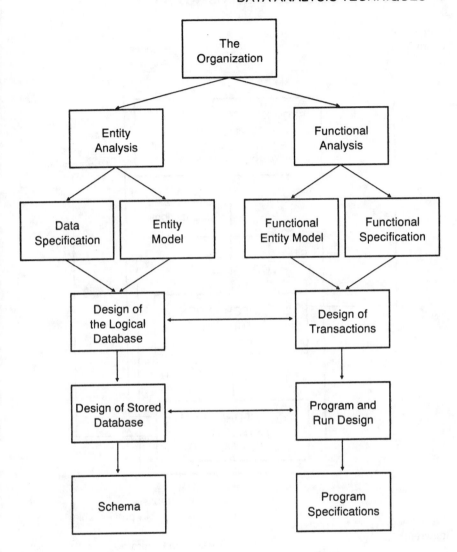

Figure 1.1 Analysis and design

- Diagramming of the flow process with which each employee is involved
- Identify the data elements associated with that process and the interfaces between processes
- Verification that both interviewer and employee agree on the flow model

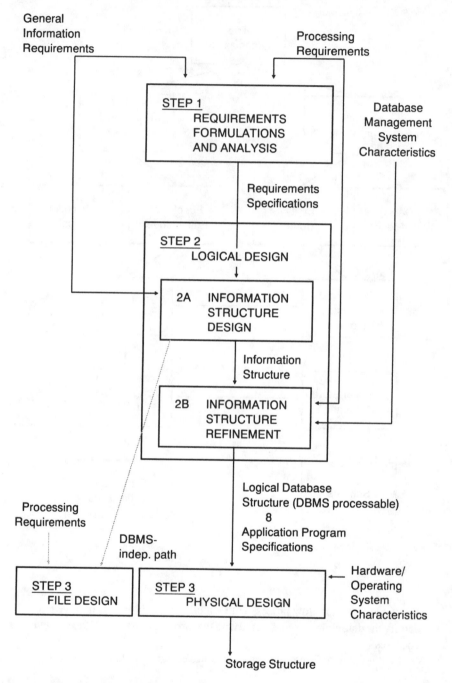

Figure 1.2   Basic database design steps

1.5   USER VIEW MODELING

User view modeling is defined as the modeling of the usage and information structure perspectives of the real world from the point of view of different users and/or applications.

View modeling involves at least the following two components:

- Extracting from the users or from persons in charge of application development the relevant parts of real-world information
- Abstracting this information into a form which completely represents the user view so that it can be consequently used in database design

There are two aspects of user view which must be modeled in order to adequately represent it. These are:

- The information structure perspective or non-process-oriented view
- The usage perspective or process-oriented view

1.5.1   Representation of View

A user view is represented in terms of entities, associations, or attributes in a view diagram.

Examples of user views:

```
EMPLOYEE = {EMP #, NAME, SCHOOL, DEGREE}
WORKS-ON = {EMP #, ASSIGNMENT #, SUPERVISOR, START-DATE}
ASSIGNMENT = {ASSIGNMENT #, ASSIGNMENT-NAME}
```

1.5.2   User View Integration

View integration is the second phase of logical database design where user views are merged to obtain a composite view of the organization or the requirements specified by data analysis.

User view integration involves:

- Merging of simple associations
- Merging of identifier associations
- Merging of entities

1.6 ANALYSIS USING DIFFERENT MODELS

Data analysis is essentially the process of producing a mental framework which will allow the viewer to describe his view or the organization's view of data. Different people will produce different mental frameworks. There are several mental frameworks, including:

- Data-structure diagrams
- Entity-relationship (E-R) model

1.6.1 Analysis Using Data-Structure Diagrams

Analysis using data-structure diagrams involves record types and data-structure sets, which are relationships between record types.

In Figure 1.3a, there are two types of conceptual records, COMPANY and PERSON, and a data-structure set representing the fact that each person is associated with exactly one company and that each company has a set of personnel.

Analysis may indicate that the personnel of the company were persons in their own right. This fact may be discovered at the merger of several companies that some of the personnel held two jobs and were personnel to two of the merged companies (Figure 1.3b). Basically, the old personnel-type record has been split into two record types, PERSONNEL and PERSON.

Further analysis may indicate that the address of residence should not be in the person's record. This requires the creation of a PLACE conceptual record type and a new data-structure-set type (Figure 1.3c). It must be assumed that each person has a unique address.

It is now recognized that people move from place to place and that it is desirable to know current address as well as past addresses. Another reason may be: it is discovered that a person may have more than one address. In either case, a new conceptual record-type ADDRESS is added to the structure (Figure 1.3d).

1.6.2 Analysis Using Entity-Relationship Diagrams

In the following, we shall use entity-relationship (E-R) diagrams to explain the above example in which data-structures were used.

The E-R diagram (Figure 1.4) corresponds to the data-structure diagram in Figure 1.3a. There are two types of entities, PERSON and COMPANY, in the user view. The data-structure set is replaced by the relationship set WORKS FOR.

Analysis shows that a new entity PLACE should be introduced into the schema. Since many persons can have the same address, a new entity is introduced called ADDRESS. The final E-R diagram is detailed in Figure 1.4b.

In general, the E-R diagram is easier to use to analyze the changes in the user view than data-structure diagrams.

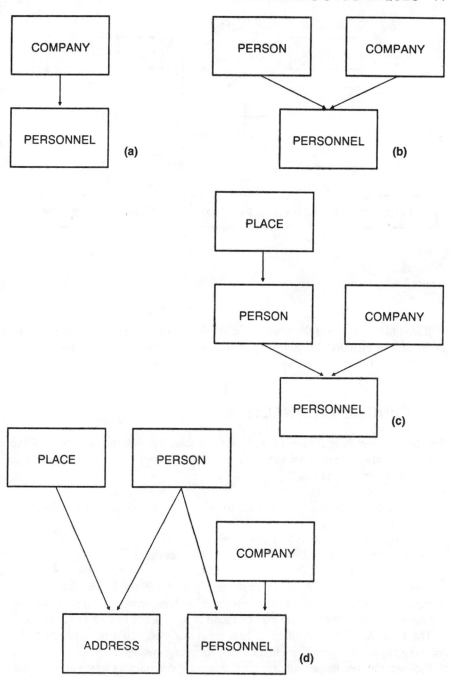

Figure 1.3   Analysis using data structures

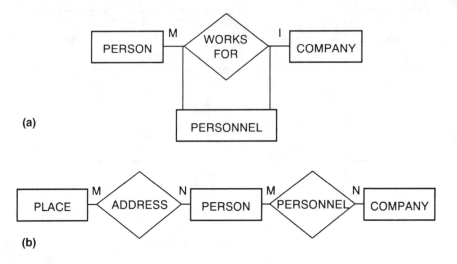

(a)

(b)

Figure 1.4

It should be noted that the relationship WORKS FOR can be materialized into an entity called PERSONNEL. Similarly, the relationship LIVES AT can be materialized into an entity called ADDRESS.

1.7 FUNCTIONAL ANALYSIS

Functional analysis is concerned with an understanding and documentation of the basic business activities with which the organization is concerned. Functional analysis has the following objectives:

- To determine how entities are used so as to increase understanding of the entity model
- To provide a firm basis for transaction design
- To gather estimates of data usage for database design

Functional analysis may reveal attribute types of entities which had not been detected during entity analysis. Similarly, relationships between entities which had not been considered meaningful may be found to be required by certain functions.

The basic functions identified in functional analysis would be expected to be translated into transaction types in the data-processing system.

Estimates of data usage will provide a means for determining which access paths should be made most efficient.

Functional analysis can be divided into the following phases:

- Preliminary
- Develop a framework
- Access path analysis

In functional analysis the application area to be analyzed must be defined. The application area may coincide with the data area examined in data analysis or it may cross several data areas. Here data area may be defined as the data utilized in areas determined by the organizational structure; e.g., accounting, personnel, manufacturing, marketing, and purchasing.

In the process of developing a framework, the analyst identifies the events and functions. Typically, there is a hierarchy of functions, but the basic activities at the foot of the hierarchy are initiated by events recurring in the organization.

An event may be defined as a stimulus to the organization and functions may be defined as tasks that must be carried out as a direct result of the event.

For example, an *order is placed* is an event, while *record the order* or *produce the invoice* are functions.

1.7.1   Functional Analysis Example

One of the functions identified as being carried out in the order processing area is *order entry*. An order is received from a DELIVERY POINT. The depot that will make the delivery is selected depending on whether the goods are bulk or packaged. The order is recorded and related to the delivery point and the depot. The goods specified in each order line are validated, and the stocks of the goods on hand are amended. Where stocks are insufficient to meet the quantities in one or more lines on the order, a back order is created. The order lines are recorded and linked to the goods and to the order, or back order as appropriate.

The functional entity model resulting from the above description is shown in Figure 1.5.

1.8   DATA ANALYSIS DOCUMENTATION

An essential outcome of data analysis is the documentation for entity types, relationship types, attribute types, functions, and events. *This documentation is in addition to the entity model and functional entity model.* Where the volumes and complexity are low, a clerical system has been found to be adequate, but in the longer term and in a dynamic environment, the use of a good data dictionary is advisable.

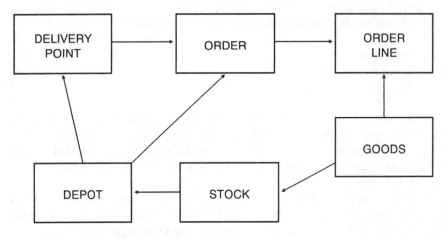

Figure 1.5   Functional entity model for order entry

1.8.1   Analysis Documentation Examples

An example of a data dictionary which makes the distribution between the constructs of the entity model and those of the logical database and between the functions of the organization and the transaction which handles them will be discussed in another section.

Examples of the types of forms that could be employed for a clerical system of documentation for data analysis are shown below. The forms are used to document an entity, an attribute, and a relationship. (See Figures 1.6 through 1.8.)

For functional analysis, the access path is documented. In addition, while no information concerning attributes is included in the functional entity model, the grouping of attributes as needed by different functions are normally shown in an attribute usage matrix, where for each entity the attributes are matched against the functions which retrieve, modify, store, or delete their values.

Similarly, the entity usage matrix summarizes overall functions the way a particular entity is accessed, whether by value of a particular attribute or by means of relationships.

1.9   THE ENTITY MODEL

The major output of the data analysis phase of database design is the entity model. The entity model is a DIAGRAMMATICAL REPRESENTATION of the relationships between the entities. The representation allows us to include only those entities that are required to solve the particular data processing problem.

DATA ANALYSIS DOCUMENTATION ENTITY TYPE	ANALYST: K. Brathwaite
NAME: Order	DATE: 22.11.89 VERSION: 1
SYNONYMS:	STATUS: Preliminary

DEFINITION: Request for delivery of a stated number of different goods

IDENTIFIERS: Order Number

OCCURRENCES: MINIMUM   AVERAGE   240,000 per year   MAXIMUM
SPECIAL VARIATIONS: GROWTH: 10% per year

AUTHORIZED TO
CREATE: Order   DELETE: Order   COUNT: Marketing
             Processing   Processing   Research
             Department   Department

CONFIDENTIALITY: Type 3   SECURITY:

ENTITY SUBTYPES:	IDENTIFIERS:
Filled Order Back Order	F B

DEFAULT FOR ATTRIBUTE DETAILS:
 	
        AVAILABILITY
        TIMELINESS
        STORAGE

Figure 1.6   Data analysis documentation — entity type

The entity model is essentially a real-world view of the data in terms of entities, attributes, and relationships.

The model is used by the data analysis team to:

- Reduce redundancy in the relationships
- Determine which entities are significant to the model and the requirement of the problem

DATA ANALYSIS DOCUMENTATION ATTRIBUTE TYPE	ANALYST: K. Brathwaite
NAME: Credit Limit	DATE: 22.11.89
SYNONYMS:	VERSION: 1
DEFINITION: If the customer's balance exceeds this value, no further orders will	STATUS: Preliminary

be accepted unless paid in advance.
ENTITY DESCRIBED: Customer
AUTHORIZED TO CREATE: Accounts Receivable   MODIFY: Finance   RETRIEVE: Salesman

PERMITTED VALUES $10,000 to   MEANING: FORMAT: 5 numeric digits   RANGE: $25,000
CONSISTENCY: Only for customers with over 3   AVAILABILITY: On-line   previous orders
STORAGE: TIMELINESS: Updated daily

Figure 1.7   Data analysis documentation — attribute type

Once the entity model is produced, the analysis team sets about the task of making revisions to the model. This is done in order to:

- Produce the optimum model
- Normalize the entities
- Synthesize the relationships

1.10   ENTITY MODEL PRODUCTION

The entity model can be produced using either a bottom-up or top-down approach. The bottom-up approach produces a composite or global view of the organization's

DATA ANALYSIS DOCUMENTATION RELATIONSHIP TYPE	ANALYST: K. Brathwaite
NAME: Places	DATE: 22.11.89
SYNONYMS:	VERSION: 1 STATUS: Preliminary

DEFINITION: The customer has indicated by phone or by mail that he wishes to buy a product

RELATED TO   ENTITY: Order   ENTITY: Delivery Point

AUTHORIZED TO CONNECT: Order Processing   DISCONNECT: Order Processing   Department   Department

CONFIDENTIALITY: Type 3

CONSISTENCY: AVAILABILITY: On-line

REPRESENTATION: TIMELINESS: Contiguity in the customer file   Update daily

Figure 1.8(a)   Data analysis documentation — relationship type

data based on the integration of several user views of the immediate problems requirements and not on the inherent structure of the data. The resulting model is limited to the immediate problem and cannot reflect the entire business activities of the corporation.

The top-down approach produces a global, corporate, or organizational view of the data before the application views are identified. The entities and relationships which are of interest to the organization are identified from the business activities of the total organization and independent of any particular application.

The bottom-up approach is the one most often used in data analysis. This approach produces a model with more clearly defined boundaries than the top-down approach. The processing requirements can be used by the data analysis team to precisely determine what entities are required and the composition of those entities. The

FUNCTIONAL ANALYSIS DOCUMENTATION					
ACCESS PATH					
FUNCTION NAME: Order Entry	REPONSE REQUIRED 5 sec Avg 10 sec Max		ANALYST: KSB DATE: 22.11.89		
FREQUENCY ASSUMPTIONS: Per Day Avg: 4000 Max: 6000 Growth: 10%					

Entity (E) Relationship (R) Accessed	E/R	Selection Criteria	Action	Volume Avg	Max
Delivery Point	E	Delivery Point Name	R	1	1
Bulk/Package	R	Bulk/Packaged	R	1	1
Depot	E	Via Relationship	R	1	1
Order	E		S	1	1
Order/Delivery Point	R	Order No. Delivery Point Name	Con	1	1
Order/Depot	R	Order No. Depot Name	Con	11	
Goods	E	Goods Code	R	10	30
Goods/Stock	R	Goods Code	R	10	30
Depot/Stock	R	Depot Name	R	10	30
Stock	E	Depot/Goods	M	9.5	28.5
Back Order	E	Back Order No.	S	0.5	1.5
Order/Delivery Point	R	Back Order No. Delivery Point Name	Con	0.5	1.5
Order/Depot	R	Back Order No. Depot Name	Con	0.5	1.5
Order Line	E	Order No. Goods Name	S	10	30

ACTION (ENTITY) RETRIEVE, MODIFY, STORE,
DELETE ACTION (RELATIONSHIP), RETRIEVE, CREATE, CONNECT,
DISCONNECT

Figure 1.8(b)   Data analysis documentation — relationship type

clustering of attributes into their respective entities or the splitting of entities can be done with more precision. It is easier with this approach to determine whether an attribute is indeed an attribute of an existing entity or is itself an entity with relationships to other entities.

FUNCTIONAL ANALYSIS DOCUMENTATION								
SUMMARY OF ACCESS TO AN ENTITY TYPE								
ENTITY NAME: Goods TIME PERIOD: Per Day ANALYST: KSB DATE: 22.11.89								
DIRECT ACCESS			FREQUENCY OF ACCESS					
ATTRIBUTES	SELECTION CRITERIA	RETRIEVE AVG	MAX	STORE AVG	MAX	DELETE AVG	MAX	
DESCRIPTION	GOODS CODE	8×10^4	10^5	50	100			
UNIT OF ISSUE	GOODS CODE			10	15			
COST PRICE	GOODS CODE	260	300	50	80			
SALES PRICE	GOODS CODE	8×10^4	10^5	50	100			
VIA RELATIONSHIP			ACTION PERFORMED					
RELATIONSHIP	SELECTION CRITIERIA	RETRIEVE AVG	MAX	TRANSFER AVG	MAX	CONNECT AVG	MAX	
Stock/Goods	Goods delivered	4×10^4	5×10^4	20	30			
Order Line/Goods	Goods of amended							
Order Line/Goods	order			80	100			
	Goods of cancelled							
	order							

Figure 1.8(c)   Data analysis documentation — attribute type

1.11   TRANSLATION OF USER VIEW TO ENTITY MODEL

A significant difficulty in defining the relationships and representing them in the entity model is determining which relationships are directly significant and which are redundant. This can be done only with a detailed understanding of the environment as there are no mathematical rules that can be applied, but merely patterns in the entity model which prompt further investigation.

To determine the existence of relationships, the following procedure can be employed:

- Take each attribute type and determine which entity type it describes, whether it could describe any other entity type, and if these entity types are related
- Take each entity type and pair it with another, and determine if a meaningful question can be asked
- Determine if the relationship is relevant

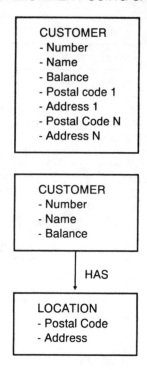

Figure 1.9   Replacing attributes by entities and relationships

No less difficult is the decision concerning each element, as to whether it should be treated as an attribute type of an entity type or as a second entity type related to the first. As a guideline, it has been found that an attribute of an entity-1 is best treated instead as entity-2 related to entity-1 if:

- The attribute itself is found to have further relevant attributes
- The resulting entity-2 is itself of significance to the organization
- The attribute in fact identifies entity-2
- Entity-2 could be related to several occurrences of entity-1
- Entity-2 is seen to be related to entity types other than entity-1

Thus, in Figure 1.9, *customer location* is seen not to be an attribute of *customer*, as a customer may have several locations and as each location has its own attributes, such as postal code.

During the translation of the user view to the entity model, the most significant entity types and relationship types are defined. But inevitably a model will be extended or modified during the detailed data analysis phase as a result of reexamining the attributes.

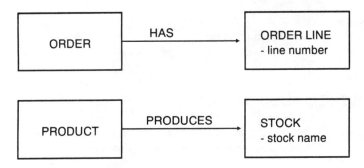

Figure 1.10   Entity identification by relationships

1.12 SELECTION AND IDENTIFICATION OF ENTITIES

Data analysis permits the selection and identification of entities in the following three ways:

- By one or more attributes
- By the combination of a relationship with one or more attributes
- By two or more relationships

The simplest case of entity identification is where each occurrence of the attribute has a unique value which is used to identify the entity. Combinations of attributes may also be used, such as when employees are identified by their name, together with the date they joined the company.

The members of the relationship are often uniquely identified within that relationship by the values of the attribute type, but for uniqueness within the system the owner of the relationship also needs to be known. In effect, it is the relationship occurrence as identified by its owner which is contributing to the unique identification of its members.

Entity identification by relationships and attributes is illustrated in Figure 1.10.

1.13 ENTITY SUBTYPES

A problem arises when different functions wish to use clearly identifiable subsets of the total population of attributes of an entity type. The question then arises as to whether the entity type, as defined, is taking too global a view and is better considered as being several entity types. In general, it may be preferable to treat entities as being of different types if they have either:

- Significant differences in their attributes
- Different means of identification
- Participation in different types of relationships

1.14 SCHEMA DEVELOPMENT

The process of developing a database structure from user requirements is called database design. The database design process consists of two phases:

- Design of a logical database structure (schema development) that is processable by the database management system (DBMS) and describes the user's view of the data
- Selection of a physical structure (physical database design) that is available within the DBMS

There are four basic components necessary to achieve a database design methodology:

- A structured design process that consists of a series of design steps where one alternative among many is chosen
- Design techniques to perform the required selection and evaluation of alternatives at each step
- Information requirements for input to the design process as a whole and to each step
- A descriptive mechanism to represent the information input and the results at each design step.

The result of the logical design step is a database definition or schema.

1.15 FORMULATING THE DBMS-SPECIFIC LOGICAL DATABASE SCHEMA

Using the entity-relationship diagrams developed during the user view modeling phase of database design, a processing matrix which links specific applications and entities identified in the processing requirements, and allowable DBMS characteristics, a logical database schema can be formulated.

In the simplest case, entities become record types and attributes become item types or entities become logical databases.

In the more complex cases entities can split or merge to form record types. This step begins the phase where consideration of the DBMS-specific rules and constraints must be given.

1.16 REFINING THE LOGICAL DATABASE SCHEMA FOR PROCESSING CONSIDERATIONS

The logical database schema can now be revised on the basis of quantitative information and performance measures.

Processing volume is defined as the combination of two parameters:

- Processing frequency
- Data volume

Processing frequency is the frequency at which an individual application is required to be run. Data volume is the number of occurrences of each record type currently stored or to be stored in the database.

Performance measures at the logical design step are limited to:

- Logical record access counts
- Total bytes transferred to satisfying an application
- Total bytes in the database

These measures attempt to predict physical database performance in terms of elapsed time and physical storage space as closely as possible.

1.17 DOCUMENTING THE DATABASE DESIGN

Documentation is the recording of facts about objects or events of concern to facilitate communication and to provide a permanent record.

In a database environment, documentation is based on giving information about the database itself, its contents, and its structure. The documentation focuses primarily on data-related components, such as:

- Data elements
- Data groups (records or segments)
- Data structures
- Databases

Database documentation covers several types of information and is intended to support the needs of several classes of users.

Seven types of documentation can be compiled for the database environment:

- Name/Meaning — a unique identifier and descriptive information that conveys the full meaning of the component. The name is used for reference and retrieval purposes, while the description is valuable to managers and users

- Physical Description — the physical characteristics of the components, such as the size of a data element or the length of a data record
- Edit/Authorization Criteria — criteria used to test the validity of instances of the component, such as acceptable range of values for data elements or passwords for update of a database
- Usage — information on where and by whom or by what a component is used, such as the programs within a system that reference a given data element
- Logical Description — the characteristics and structure of each user view of the database, such as logical relationships among data records
- Procedures — guidelines for human interaction with the database, such as for backup, recovery, and system restart
- Responsibility — a record of the individual or organizational unit responsible for the generation and maintenance of the database component

1.18 THE ROLE OF DATA DICTIONARY/DIRECTORY SYSTEMS

Data dictionary/directory systems (DD/DS) are valuable tools for assisting generally in the collection and management of data about the database. This data about the database is called metadata.

The major objective of a DD/D system is to support the integration of metadata in much the same way that a DBMS supports the integration of an organization's data.

The benefits achieved are as follows:

- Minimum redundancy
- Consistency
- Standardization
- Data sharing
- Monitoring of database content
- Effectively enforcing security and integrity policies

1.19 FEATURES AND FUNCTIONS OF DD/D SYSTEMS

All data dictionary/directory systems provide the basic functions necessary to capture and maintain metadata and to generate reports from that store of metadata. Data capture implies the initial loading of the data dictionary with metadata of entry types. This capability may be provided through fixed — or free — format transactions in either batch or on-line mode. Very often, all or part of a data dictionary entry may be generated directly from source program data descriptions.

Reporting is a primary function of any DD/D system. Basically, two types of reports are provided:

- List of dictionary entries, either alphabetically or by entry type
- A cross-reference report

In a cross-reference report, entries in the dictionary are associated by the relationships in which they participate. Since these relationships are bidirectional, the cross-reference may be either top-down or bottom-up. For example, one may ask to see a top-down listing of entries associated with a particular application or might ask for a trace of all entries with which a particular element is associated, a bottom-up view.

Other DD/D system features may include:

- Selectivity — entries associated with a particular element
- Query languages — for users to formulate reports of their own choosing
- Program code generation
- Directory — indicating the physical location of data in the database
- Maintenance of archival definitions

1.20 THE NORMALIZATION PROCESS

During data analysis the relevant attributes are recorded and defined for each entity type. This may lead to identification of new entity types or to the subdivisions of existing entities. It also enables the boundaries of the data area to be defined more precisely. Once the entity model is reasonably complete, explicit checks need to be made to detect redundant relationships. These checks may include the process called normalization.

1.21 NORMALIZATION

Normalization requires three actions to be performed on the attributes of an entity. These are as follows:

- First Normal Form — repeating groups are removed
- Second Normal Form — attributes are removed which are dependent on only some of the identifying attributes
- Third Normal Form — attributes are removed which are not directly dependent upon the identifying attributes

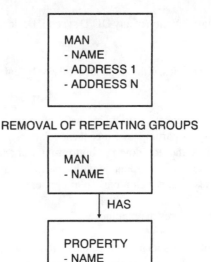

Figure 1.11 First normal form

1.21.1 First Normal Form

During data analysis *man* was identified as one of the entity types of interest to the organization, and *address* was identified as one of the attributes of *man*. During the first normalization process it will be shown that there are hidden relationships inside the entity type since several men may reside at the same address or a man may have several addresses (Figure 1.11).

First normal form normalization would produce a new entity type *property* (say).

1.21.2 Second Normal Form

A normalized relation (entity) is said to be in second normal form if all its nonprime (attributes which do not serve to identify the relation) are fully functionally dependent on each candidate key (attributes which uniquely identify the relation).

Second normal form example:

CUSTOMER (ORDER #	CUSTOMER #	CUSTOMER NAME)
1	241	H. Pratt
2	250	M. Hall
3	241	H. Pratt

In the above example the nonprime attribute CUSTOMER NAME is fully dependent on the candidate key, ORDER #. That is, for each value of ORDER # there is one and only one value of CUSTOMER NAME.

Unnormalized Relation:

CUSTOMER (ORDER #	ITEM CODE	UNIT PRICE	QUANTITY)
1	A10	5	10
1	C13	3	20
2	A10	5	15
2	B16	12	2
3	B16	12	11

In the above unnormalized relation, the attribute UNIT PRICE is not fully dependent on the candidate key ORDER #/ITEM CODE.

A removal of partial dependence in the unnormalized relation CUSTOMER will produce two relations ORDER and PRICE which are in second normal form.

Second normal form example:

ORDER (ORDER #	ITEM CODE	QUANTITY)
1	A10	10
1	C13	20
2	A10	15
2	B16	2
3	B16	11

PRICE (ITEM CODE	UNIT PRICE)
A10	5
C13	3
B16	12

Update problems with unnormalized relations:

The following update problems are experienced in unnormalized relations:

- Insertion — if we wish to introduce a new item in the CUSTOMER relation with a specific UNIT PRICE, we cannot do so unless a customer places an order, since we need an ORDER #.

- Deletion — if the information about a customer order is deleted, the information about the item; e.g., UNIT PRICE, is also deleted.
- Modification — since the information about an item appears as many times as there are orders for it, modifications on the item information would be very difficult.

1.21.3 Third Normal Form

A normalized relation is said to be in third normal form if all its nonprime attributes are fully functional and directly dependent on each candidate key.

STOCK (BIN #	PART #	QUANTITY	LEAD TIME	REORDER LEVEL)
210	30	5	10	5
211	30	10	10	5
225	50	7	7	6
231	81	3	15	10
232	81	12	15	10

In the above relation we assume that a bin cannot hold stock of more than one part number (PART #). If BIN # is the candidate key, then the relation is not in THIRD NORMAL FORM, since the nonprime attributes LEAD TIME and REORDER LEVEL are not directly dependent on BIN #.

Third normal form example:

STOCK	(BIN #	PART #	QUANTITY)
	211	30	5
	211	30	10
	225	50	7
	231	81	3
	232	81	12

STOCK B	(PART #	LEAD TIME	REORDER LEVEL)
	30	10	5
	50	7	6
	81	15	10

1.22   PHYSICAL DATABASE DESIGN

This section discusses the objectives and procedures of physical database design.

1.22.1   Objectives of Physical Database Design

The aim of physical database design is to produce a physical database which achieves the best performance at the least cost. The physical design process assumes that the logical design has been completed and that the logical schema presented is a true and complete representation of the real world. It also assumes that a database which follows the schema will be capable of supporting the user's needs.

1.22.2   Steps in the Physical Design Process

Physical database design can be broken into four main steps:

- Determining and documenting data representation
- Selecting and documenting access modes
- Allocating data to devices
- Loading and reorganizing the database

1.23   DETERMINING DATA REPRESENTATION

Starting with the logical schema produced by logical data design, the physical designer must determine how each data element, record, and file is to be represented. For each element, the data type and size must be determined. The size and expected number of occurrences must be determined for each record.

Requirements for data types and size estimates may have been collected during the initial stage of logical design.

The physical designers can provide feedback to users and system developers concerning the storage implications of their database design.

1.24   SELECTING ACCESS METHODS

The selection of access methods depends on the organization's DBMS. However, in all cases the way in which each record type in the database will be accessed must be determined. Record types which will be directly accessible by their keys must be distinguished.

The access path; i.e., the sequence of records that must be retrieved to achieve a given process, must be described.

1.25 ALLOCATING DATA TO DEVICES

Each record and file defined by the access method must be assigned to storage locations on physical devices. This assignment completes the physical design process. During this step, performance benefits can be gained by allocating the database to physical devices in a way that gives priority to frequently used data or maximizes the likelihood that related data will be stored close together. This process is called clustering.

Clustering can take place at three levels:

- Records consisting of many attributes can be divided and subsets of the attribute stored together
- Different records that are likely to be accessed simultaneously should be clustered together
- Assign most frequently used portions of the database to faster or more cost-effective storage medium

1.26 LOADING AND REORGANIZING THE DATABASE

In addition to developing the initial design, the physical designer is also responsible for seeing that the database is loaded properly and for any reorganization that may be required during the life of the database.

Reorganization of the database may imply changes in content, structure, access methods, or device allocation. Such changes may be required as a result of the introduction of new data elements or record types, as a result of new processing requirements, or simply to rectify the degradation in storage and processing efficiency.

1.27 SUMMARY OF PHYSICAL DATABASE DESIGN PROCESSES

The implementation of databases from logical schemas require the following selections:

- Types of logical relationships
- Access methods
- Secondary indices
- Types of pointers in relationships
- Allocation to storage devices
- Loading and reorganization of the database

2

STRUCTURED DESIGN
METHODOLOGIES
FOR CASE

This chapter presents an overview of database design and development methodologies and a detailed discussion of one of these methodologies — the entity-relationship (E-R) approach.

Database design refers to the process of arranging the data fields needed by one or more applications into an organized structure. That structure must foster the required relationships among the fields, while conforming to the physical constraints of the particular database management system in use. There are really two parts to the process: logical database design, followed by physical database design.

Logical database design is an implementation-independent exercise that is performed on the fields and relationships needed for one or more applications. Physical database design is an implementation-dependent exercise that takes the results of logical database design and further refines them, according to the characteristics of the particular database management system in use.

A variety of reasons make careful database design essential. These include data redundancy, application performance, data independence, data security, and ease of programming. All are important factors in the data processing environment, and all can be adversely affected by a poor database design.

2.1 REVIEW OF EXISTING METHODOLOGIES

This section will present two of the most common database design methodologies. In the case of the first methodology we will give only a brief introduction, whereas for the second we will give a more detailed discussion.

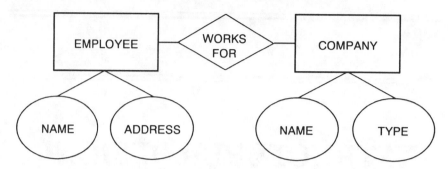

Figure 2.1   The entity-relationship diagram

The first method, data normalization and data structuring, is representative of the class of methods that take as input a list of fields and the associations among those fields. The second method, the entity-relationship method, is representative of the class of methods that take entities and relationships as input.

Database design using the entity-relationship model begins with a list of the entity types involved and the relationships among them. The philosophy of assuming that the designer knows what the entity types are at the outset is significantly different from the philosophy behind the normalization-based approach.

The entity-relationship approach uses entity-relationship diagrams as illustrated in Figure 2.1. The rectangular boxes represent entity types, the diamond-shaped box represents a relationship between entities, and the circular figures represent attributes.

A more detailed discussion of the entity-relationship method is given in the following sections.

2.2   DETAILED DISCUSSION OF DATABASE DESIGN

The process of developing a database structure from user requirements is called database design. Most practitioners agree that there are two separate phases to the database design process: the design of a logical database structure that is processable by the database management system (DBMS) and describes the user's view of data, and the selection of a physical structure such as the indexed sequential or direct access method of the intended DBMS. Other than the logical/physical delineation, the overall structure of the design is not well defined.

Novak defined four basic components necessary to achieve a database design methodology:

- A structured design process that consists of a series of steps where one alternative among many is chosen
- Design techniques to perform the enumeration required as stated previously and evaluation criteria to select an alternative at each step
- Information requirements for input to the design process as a whole and to each step of the design process
- A descriptive mechanism to represent the information input and the results at each design step

Current database design technology shows many residual effects of its outgrowth from single-record file design methods. File design is primarily application-program dependent since the data has been defined and structured in terms of individual applications that use them. The advent of DBMS revised the emphasis in data and program design approaches. The concept of the integrated database spanning multiple users was a direct result of the complex data structuring capabilities which the DBMS afforded. Data can now be viewed as a corporate resource instead of as an adjunct to a program, and consequently should have an integrated requirements orientation instead of a single-program orientation.

Achieving a design which results in an acceptable level of database performance for all users has become a complex task. The database designer must be ever conscious of the cost/performance trade-offs associated with multiple users of a single integrated database. Potential savings of storage space and expanded applicability of databases into corporate decision making should be accompanied by a critical analysis of potential degradation of service to some users. Such degradation is to be avoided if possible. Acceptable performance for all users should be the goal.

Another aspect of database design is flexibility. Databases that are too tightly bound to current applications may have too limited a scope for many corporate enterprises.

Rapidly changing requirements and new data elements may result in costly program maintenance, a proliferation of temporary files, and increasingly poor performance. A meaningful overall database design process should account for both integration and flexibility.

2.2.1   Inputs to Design Process

The major classes of inputs to and results from the database design process are:
   Inputs:

- General information requirements
- Processing requirements
- DBMS specifications
- Operating system/hardware configuration
- Application program specifications

Results:

- Logical database structure (user view)
- Storage structure (physical design)

The general information requirements represent various users' descriptions of the organization for which data are to be collected, the objectives of the database, and the users' views of which data should be collected and stored in the database. These requirements are considered to be process-independent because they are not tied to any specific database management system or application. Database design based on these requirements is considered to be advantageous for long-term databases that must be adaptable to changing processing requirements.

Processing requirements consist of three distinguishable components: specific data items required for each application, the data volume and expected growth, and processing frequencies in terms of the number of times each application must be run per unit time. Each of these components is very important to a particular stage or step of the database design process.

Performance measures and performance constraints are also imposed on the database design. Typical constraints include upper bounds on response times to queries, recovery times from system crashes, or specific data needed to support certain security or integrity requirements.

Specific performance measures used to evaluate the final structure might include update, storage, and reorganization costs in addition to response requirements.

The three major outputs of the database design process are the logical database structures, the physical storage structure, and specifications for application programs based on these database structures and processing requirements. As a whole, these results may be considered the specification for the final database implementation.

2.2.2 The Entity-Relationship (E-R) Approach

As more and more organizations implement systems employing database technology, the need arises for better methodologies to design these databases. The methodology described here provides a means of mapping the entity model produced from the data analysis phase to the database management system-supported structure.

The E-R approach requires several steps to produce a structure that is acceptable by the particular DBMS. These steps are:

- Data analysis
- Producing and optimizing the entity model
- Logical schema development
- Physical database design process

Definitions and Terminologies   The following definitions and terminologies are frequently used in E-R theory and are basic to an understanding of the methodology. A more complete description of the process is available in existing literature.

1. An *entity* is a fundamental thing of interest to an organization.

    An entity may be a person, place, thing, concept or event that is real or abstract.

    Entity and *entity class* are used interchangeably in some of the literature, whereas some researchers define an entity as an occurrence of an entity class. For example, EMPLOYEE is an entity class, whereas S.T. LOCKE, an occurrence of the entity class EMPLOYEE, is an entity.

2. An *attribute* is a descriptive value or property associated with an individual entity.

    Attributes can be classified by one or more rules as follows:

    • Describe an entity
    • Uniquely identify an entity
    • Describe relationships between entities
    • Use to derive other attributes

3. A *relationship* is an association between two or more entities.

    For example, EMPLOYED BY is a relationship between an employee and his employer.

4. An *access group* is a physical clustering of attributes based on common usage, access requirements, and same data security or privacy requirements.

    In a database environment using the Information Management System (IMS) database management system, an access group could be attributes from one or more IMS segments. For example, a user may form an access group consisting of Employee name and Employment history taken from two segments, Employee and Position, respectively.

    The concept of access groups in an IMS environment which uses the current retrieval language (DL/1) to retrieve segments is not readily accepted. However, many organizations are using user-written routines to retrieve access groups.

5. *Access statistics* may be defined as data collected about the frequency of retrieval of a particular stored attribute over a given period of time.

    These statistics provide a means of making performance-oriented judgments when designing physical databases. In particular, these statistics assist in the choice of physical and logical parents and the left-to-right ordering of segments. They are useful in the selection of secondary indices since attributes that are updated frequently make poor target fields.

    Access statistics can have a major effect on the placing of dependent segments in relation to their root and on the decision to combine segments in preference to decreasing data independence.

2.2.3   The Data Analysis Phase

A fundamental part of the E-R methodology is the data analysis phase. This phase is concerned with identifying the data resources of an organization. Although methodologies for data analysis have stemmed from the need for a new approach to system design in a database environment, experience has shown that the concept of data analysis has a wider applicability, whether or not database software is involved. The approach to data analysis, the same scale involved, and the emphasis placed on the various tasks that must be done depend very much on the objectives of the project.

Davenport indicates that data analysis is used to:

- Determine the fundamental data resources of an organization
- Permit the design of flexible file structures capable of supporting a number of related applications
- Aid application development or conversion by providing a fundamental understanding of the data involved
- Form a basis for data control, security, and auditing of the resulting applications and systems
- Organize all relevant facts concerning the organization's data
- Aid the unification of an organization by indicating the commonality between its departments and data requirements
- Provide a basis for evaluating the structuring capability of competing database management systems

Further uses of data analysis are to:

- Identify the entities that are relevant to solve the existing data processing problem
- Determine the relationships among those entities
- Establish data and process definitions in a data dictionary
- Produce the entity model

The primary interest in data analysis tends to be in providing a sound basis for database design. It provides a disciplined approach toward cataloging the existing data in terms of the entities and relationships it represents. Without such an understanding of that part of the organization being analyzed, it is more difficult to establish whether and where a database could be efficiently installed. Data analysis provides a very effective means of communicating with non-data processing users as it deals only with things that the users are familiar with and not with objects such as files and records.

The data analysis phase is sometimes referred to as requirements formulation and analysis, which involve the establishment of organization objectives, derivation of specific database requirements from these objectives or directly from management personnel, and documentation of these requirements in a form that is agreeable to management and database designers.

2.2.4   Conducting the Data Analysis Phase

Data analysis is best conducted by a team of individuals drawn from the user community, the systems development department, data administration group, and corporate standards department.

The data analysis team may not be involved in the requirement analysis phase of the project, if that phase is limited to personal interviews with various levels of management and key employees involved in the processing of goods, services, and data in the organization. The result of such interviews should be flow diagrams of the process; e.g., illustrations of steps required to process an invoice and where in the organization these steps are undertaken, with which each employee is involved, and identification of the data elements associated with each process, interfaces between processes, and a verification that both the interviewer and employee agree on the flow model semantics. Specific objectives and database requirements should be obtained at the highest possible level in the organization.

The data analysis team first identifies the entities needed to solve the problem defined by the users. During the initial stages of data analysis, all of the attributes of each entity may not be known. However, as each attribute is determined, the team should document the attribute definition and role in an appropriate data dictionary.

2.2.5   The Entity Model

During the data analysis phase the major entities and their relationships are determined. These entities and their relationships are represented by models called entity models. The model is a diagrammatical representation of the relationship between the entity classes.

The representation allows us to include only those entities that are required to solve the particular data processing problem. The entity model is essentially a real-world view of the organizational data in terms of the entities, attributes, and relationships.

During the entity modeling phase, the most significant entity classes and relationships are defined. But inevitably a model will be revised, modified, or extended as a result of new knowledge about the entities being discovered. The model is used by the analysis team to:

- Reduce redundancy in the relationships
- Determine which entities are significant to the model and user requirement
- Resolve nonbinary relationships between entities

2.2.6 Approaches to Entity Modeling

There are two main approaches to entity modeling:

- Top-down approach
- Bottom-up approach

The top-down approach produces a global, corporate, or organizational view of the data before the application or user views are identified. The entities and relationships of interest to the organization are identified from the point of view of the organization and independent of any particular application.

The bottom-up approach produces a composite or global view of the data based on the integration of several application views of the immediate problem requirements. The resulting model is limited to the immediate problem and cannot reflect the entire business activity of the corporation.

The bottom-up approach is the one most often used in entity modeling. This approach produces a model with more clearly defined boundaries than the top-down approach. The processing requirements can be used by the analysis team to determine precisely what entities are required and the composition of those entities. The clustering of attributes into their respective entities or the splitting of entities can now be done with more precision. It is also easier to determine whether an attribute is indeed an attribute of an existing entity or is itself an entity with relationships to other entities when using this approach.

The bottom-up approach produces entity models for each data area analyzed, but these models can be merged together to produce an integrated model which will satisfy all data areas or the whole corporation. This integration phase initially involves some editing to remove inconsistencies in the type of attributes, entities, or relationships. These inconsistencies may be in the form of one name referring to different components of the model (homonyms) or different names referring to the same component (synonyms).

2.2.7 Stages of Integration of Entity Models

The stages required to integrate entity models are as follows:

- Identify any synonyms or homonyms in the different models. This task is made easier if a data dictionary is used. Components with homonyms will have to be renamed. Components with synonyms will have to be referred to by a single name.
- Entity models for two data areas are integrated by superimposing the identical or similar entity types in the different entity models. This may increase the total number of attributes in the entity type, as identical entity types in each model have been concerned with different subsets of the total group of properties.

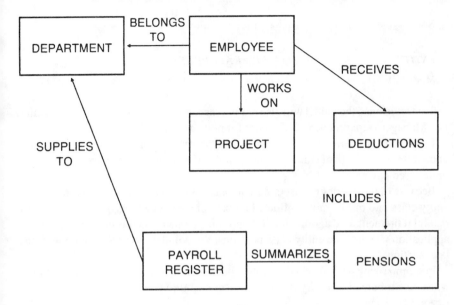

Figure 2.2   Entity model for paycheck processing

- As a result of the integration, the composite entity model may contain redundant relationships. The redundant relationships may be eliminated. However, determining which relationships are directly significant and which are redundant can present difficulties which can only be solved by an understanding of the environment.

2.2.8 Entity Modeling Case Study

The following case study will serve to illustrate the use of entity modeling in database design. The database application is a general payroll system. The relevant department consists of a number of employees for whom paychecks must be processed. The employees' pensions can be paid in a lump sum or by installments upon retirement, death of employee, or resignation. The department also wishes to make inquiries about projects a particular employee has worked on.

The entities and relationships from the above case study are represented in the entity model (Figure 2.2).

The model shown in Figure 2.2 will require several revisions as the data analysis phase continues and the requirements are more clearly identified. Some researchers indicate that anywhere from 4 to 20 revisions to the model may be required.

In the department and employee entity classes, the attributes head and supervisor best describe another entity class. We can now create a new entity class, Manager, for example, and replace the two attributes with pointers or relationship codes to the original entity classes. We can also add new attributes to the entity class, Manager.

Some typical attributes of Manager are as follows:

ENTITY	TYPICAL ATTRIBUTES
MANAGER	Manager identifier, description, authority

This revision to the model will also require that we establish two more relationships; i.e., Manager/Department and Manager/Employee relationships.

In the pensions entity class, the attribute "type" indicates that pensions can be paid upon retirement, death of employee, resignation of employee, in a lump sum, annually or deferred payment.

Because of the queries the users want to make, one may decide to split the pensions entity class into one or more entities. For example, we may have one entity class for natural retirements and another for all lump sum payments. In this case the entities are application views of the entity class pensions. We will discuss application views in a later section.

In summarizing revisions to the entity model, we may list a few rules in determining when an attribute of an entity is best treated as an entity in its own right related to the first entity. The rules are:

- Determine if the attribute itself has any other related attributes
- Determine if the new entity is required in order to solve the data processing problem
- Determine if the attribute in fact identifies the second entity
- Determine if the new entity is related to the original entity
- Determine if the new entity is related to any other entities in the model

2.3   DERIVING ENTITY MODELS FROM TRADITIONAL OR FLAT FILES

This section discusses some approaches for deriving entity models from flat files or databases that were not designed using E-R methodology. There are no hard and fast rules for this derivation. One would have liked to say that there is a one-to-one correspondence between the entity classes in a model and the number of files/descriptions (FD) in a program.

However, the clustering of data items from which the logical files were constructed may not be the same clustering required for the respective entity classes. Nevertheless, the following simple rules can be followed when converting from flat files to the entity model of that application.

- List all the file types in the relevant programs
- List all the logical records in the files

- List all the data items in the records
- Eliminate redundancies and inconsistencies in the data items and logical records
- List all possible combinations of entity classes from the logical records. The record name is an indicator of the entity class.
- List all codes in the records which can give the relationships of the entity model
- Conduct a preliminary data analysis of the data items
- Cluster the attributes into their respective entity classes

This procedure will result in a baseline entity model that will serve as a framework for making further revisions, which will become necessary due to more detailed data analysis.

The procedure to follow for old databases created by methods other than E-R methodology will depend largely on how the data was physically clustered for data retrieval. Very often if the physical clustering was performance oriented, the logical clustering into entity classes becomes a very complex, if not impossible task.

It is my experience that the most productive method is still to obtain data definitions for all the data items in the databases, take the applications that use those data items, and cluster the data items into entity classes using any known data analysis techniques.

The entity model for the particular user area can then be obtained by an integration or superimposition of the individual program-oriented models.

2.3.1   Superimposition of Entity Models

In the conversion of existing physical databases back to their entity model equivalents, the designer may arrive at several different models depending on the programs or applications from which the models were derived. He should then attempt to remove redundancies and inconsistencies by superimposing the models from several programs to arrive at one integrated model.

The superimposition of entity models would allow the designer to determine:

- What are the common entity classes and attributes. These can be recognized on the basis of names only.
- The inconsistencies in the naming and use of attributes. These inconsistencies exist when two entities with different names are clearly shown to be one and the same entity.
- The adequacy of the model in terms of meeting the needs of the user
- Whether attributes clustered into an entity class are indeed members of another entity class or new entity classes themselves
- The existence of inconsistencies in the relationships

The superimposed entity model can now be used as a framework for further revisions to arrive at an integrated entity model that will serve a larger data area than several smaller application-oriented models.

2.3.2   Clustering of Entity Classes

Clustering of entity classes in database design may occur in the logical or physical design stage. In the physical design stage the clustering of the entity classes may be done solely on the basis of performance considerations. The entity classes may be merged or split into different physical databases depending upon the access requirements.

The logical clustering of entity classes is dependent upon the inherent nature of the data and data structure, whereas physical clustering is not. It is necessary, but not a sufficient rule to say that attributes are clustered within an entity class because they best identify and describe that entity class, and entity classes are clustered into an entity model to satisfy a user's data processing requirement.

The logical clustering of entity classes is done to satisfy the following:

- The area served by the data or from which the data originated
- The inherent data structure
- The local view of the user
- The usage of the data
- The queries against the data
- The data processing needs of the user

The clustering of entity classes on the basis of data area is essentially that all data for which the accounting department has a functional responsibility will be clustered as accounting data. Similarly, all data for which the personnel department has that responsibility will be clustered as personnel data. The data areas are usually determined by the same methods that were used to create the organizational structure or boundaries.

The inherent data structure of an organization would indicate that employees are assigned to departments, assigned to projects; customers place orders; and orders are for products. Thus, in clustering of entity classes, the cluster must reflect that inherent data structure. The inherent data structure now reflects the business practices of the organizations, and the clustering would also reflect those practices.

The clustering of entity classes on the basis of the local view of the user can be translated to mean that only those entities in which the user has some interest are assembled. The cluster may be part of a larger cluster or an amalgamation of several clusters. Thus, if the user wanted to determine the projects an employee worked on, his local views would consist of the cluster of the employee and project entity classes.

The attributes within an entity class and the clustering of the entity classes must satisfy the queries made against them. For example, one could not satisfy a query about employees' skill and education if these attributes are not in the entity class. Similarly, a query about the percentage of an employee's time spent on a project could not be answered if there was not a clustering of employee and project entity classes.

As in entity modeling, so in clustering of entity classes the object of the exercise is to satisfy the data processing need of the user. The adequacy of the model is measured in relation to how well those needs are met. The entity classes will be clustered in accordance with those needs.

2.3.3   Application View and Logical Schema Design

An application view may be defined as the set of data required by that particular application to fulfill a specific data processing need. For example, one application may be interested in materializing employee name and social security number as its employee entity class while another may materialize employee name, social security number, and salary as its employee entity class. In turn, these two entity classes may be just a subset of a larger set of attributes which make up a corporate or global entity class called employee entity class.

We may have application views of:

- Entity class
- Cluster of entity classes
- Cluster of entity classes and physical databases
- Cluster of physical databases

The logical schema may be defined as the mapping of the entity model into the constructs provided by the database management system (DBMS), for example, the mapping of the entity model into an IMS construct. In general, the logical schema indicates how the model will be stored and accessed. In the design of the logical schema, some restructuring of the model and changes to conform to the DBMS may be necessary.

The entity model is not the logical schema. The entity model is:

- A representation of real-world view of the data
- The building blocks used for further data analysis and database design
- Not restricted to any database management systems (DBMS)
- Not directly implementable
- A stable framework or frame of reference into which new entities, attributes, and relationships can fit as more organizational database needs evolve

2.3.4   Logical Schema — Case Study

In this section, I will endeavor to construct a logical schema from the entity model shown in Figure 2.2. Due to space limitations, I will not do the schema for the entire model as shown. A partial logical schema for Figure 2.2 is shown in Figure 2.3.

In the logical schema of Figure 2.3 we should note that the hierarchical data structure of IMS is now applied to the entity model. We also see that the pointers and unique keys are imposed on the entity model.

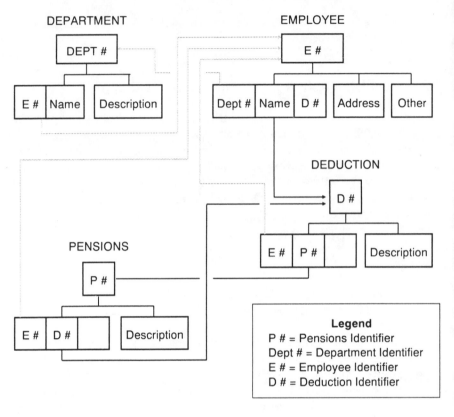

Figure 2.3   Logical schema for paycheck entity model

If other relationships than those shown in the logical schema are required, these are shown including all materialized attributes of relationships and their pointers. The logical schema should also show the occurrences of major groups of data or segments.

It should be noted that the logical schema for RELATIONAL and NETWORK databases will exhibit the constructs provided by their respective database management system.

2.3.5   Translation of the Logical Schema into Physical Databases

The details of this phase depend very much on the characteristics of the database management system (DBMS) chosen for the database design.

In an IMS environment, the translation from the logical schema to physical databases requires the following selections:

- Physical databases and types of logical relationships, whether unidirectional or bidirectional physically paired
- Access methods, whether HISAM, HIDAM, or HDAM
- Segments and hierarchial structures and data representation, including type and size
- Secondary indices
- Types of pointers in relationship

In addition to the selections mentioned above, the implementation of the physical databases includes:

- Allocation to storage devices
- Loading and organization of the databases

The logical schema should be so developed by the logical database designers that the only selection requirements left to be done by the physical designers would be the selection of access methods and secondary indices.

The translation of logical schemas into physical databases is dealt with at considerable length in the current literature.

Finally, Hubbard indicates that the following rules should be followed during the physical design process:

- Each entity class should be treated as a physical database
- If two entity classes share a relationship between at least one attribute and the primary key, then the structures should consist of two physical databases with physical or virtual pairing between them
- Parent-child relationship should be defined in a single physical database
- Frequently accessed segments should be kept as close to their root as possible
- Reduce the time for searching large data groups by using secondary indexing
- Segments of varying sizes should not be placed in the same data set or group if frequent inserts or deletes are to be performed.

2.4 OTHER STRUCTURED TECHNIQUES

CASE tools aim to support all the activities of a systems development life cycle. The development techniques supported are as follows:

- Data-model diagrams, of which E-R diagrams are a subset
- Data-flow diagrams
- Activity-decomposition diagrams
- Activity-dependency diagrams
- Activity-process-logic diagrams

- Data-flow-content diagrams
- State-change diagrams

2.4.1 Data Models

Data models aim to show pictorially what data a business needs in order to complete its activities. It may be represented in one picture or more than one picture. Data models diagrammatically represent the concepts of entity and relationships.

2.4.2 Data-Flow Diagrams

A data-flow diagram aims to show pictorially the activities of a business, the static data that is used by the activities, and the dynamic data that is passed between activities. It also shows sources and sinks; that is, people, organizations, types of organizations, or people outside the scope and what collections of data come from or go to them. It does not show the sequence, selection, or interaction of one activity in relation to another. Its prime purpose is to depict the use of data — stored or flowing.

2.4.3 Activity-Dependency Diagrams

Activity-dependency diagrams aim to show pictorially the sequence, selection, and iteration of one activity with respect to others — the dependency of one activity upon another.

Activity-dependency diagrams have been enhanced to show more than this base representation. Some show data as well. Some show "extends" to the system. With a few notable exceptions, this has not always worked diagramatically, as control flow and data flow become confused.

2.4.4 Activity-Decomposition Diagrams

These diagrams aim to show the breakdown of activities into more and more detail. The purpose of the diagram is to first provide a picture to summarize all the activities in the scope and how they have been broken down. A second purpose is to enable sequence, selection, and iteration of activities to be recorded on a diagram other than the activity-dependency diagram.

2.4.5 Process-Logic Diagrams

Process-logic diagrams aim to show, in a structured way, the detailed logic of an elementary process or activity.

Process-logic diagrams also show the selection, sequence, and iteration of detailed logic and parallel activity. They may also show how the data-model components-entities, attributes, and relationships are used by the logic.

2.4.6   Data-Flow-Content Diagrams

A data-flow-content diagram aims to show the "content" of a data flow. It shows the sequence optionality and repeating nature of the data in the data flow. Normally, this data corresponds to the data in the data model — primarily entities and attributes, but also occasionally permitted values.

2.4.7   State-Change Diagrams

True state-change diagrams — normally expressed as a form of decision table — show the permissible changes of state of entities as a result of an event or activity. They also show the definition of each state in terms of the entity's attribute values and relationship values.

Within this general category, however, other sorts of state changes can be shown. The entity life history shows the permissible sequence of events in relation to an entity. The state transition diagram shows the state of the system and the permissible sequence of activities that can change those states.

3

LOGICAL AND PHYSICAL DATABASE DESIGN

3.1 INTRODUCTION

This chapter discusses the two major phases of database development. In the first phase, logical database design, we take the user requirements as represented by a data model, superimpose the constructs of the database management system, and obtain input to the second phase, physical database design. In the second phase, we are primarily concerned with storing the data as defined in the logical data model and defining access paths to the stored data.

3.2 THE SYSTEMS DEVELOPMENT LIFE CYCLE

In Chapter 1, we discussed two development life cycles for the development of databases. In both cycles, we placed a lot of emphasis on the processes and functions that were required to satisfy the user requirements. We want to move away somewhat from that approach and adopt an approach where the data is the driving force behind the database development activities. The phases of this approach are shown in Figure 3.1.

3.2.1 The User Requirements Phase

The user requirements phase has been discussed at some length in Chapter 1. However, in this section, we will concentrate on those areas that are more data related.

During the initial survey subphase, the analyst seeks to determine the entities and relationships that are of interest to the users.

TRADITIONAL	DATA-DRIVEN
1. Identification Phase	1. User Requirements
• Initiation	• Initial Survey
• Initial Survey	• Data Definitions
	• Feasibility Study
	• Project Scope
	• Security Plans
2. Systems Study Phase	2. Logical Design
• Feasibility Study	• Data Model
• General Systems Study	• Dictionary Population
	• Process Definitions
	• Program Specifications
	• Systems Test Plans
	• Normalization
3. Systems Development Phase	3. Physical Design
• Detail Systems Design	• Program Development
• Data Conversion Plan	• Physical DB Design
• Program Specification	• Database Loading
• System Test Plan	• Testing
• Manual Practices	• Training
4. Systems Implementation	4. Evaluation
• Program Development	• Monitoring
• Data Conversion	• Performance Tuning
• Systems Testing	• Reorganization
• Training	• Auditing
• Parallel Operations	
5. Evaluation	

Figure 3.1   The phases of a data-driven SDLC

In the data definition subphase, the analyst obtains descriptions, functions, data characteristics, and editing rules about the entities and all known attributes.

In the project scope subphase, the analyst obtains metadata about the boundaries of the data model, the common usage of items in the user views, and information on what should not be included in the project.

In the security plans subphase, the analyst obtains information on the security, privacy, and integrity requirements of the data that will be processed by the system. He begins to formulate plans and policies for the protection of that data.

3.2.2   The Logical Design Phase

In the data model subphase of logical database design, the analyst creates a data model of the entities and relationships that were described to him in the user requirements phase. The model is superimposed with the constructs of the relevant database management system. It is during this phase that some attention is paid to key selections and access methods.

In the usage statistics subphase, the analyst collects information about the volume of data to be processed, the processing frequencies, the variations in volumes, the volatility of the data, and plans for access to the data other than by unique keys.

In the normalization subphase, the analyst seeks to ensure that all attributes clearly belong to the entities they best describe. He ensures that existing entities cannot be further collapsed into other entities and that attributes cannot be further grouped into other entities.

In the data dictionary population subphase, the analyst begins to enter all collected metadata about the entities, attributes, relationships, data models, and processes into the corporate data dictionary. This process is usually started in the data definitions subphase but must be emphasized in this subphase.

3.2.3   The Physical Design Phase

In the physical design phase, the analyst takes the data model from the logical design phase as input, selects the best storage and accessing methods, and produces the physical data model.

It is during this phase that storage and time estimates for the chosen database management system are calculated.

The analyst may split existing entities in the logical data model or collapse entities in order to improve performance, reduce redundancy in storage, or to adhere to access methods requirements. The resulting physical model may differ greatly from the input logical model.

In the database loading subphase, the analyst uses a database-specific utility to load data into storage areas on the relevant storage devices.

3.2.4   The Evaluation Phase

During the evaluation phase, the performance of the database management system is monitored to determine if it meets the user's expectations for response time and throughput. The database is stress-tested for large volumes of data. The pointers and chains are tested to prove ability to return data items from the lowest levels of the hierarchy.

In the performance tuning step, utilities are run against the database to repair broken pointers and chains. Transaction rates, mixes, and processing regions are examined to ensure that the system is performing adequately. The analyst must reexamine main storage space, DASD space, channels, and teleprocessing lines to ensure that the database is doing the work required of it.

In the reorganization phase, the analyst reorganizes or restructures the database in order to recapture all unused space between the valid records as a result of the deletion of some records. He also reorganizes the database to prevent fragmentation of space, the creation of long chains and excessive fetch times. He may also want to rearrange the records so that, for most of them, their physical sequence is the same as their logical sequence. He may also want to reorganize the database so that the frequently accessed records may be stored on a high-speed medium, whereas the rarely accessed records are stored on a slower-speed medium.

In the case of a sequentially organized database, reorganization may take the form of combining the old database records with the transaction log file to form a new database. In an indexed sequentially organized database, reorganization means taking all the database records from the prime and overflow areas and reloading the database without any records going into the overflow area.

In the auditing phase, the Internal Auditors examine the audit trails, the transaction log file, the backup and recovery procedures, and all relevant standards and procedures that have been developed during the database development period to determine their adequacy and their ability to ensure the security, privacy, and integrity of the stored data.

3.2.5 Data-Related Activities During the SDLC

In a data-driven systems development life cycle, the analyst, data administrator, database administrator, and system designer carry out activities and produce deliverables, some of which are distinctly data related. These activities and deliverables differ greatly from those that are strictly process driven or process related. I have summarized these activities and deliverables in Figure 3.2.

3.3 LOGICAL DESIGN OF DATABASES

The logical design of databases is mainly concerned with superimposing the constructs of the database management system on the logical data model. As stated earlier, these constructs fall into three categories: hierarchical, relational, and network.

In this section of the chapter, we will develop various logical models of a database using these structures.

3.3.1 Mapping to a Hierarchical Data Model

The steps to follow in deriving a logical hierarchical database from the logical data model are as follows:

TRADITIONAL	*DATA ACTIVITIES*	*DATA DELIVERABLES*

1. Identification
  • Initiation
  • Initial Survey
	1. User Requirement
	  • Define the entities that will be included in project scope
		• Data dictionary containing data items, validation rules and other definitions

2. Systems Study
  • Feasibility Study
  • Data Conversion Plan
  • Program Specifications
  • Systems Test Plan
  • Manual Practices
	2. Logical Design
	  • Identify relationships among data items
	  • Normalize user views
	  • Produce logical data model
		• Logical database and data model

3. Systems Development
  • Detail Systems Design
  • Data Conversion Plan
  • Program Specification
  • Systems Test Plan
  • Manual Practices
	3. Physical Design
	  • Develop physical database from logical model
	  • Verify adequacy of physical design
		• Data dictionary with all physical data flows

4. Systems Implementation
  • Program Development
  • Data Conversion
  • Systems Testing
  • Training
  • Parallel Operations
	4. Evaluation
	  • Assist DBA in setting procedures for monitoring the database
	  • Assist auditors in setting procedures for auditing the database	

5. Evaluation		

Figure 3.2   Data-related activities and deliverables

- Derive a hierarchical data model including the constructs of the database management system (DBMS)
- Refine the data model according to performance requirements

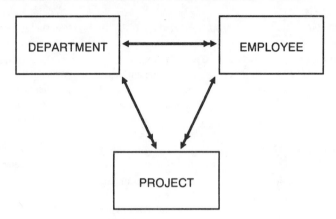

Figure 3.3   Superfluous relationships

- Select key names
- Add relationships, association, and characteristic entities as required by the particular DBMS

In deriving a hierarchical data model which includes the constructs of the DBMS, we may want to:

- Eliminate superfluous relationships
- Derive all parent–child relationships
- Resolve multiple parentage

Let's examine the relationships represented in Figures 3.3 and 3.4. The relationship between DEPARTMENT and EMPLOYEE is superfluous since it can be derived from the relationship shown in Figure 3.4.

In deriving relationships, we may want to derive a parent–child relationship from a given relationship. Let us examine the relationships represented in Figures 3.5 and 3.6.

We can derive a new relationship where either DEPARTMENT or EMPLOYEE is the parent. The significance of creating the parent–child relationship is illustrated as follows. Let's store some information on the date the employee joined the department, the results of performance reviews, promotions within the department, and job functions. We can see that all of these stored attributes do not identify either the DEPARTMENT or EMPLOYEE entity but identify the relationship between DE-PARTMENT and EMPLOYEE. When this situation occurs, the key of the new entity is a combination of the keys of the two original entities.

The resolution of multiple parentage depends upon whether some parents are third normal form relations or a created one. Very often, created entities are needed mainly for the physical implementation of the data model. When this is the case, and no data

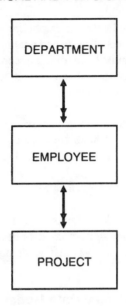

Figure 3.4 Modify relationships

Figure 3.5 Relationship between department and employee

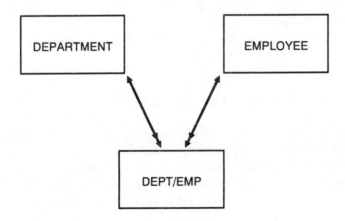

Figure 3.6 Representation of parent–child relationship

is lost by eliminating the created entity or combining it with another entity, we can safely opt for eliminating the created entity and not the third normal form one.

Very often, the data model must be modified to conform to the constraints of the DBMS. For example, if the DBMS was an information management system (IMS), we would have the following constraints:

- There can be no more than 255 node types or segment types
- There can be no more than 15 hierarchical levels
- A child segment type can have no more than two parents: a "physical" parent and a "logical" parent
- A logical child cannot have a logical child

On occasion, we may want to add relationships to the data model. The reason may be to add entities that may better support the data needs of the organization in the future. These should not be done in a way that would degrade the performance of the system.

3.3.2   Mapping to a Relational Data Model

As we have discussed before, the relational model consists of a number of relations or tables. In mapping the data model onto the constructs of the relational DBMS, we would produce a table for each entity in the model. The relationships between entities would show up as foreign keys in one of the related entities.

Mapping into a relational DBMS is a relatively easy process.

3.3.3   Mapping to a Network Data Model

In mapping a data model onto the constructs of the network DBMS, we derive owner-member relationships within set types. We may collapse some of the set types by combining entities or eliminating them after the normalization process.

The logical database designers will have to pay more attention to performance considerations when mapping to a network database than during similar phases of hierarchical or relational database design.

3.4   PHYSICAL DESIGN OF DATABASES

The physical model is a framework of the database to be stored on physical devices. The model must be constructed with every regard given to the performance of the resulting database. One should carry out an analysis of the physical model with average frequencies of occurrences of the groupings of the data elements, with expected space estimates, and with respect to time estimates for retrieving and maintaining the data.

The database designer may find it necessary to have multiple entry points into a database or to access a particular segment type with more than one key. To provide this type of access, it may be necessary to invert the segment on the keys, thereby posing some overhead on space and/or time. This is very often the price that must be paid to satisfy this particular business requirement.

The physical designer must have expertise in at least three areas:

- Knowledge of the DBMS functions
- Understanding of the characteristics of direct-access devices
- Knowledge of the applications

The physical designer must know how the DBMS performs its specific functions. For example, in IBM's information management system (IMS), he must know the following:

1. That access to all segments, except when using secondary indexing, is through the root segment. Hence, remote segments should be confined to few levels and not spread out from left to right.
2. That retrieval from the database is by segments. This means that a programmer may be presented with more data than is necessary. This often poses security problems for the installation. In this case, the trade-off is between too few and too many segments.
3. That frequently accessed segments should be kept at the top of the hierarchy, since all access is through the root of the hierarchy.
4. That one physical database is based on one root segment. Hence, if one physical database is expected to become too big, he should consider splitting it. However, he must take into consideration the operational issues of backup and recovery for several physical databases.
5. How to provide alternate paths to the data other than through the root segment. For example, we must know that with secondary indexing, IMS database records can be accessed on data elements other than the primary key.

3.5 SELECTION OF ACCESS METHODS

We often refer to the way that we store the data for subsequent retrieval as the file organization. The way that we retrieve the data is called the access method.

The types of access methods vary from manufacturer to manufacturer. The names also vary from DBMS to DBMS. The physical database designer must be familiar with several access methods. However, because of my background with IMS, I will discuss only those that are pertinent to IMS.

IMS allows us to define eight different types of databases. These are as follows:

DATABASE TYPE	GROUP	ACCESS METHOD
HSAM	Sequential	Hierarchical Sequential
SHSAM	Sequential	Simple Hierarchical Sequential
HISAM	Sequential	Hierarchical Indexed Sequential
SHISAM	Sequential	Simple Hierarchical Indexed Sequential
HDAM	Direct	Hierarchical Direct
HIDAM	Direct	Hierarchical Indexed Direct
MSDB	Direct	Main Storage
DEDB	Direct	Data Entry

3.5.1   Hierarchical Sequential Databases

HSAM databases use the sequential method of storing data. All database records and all segments within each database record are physically adjacent in storage.

HSAM data sets are loaded with root segments in ascending key sequence and dependent segments in hierarchic sequence. You don't have to define a key field in root segments. You must, however, present segments to the load program in the order in which you want them loaded. HSAM data sets use a fixed-length, unblocked record format (RECFM=F), which means that the logical record length is the same as the physical block size.

HSAM databases can only be updated by rewriting them. They are appropriate primarily for low-use files, for example, audit trails, statistical reports, or files containing historical or archival data.

Segments in an HSAM database are loaded in the order in which you present them to the load program. You should present all segments within a database record in hierarchic sequence. In the data set, a database record is stored in one or more consecutive blocks. If there is not enough space left in the block to store the next segment, the remaining space is filled with zeros and the next segment is stored in the next consecutive block.

Figure 3.7 illustrates the HSAM database records sequence. Figure 3.8 illustrates how the HSAM database records would be stored.

3.5.2   Hierarchical Indexed Sequential Databases

In a HISAM database, as with HSAM databases, segments in each database record are related through physical adjacency in storage. Unlike HSAM, however, you must define a unique sequence field in each root segment. These sequence fields are then used to construct an index to root segments in the database.

HISAM is typically used for databases that require direct access to database records and sequential processing of segments in a database record. It's a good candidate for databases with the following characteristics:

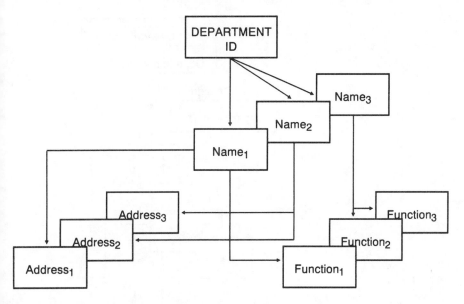

Figure 3.7 Representation of HSAM database in hierarchic sequence

- Most database records are about the same size
- The database does not consist of relatively few root segments and a large number of dependent segments
- Applications don't require a heavy volume of root segments inserted after the database is initially loaded
- Deletion of database records is minimal

HISAM database records are stored in two data sets. The first, called the primary data set, contains an index and all segments in a database record that can fit into one logical record. The index provides direct access to the root segment. The second data set, called the overflow data set, contains all segments in the database record that cannot fit in the primary data set.

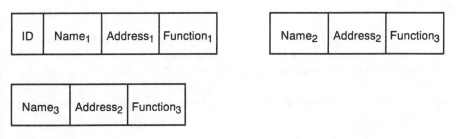

Figure 3.8 Storage of HSAM records

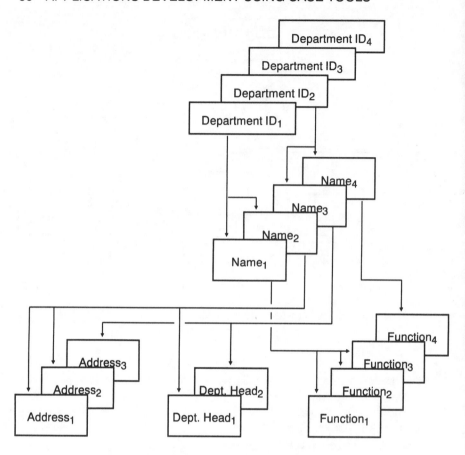

Figure 3.9   Representation of HISAM database in hierarchic sequence

Figure 3.9 illustrates the HISAM database records sequence. Figure 3.10 illustrates how HISAM database records are stored.

There are several things you need to know about storage of HISAM database records:

- You define the logical record length of both the primary and overflow data set
- You define the size of the control interval or block
- Each database record starts at the beginning of a logical record in the primary data set
- Segments in a database record cannot be split and stored across two logical records

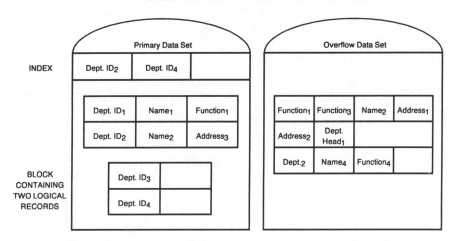

Figure 3.10 Storage of HSAM records

3.5.3 Hierarchical Direct Databases

Hierarchical direct databases differ from sequentially organized databases in two important ways. First, they use a direct method of storing data; that is, the hierarchic sequence of segments in the database is maintained by having segments point to one another. Except for a few special cases, each segment has one or more direct-address pointers in its prefix. When direct-address pointers are used, database records and segments can be stored anywhere in the database. Their position, once stored, is fixed. Instead, pointers are updated to reflect processing changes.

Hierarchical direct (HD) databases also differ from sequentially organized ones in that space in HD databases can be reused. If part or all of a database record is deleted, the deleted space can be reused when new database records or segments are inserted.

HDAM databases are used when you need direct access to database records. A randomizing module provides fast access to the root segment.

HIDAM databases are used when you need both random and sequential access to database records and random access paths or segments in a database record. Access to root segments is not as fast as with HDAM, because the HIDAM index database has to be searched for a root segment's address. However, because the index keeps the address of root segments stored in key sequence, database records can be processed sequentially.

Figures 3.11, 3.12, and 3.13 illustrate how hierarchical direct databases are stored and processed.

In hierarchic pointers, each pointer points from one segment to the next in either forward or forward and backward hierarchic sequence.

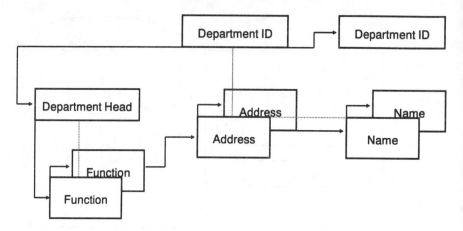

Figure 3.12 Hierarchic forward pointers

In physical child first pointers, each pointer points from a parent to the first child or dependent segment. You should notice that no pointers exist to connect occurrences of the same segment type under a parent.

In physical twin forward pointers, each segment occurrence of a given segment type under the same parent points forward to the next segment occurrence.

HDAM databases consist of two parts; a root addressable area and an overflow area. The root addressable area contains root segments and is the primary storage area for dependent segments in a database record. The overflow area is for storage of dependent segments that don't fit into the root addressable area.

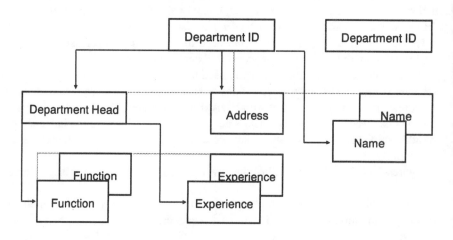

Figure 3.11 Physical child first pointers

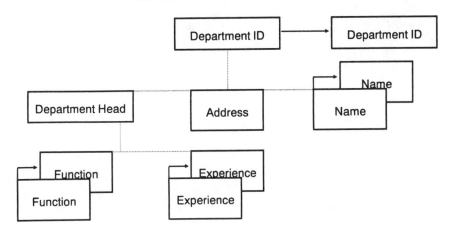

Figure 3.13   Physical twin forward pointers

Root segments in HDAM databases must have a key field, although the key field doesn't have to be unique.

A HIDAM database is actually composed of two databases. One is for storage of the database records, the other for the HIDAM index.

Root segments in HIDAM databases must have a unique key field. This is because an index entry exists for each root segment based on the root's key.

3.5.4 SUMMARY

This chapter dealt with the logical and physical design aspects of database development. In the logical design phase, we discovered that the primary deliverable was a data model with the constructs of the relevant DBMS superimposed. In the physical design phase, we indicated that the important steps were calculating space and time estimates, selecting access methods, and learning the mechanics of the database. The chapter discussed in some detail the access methods of IMS, a hierarchical DBMS.

4

DATA MODELS AND DATA STRUCTURES

4.1 INTRODUCTORY REMARKS

This chapter discusses data models and entity-relationship (E-R) diagrams and the role they play in database design.

Data models are the basic building blocks for all database design. They provide the underlying structure for the three dominant data structures of today's database management system (DBMS). In addition, data models are used by many large corporations in business systems planning, strategic systems planning, and corporate data modeling.

Entity-relationship diagrams or entity models, as they are also called, are used to define a conceptual view or real-world view of data and the data requirements of an organization. E-R diagrams were popularized by P. Chen (1976) and have since revolutionized the world of structured design.

4.2 DEFINING SOME TERMS

A data model (Figure 4.1) is a logical representation of a collection of data elements and the association among these data elements.

A data model can be used to represent data usage throughout an organization, or can represent a single database structure. A data model is to data what a logical data flow diagram is to a process.

There are three types of data models: (1) conceptual, (2) logical, and (3) internal or physical.

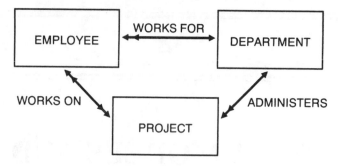

Figure 4.1   Example of a data model

The entity diagram is a representation of the relationship between entity classes. The representation allows us to include only those entities that are required to solve the particular data processing problem.

The entity diagram is essentially a real-world view of the organization data in terms of the entities, attributes, and relationships.

The entity diagram (model) is an example of a conceptual data model.

4.3 ENTITY AND ENTITY CLASSES

Entity and entity class are used interchangeably in some of the literature, whereas some researchers define the entity as an occurrence of an entity class. For example, EMPLOYEE is an entity class, whereas P. CAREY, an occurrence of the entity class EMPLOYEE, is an entity.

4.4 SUPER ENTITIES AND ENTITY SUBTYPES

An entity may be broken down into smaller subgroups on the basis of the function of each subgroup. These subgroups are often called entity subtypes. The original entity is often referred to as a super entity.

The representation of entity subtypes and super entities is shown in Figure 4.2.

4.5 TYPES OF RELATIONSHIPS

A relationship was defined earlier as an association between two or more entities. In this section, we will discuss the types of relationships and how they are represented diagrammatically.

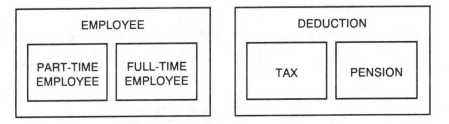

Figure 4.2   Representation of entity subtype

4.5.1 One-to-One Relationship

At a given time, one EMPLOYEE may be assigned to one DEPARTMENT. The relationship between EMPLOYEE and DEPARTMENT is termed one-to-one. This relationship is represented diagrammatically in Figure 4.3.

The single-headed arrows denote the one-to-one relationship.

4.5.2 One-to-Many Relationship

At a given time many EMPLOYEES may be assigned to one DEPARTMENT. The relationship between EMPLOYEES and DEPARTMENT is termed one-to-many. This is represented diagrammatically in Figure 4.4.

4.5.3 Many-to-Many Relationship

At a given time many EMPLOYEES may be assigned to many DEPARTMENTS. The relationship between EMPLOYEES and DEPARTMENTS is termed many-to-many. This is represented diagrammatically in Figure 4.5.

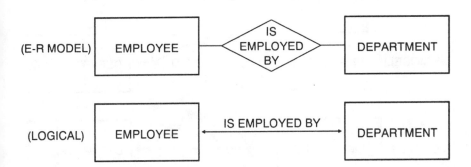

Figure 4.3   Representation of one-to-one relationship

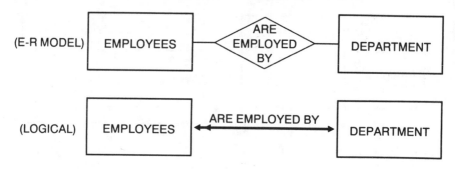

Figure 4.4   Representation of one-to-many relationship

4.5.4 Mutually Exclusive Relationship

At a given time an EMPLOYEE may be assigned to either DEPARTMENT A or B, but not to both. The relationship between EMPLOYEE and either DEPARTMENT is termed mutually exclusive. This is represented diagrammatically in Figure 4.6.

In Figure 4.6 the vertical bar in the direction of DEPARTMENT A indicates that DEPARTMENT A must always exist in the relationship. The circle indicates that DEPARTMENT B is optional. We obtain exclusivity by switching the circle and bar around in the relationship.

4.5.5 Mutually Inclusive Relationship

At a given time an EMPLOYEE may be assigned to both DEPARTMENT A and B. The relationship between EMPLOYEE and both DEPARTMENTS is termed mutually inclusive. This is represented diagrammatically in Figure 4.7.

The presence of vertical bars in the direction of both departments indicates that both must co-exist for the relationship to be completed.

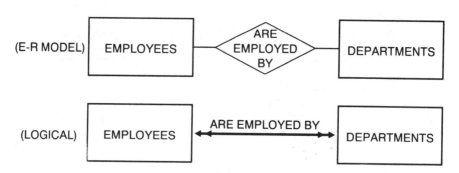

Figure 4.5   Representation of many-to-many relationship

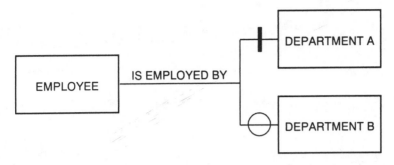

Figure 4.6   Representation of mutually exclusive relationship

4.5.6 Mandatory Relationship

Sometimes an employer may rule that a DEPARTMENT must exist before the EMPLOYEE is hired. The relationship between EMPLOYEE and DEPARTMENT is termed mandatory. This is represented diagrammatically in Figure 4.8.

The presence of a vertical bar in the direction of DEPARTMENT indicates that it must exist in the relationship.

4.5.7 Optional Relationship

Sometimes an EMPLOYEE may be hired but not assigned to a DEPARTMENT. The relationship between the EMPLOYEE and DEPARTMENT is termed optional. This is represented diagrammatically in Figure 4.9.

The presence of the circle in the direction of DEPARTMENT indicates that DEPARTMENT is not required to exist in the relationship.

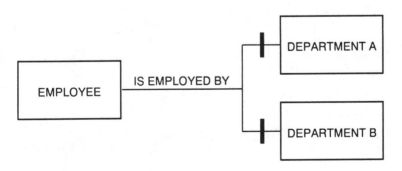

Figure 4.7   Representation of mutually inclusive relationship

Figure 4.8   Representation of a mandatory relationship

4.6 TRANSLATION OF E-R DIAGRAMS TO LOGICAL MODELS

E-R diagrams (models) are sometimes call Business Entity models since they reflect the business practices of an organization independently of any requirements for the underlying structure of a database management system (DBMS). However, in order for these diagrams to be processed by a computer, they must take on the constructs of the chosen DBMS. This section discusses the translation of E-R diagrams to logical data models.

Let's consider the following problem: A company is heavily project oriented. Each project has one or more employees assigned to it full-time, perhaps from different departments.

Office space is assigned from time to time. Employees are assigned to an office in the department where they work. Several may share an office. Each department has one employee who is a manager.

The company needs better information on projects, project costs, utilization of office space, and employee's time.

4.6.1   Identification of Business Entities

When business entities are identified, careful consideration should be given to:

- A generally acceptable *name* for the entity
- A complete definition that makes clear what is included and what is excluded from the members of the entity
- A *business-oriented* entity identifier that can be agreed upon across the enterprise

Figure 4.9   Representation of an optional relationship

Table 4.1 Business Entities

Entity Name	Abbreviation	Identifier	Description
Department	Dept	Unique ID of DEPT	An organizational unit in the company
Project	Proj	Unique ID of PROJ	A budgeted project now in progress
Employee	Emp	Unique ID of EMP	An active employee of the department. He/she may be full or part-time
Office	Office	Unique ID of OFFICE	A room allocated to a department

The business entities, with their name, abbreviation, identifier, and description, are shown in Table 4.1.

4.6.2 Determination of E-R Diagram for Problems

The determination of the E-R diagram for the problem may be carried out in a variety of ways. The simplest of these is to take all the nouns in the problem statement and declare them to be entities and the significant verbs as relationships.

The diagram resulting from the problem is shown in Figure 4.10.

The degree of the relationships between the entities may be denoted by using 1, M, single-headed or double-headed arrows.

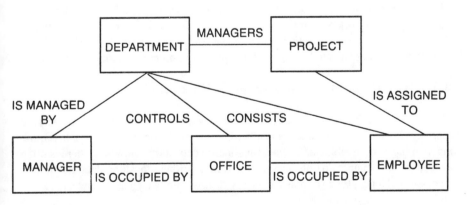

Figure 4.10 E-R diagram for illustrative problem

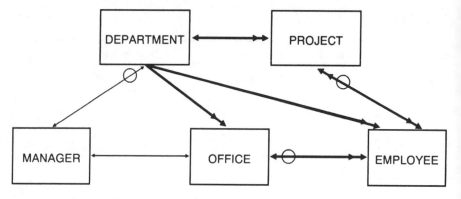

Figure 4.11 Logical data model for problem

4.6.3 Conversion of E-R Diagram to a Logical Data Model

The following steps are taken to convert E-R diagrams to logical data models:

- Convert business entities to data entities
- Represent the degree of the relationship between entities
- Convert many-to-many relationships to associations
- Look for conditional relationships
- Convert repeating groups to characteristic entities

If we apply the above steps, we can convert the E-R diagram of Figure 4.10 to a logical data model as depicted in Figure 4.11.

In Figure 4.11 the single-headed arrow in the direction of DEPT and the double-headed arrow in the direction of PROJ indicate that one DEPT may administer many PROJ's. The double-headed arrows in the two directions PROJ and EMP indicate that many employees work on many projects. The circle in the direction of PROJ indicates that there is an optional relationship between PROJ and EMP. In other words, an employee does not have to be assigned to a project in order to become an employee.

4.6.4 Conversion of Many-to-Many Relationship

Many-to-many relationships are common among business entities, but awkward to represent in a logical data model by just two entities, since completeness would require much of the same attribute data appearing in each data entity. However, there is often a need to associate two business entities and, further, to store data about that association. Hence, for each many-to-many relationship, we create a new data entity with the following characteristics:

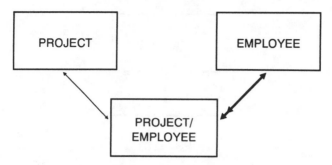

Figure 4.12   Representation of association entity

- The new data entity is called an ASSOCIATION data entity
- It has a many-to-one relationship with each of the original data entities
- It is a *child* of each of the original data entities
- The unique identifier of the new data entity will contain the unique identifier of both original data entities

The new data entities form an association with the two original entities as shown in Figure 4.12.

4.6.5   Handling of Repeating Groups

A repeating group is a group of one or more attributes of a data entity which may have multiple values for a given value of the unique identifier.
Repeating groups are undesirable because:

- There is no way to pick a single occurrence within the group
- They either impose limitations or cause more complex processing of the physical structure

In order to remove repeating groups from the logical model, we must:

- Create a new entity called a CHARACTERISTIC data entity
- Create a one-to-many relationship between the original entity and the new entity
- Use the unique identifier of the original entity as part of the identifier of the new entity

Figure 4.13 illustrates the handling of repeating groups found in the entity PROJ. Let's say that PROJ has the following attributes:

PROJ (Proj ID, name, address, cost, type)

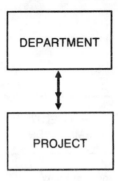

Figure 4.13 Representation of repeating groups

where cost, address and type have several values. We can now create a one-to-many relationship with PROJ and a new entity PROJ-TYPE whose attributes are: proj-type ID, type name, cost, and address. The relationship is now as shown in Figure 4.13.

4.6.6 Translation of Data Models to Logical Schemas

Logical schemas are defined as data models with the underlying structures of particular database management systems superimposed on them. At present the structures for database management systems are:

- Relational
- Hierarchical
- Network

4.7 OVERVIEW OF DBMS STRUCTURES

The hierarchical and network structures have been used for database management systems since the 1960s. The relational structure was introduced in the early 1970s.

In the relational model, the entities and their relationships are represented by two-dimensional tables. Every table represents an entity and is made up of rows and columns. Relationships between entities are represented by common columns containing identical values from a domain or range of possible values. Some of the commercially available relational database management systems are:

VENDOR	DBMS
IBM	SQL/DS, DB2
TYMSHARE	MAGNUM
CINCOM	SUPRA
RELATIONAL TECHNOLOGY	INGRES

The hierarchical model is made up of a hierarchy of entity types involving a parent entity type at the higher level and one or more dependent entity types at the lower levels. The relationship established between a parent and a child entity type is one-to-many. At the same time, for a given parent entity occurrence, there can be many occurrences of the child entity type. Some examples of the hierarchical models are:

VENDOR	DBMS
IBM	IMS
SAS	SYSTEM 2000

In the network model, the concept of parent and child is expanded in that any child can be subordinate to many different parent entities or owners. In addition, an entity can function as an owner and/or member at the same time. There are several commercially available DBMS based on the network model. Some are:

VENDOR	DBMS
CULLINET	IDMS
HONEYWELL	IDS
UNIVAC	DMS 1100

4.8 THE RELATIONAL DATA MODEL

We will use the example discussed in earlier sections of this chapter to illustrate the various relationships between the entities of an organization. The example will also serve to illustrate the various approaches to creating a relational database.

Consider the example shown in Figure 4.14. This data is represented in a two-dimensional table, which is called a relational model of the data. The data represented in the figure is called a "relation." Each column in the table is an "attribute." The values in the column are drawn from a domain or set of all possible values. The rows of the table are called "tuples."

In Figure 4.14, the DEPARTMENT ID, 101, is the value of the key that uniquely identifies the first row of the table. This key is called PRIMARY key.

We can now show how the relationship between DEPT and MANAGER in Figure 4.11 can be represented in the relational model. Let us say that the MANAGER relation is shown (MGR. ID, TITLE, NAME) where MGR. ID is the PRIMARY key of the relation. We can now represent the relationship as shown in Figure 4.15.

In Figure 4.15, column MANAGER ID is called the PRIMARY key and DEPARTMENT ID is called FOREIGN key. We can also have a column or set of columns identifying the rows of the table. This column is called a CANDIDATE key.

The creation of a table to represent the many-to-many relationship can be accomplished as follows:

DEPARTMENT TABLE

DEPARTMENT ID	DEPARTMENT NAME	DEPARTMENT ADDRESS
101	Engineering	Building A
102	Computer Science	Building B
103	Biology	Building C
104	Medical Technology	Building D

Figure 4.14   Representation of data in a relational model

- Create the ASSOCIATION entity as outlined earlier
- Create the ASSOCIATION entity table in a similar manner as the MANAGER table above.

4.8.1 Advantages of a Relational Data Model

1. Simplicity

   The end user is presented with a simple data model. His or her requests are formulated in terms of the information content and do not reflect any complexities due to system-oriented aspects. A relational data model is what the user sees, but it is not necessarily what will be implemented physically.

2. Nonprocedural Requests

   Because there is no positional dependency between the relations, requests do not have to reflect any preferred structure and therefore can be nonprocedural.

3. Data Independence

   This should be one of the major objectives of any DBMS. The relational data model removes the details of storage structure and access strategy from the user interface. The model provides a relatively higher degree of data

MANAGER TABLE

MANAGER ID	DEPARTMENT ID	TITLE	NAME
MG101	101	Chief Scientist	Mr. Brown
MG102	102	Systems Designer	Mr. Charles
MG103	103	Sr. Biologist	Dr. Green
MG104	104	Sr. Technologist	Mr. Cave

Figure 4.15   Representation of a relationship in a relational model

independence than do the next to models to be discussed. To be able to make use of this property of the relational data model, however, the design of the relations must be complete and accurate.

4.8.2 Disadvantages of a Relational Data Model

Although some DBMSs based on the relational data model are commercially available today, the performance of a relational DBMS has not been comparable with the performance of a DBMS based on a hierarchical data model or a network data model. As a result, the major question yet to be answered concerns performance. Can a relational data model be used for a DBMS that can provide a complete set of operational capabilities with required efficiency on a large scale? It appears today that technological improvements in providing faster and more reliable hardware may answer the question positively.

4.9 THE HIERARCHICAL DATA MODEL

The hierarchical data model is based on a treelike structure made up of nodes and branches. A node is a collection of data attributes describing the entity at that point. The highest node of the hierarchical tree structure is called a "root." The nodes at succeeding lower levels are called "children."

A hierarchical tree structure has to satisfy the following conditions:

- A hierarchical data model always starts with a "root" node.
- Every node consists of one or more attributes describing the entity at that node.
- Dependent nodes can follow the succeeding levels. The node in the preceding level becomes the "parent" node of the new "dependent" nodes.
- Every node occurring at level 2 has to be connected with one and only one node occurring at level 1
- A parent node can have one child node as a dependent or many children nodes.
- Every node except, of course, the root has to be accessed through its parent node.
- There can be a number of occurrences of each node at each level.

Consider the two data entities discussed earlier in the chapter DEPT and EMP. The data model for these two entities is shown in Figure 4.16. Dept ID is the root node and NAME and ADDRESS the dependent or "child" nodes. In the hierarchical data model, DEPT ID and all occurrences of NAME and ADDRESS will constitute a database record.

4.9.1 Representation of Relationships

As in the relational data model, the representation of relationships in the hierarchical data model is accomplished by making the unique identifier of one entity in the

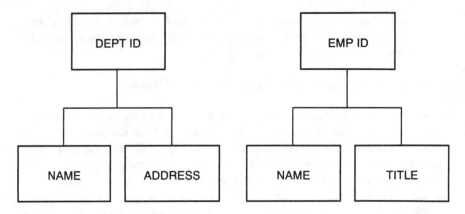

Figure 4.16 Representation of entities in the hierarchical data model

relationship part of the unique identifier of the other entity. The relationship between DEPT and EMP is shown in Figure 4.17.

4.9.2 Storage Operations

In the hierarchical data model, insertion and deletion of nodes operate as follows:

- Insertion — a child node occurrence cannot exist without a parent node occurrence.
- Deletion — when a parent node is deleted, the child occurrence is deleted, too.

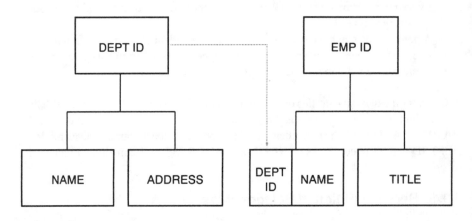

Figure 4.17 Representation of relationships in the hierarchical data model

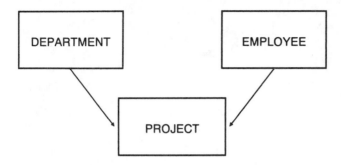

Figure 4.18   Representation of the network data model

4.9.3   Advantages of a Hierarchical Data Model

- The major advantage of the hierarchical data model is the existence of proven database management systems that use the hierarchical data model as the basic structure.
- The relative simplicity and ease of use of the hierarchical data model and the familiarity of data processing users with a hierarchy are major advantages.
- There is a reduction of data dependency.
- Performance prediction is simplified through predefined relationships.

4.9.4   Disadvantages of a Hierarchical Data Model

- The many-to-many relationship can be implemented only in a clumsy way. This often results in redundancy of stored data.
- As a result of strict hierarchical ordering, the operations of insertion and deletion become very complex.
- Deletion of parent results in the deletion of children.
- Any child node is accessible only through its parent node.

4.10   THE NETWORK DATA MODEL

The components of a database with a network data model as the underlying structure are shown in Figure 4.18. The network data model interconnects the entities of an enterprise into a network.

In the figure, the blocks represent the entity types. It should be noted that the entity EMPLOYEE is owned by two entities, DEPARTMENT and PROJECT. It is this fact that distinguishes the network data model from the hierarchical data model, where the dependent entity has one and only one owner.

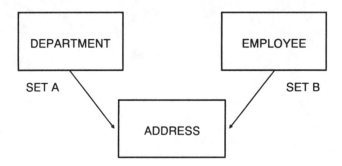

Figure 4.19   Representation of sets in the network data model

In the network data model, a database consists of a number of areas. An area contains records. In turn, a record may consist of fields. A set, which is a grouping of records, may reside in an area or span a number of areas.

A set type is based on the owner record type and the member record type. For example, if the entity DEPARTMENT had an attribute ADDRESS with several values, we may want to create a new entity ADDRESS. In turn, this new entity ADDRESS may have a relationship with the entity EMPLOYEE, hence we will have a set made up of the DEPARTMENT and ADDRESS relationship and another set made up of the EMPLOYEE and ADDRESS relationship.

These two sets are shown in Figure 4.19.

4.10.1   Advantages of the Network Data Model

- The major advantage of the network data model is that there are successful DBMSs that use the network data model as the basic structure.
- The many-to-many relationship, which occurs quite frequently in real life, can be implemented easily.

4.10.2   Disadvantages of the Network Data Model

- The main disadvantage of the network data model is its complexity.
- The application programmer must be familiar with the logical structure of the database.
- The programmer has to know his position in set occurrences when moving through the database.

4.11   CONCLUDING REMARKS

This chapter dealt in great detail with the three major data models: RELATIONAL, HIERARCHICAL, and NETWORK. It was shown how those three form the underlying structure for the three major database management systems bearing their names.

We developed some ideas about normalization, logical database design, and physical database design. These ideas will be further cemented in the next two chapters.

5

MODELING THE SOFTWARE DEVELOPMENT PROCESS

5.1 INTRODUCTORY REMARKS

This chapter provides a brief overview of a typical software development cycle. You might find it helpful to read this material before proceeding to the other chapters on application development and the CASE tool environment. This overview defines many of the concepts and terms that will be referenced in subsequent chapters.

There are many ways to organize a software project. The factors, or characteristics, that influence the organizational approach include such variables as:

- Number of people involved in the project
- Experience and skill level of the participants
- Technical complexity of the product
- Degree of new technology required; e.g., CASE tools
- Total lines of code to be developed
- Number of products involved
- Languages used to write the code
- Availability of both product and tools
- Proximity of the people to one another
- Number of locations and companies involved
- Single or multiple customers

The organization chosen for a five-person project will be significantly different from that for a project of 500 persons. However, regardless of the size of the projects and the organization chosen, there is a sequence of major activities that, if followed, can greatly reduce the problems that often plague a software project. These activities

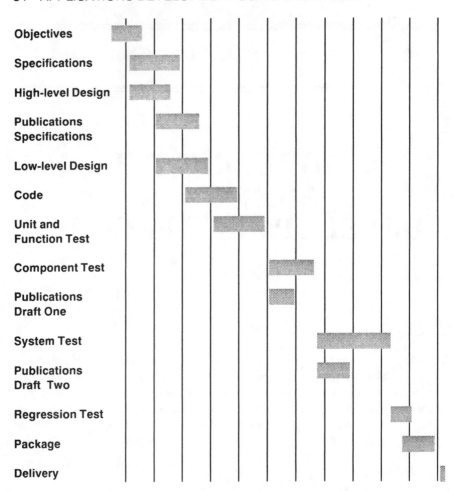

Figure 5.1 The product development cycle

are shown in Figure 5.1. They range from providing product objectives to performing final regression tests just prior to packaging the products and delivering it to a customer. Notice that the relative relationship among the activities is shown in Figure 5.1, yet no durations are specified for any of the activities. The durations depend on the size and characteristics of the project.

The product development cycle model is illustrated in Figure 5.1. This model was chosen because many existing development cycle models can be mapped to it. The model should aid you in relating your personal knowledge and experience to the concepts and ideas expressed throughout this chapter. However, not all project activities are shown in this model. Only the more essential activities that make up the foundation for the model are identified. Several additional activities, however, can be found in the current literature.

The following sections describe the primary activities of the product development cycle shown in Figure 5.1. As with any rapidly growing and changing industry, it is important to define a common terminology in order to impart knowledge and share ideas. The terminology chosen in Figure 5.1 is an attempt to reach, and benefit, the broadest audience possible.

5.2 PRODUCT OBJECTIVES

The product objectives is a document that defines the requirements and operational need that must be satisfied for a new or enhanced product. This document defines a product that will satisfy a marketing opportunity and focuses on the perceived needs of the targeted customer. The project objectives document will also provide the underlying direction to be followed by the project as functional and design trade-offs are made throughout the product development cycle. Direction for both the programming and publications pieces of the product are addressed in the product objectives.

5.3 PRODUCT SPECIFICATIONS

The product specifications describe, in detail, the externals of the product. That is, they describe what the product will look like to the product's user. Every function, command, screen, prompt and so on must be documented here so that all the participants involved in the product development cycle know the product they are to build, test, document, and support. Since the product objectives provide the direction and basis for the new product, writing the product specifications should begin after the objectives have been started. However, the product objectives should be finalized before the product specifications are completed.

Also, the high-level design should be completed before the product specifications are finished. This helps to ensure that any high-level design considerations that could impact the externals of the product are properly reflected in the product specifications.

5.4 HIGH-LEVEL DESIGN

High-level design is the level of design required to understand how the components of the product will work technically with one another and with the surrounding hardware and software environment with which they must operate. This design identifies the components that make up the product, defines the functional mission for each component, and defines the interface across these components and externally to the operating environment. In some development shops, what is defined here as high-level design is called architecture.

The high-level design should begin shortly after the product objectives have been started. However, the high-level design should be reasonably understood before the product objectives are completed. This overlap between the development of the product objectives and the preliminary high-level design will prevent the product objectives from defining a product that could not technically be built in a satisfactory manner. There must be confidence that a high-level design supports the objectives before the product objectives are completed.

5.5   PUBLICATIONS SPECIFICATIONS

The publications specifications may also be called a publications content plan. These plans describe the content and layout of each publication to be delivered with the product. Content plans include the table of contents for each publication and the basic content and structure of each chapter. The writing of the content plans cannot begin until the product specifications activity has been started. Otherwise, there would be too little product externals data available to plan the publications to a chapter level. Similarly, the contents plans cannot be completed until after the product specifications have been completed.

The publications specifications document is especially important for two reasons. Both reasons center around the importance of providing information to the user in an expedient, easy-to-use, and understandable fashion. First, most products require the user to reference the publications that accompany the product. Without a good set of publications, the product will have far less chance for success.

The second reason for the importance of the publications specifications is in support of an industry direction. This direction is to provide publications-related information online for the product's users and to make the use of products users and to make the use of products more intuitive. Online information directly from the computer workstations rather than through documents and intuitive man-machine interfaces both require careful, advanced planning. The publications specifications document is a vehicle to help define this direction early in the product development cycle.

5.6   TEST PLANS

Test plans are documents that describe the who, what, when, where, and how for a designated test. A test plan is written for each test activity, such as a unit test, function test, component test, and system test. Test plans cannot be started until after the product specifications have been started. Also, the test plans cannot be finished until after the product specifications have been completed. Otherwise, the test plans would be incomplete, since the externals of the product would not yet be fully known and documented.

5.7 LOW-LEVEL DESIGN

Low-level design actually represents two levels of design. The first level is the design required to understand how modules within each component will work technically with one another. A component is typically made up of one or more modules. This design identifies the modules that make up each component, the functional mission for each module, and the interface across these modules. In some development shops, this level of design is called high-level design, not to be confused with the same term introduced earlier in this chapter.

The next level of design deals with the internal design of each module of a component. This design identifies each programming decision path and may be documented by using a design language, graphic flows, and so on, or simply by writing English narratives. There is no requirement to complete all high-level design before low-level design can be started. Notice from Figure 5.1 that some overlap of low-level design activity and high-level design is typical. Once the high-level design has been completed for a component or a major portion of a component, the low-level design can begin on the modules for that portion.

5.8 CODE

Coding is the act of writing instructions that are immediately computer recognizable or can be assembled or compiled to form computer recognizable instructions. Coding can begin on those areas of components that have already been designed to a low level. Consequently, as shown in Figure 5.1, a large overlap can occur within a project between the coding activity and the low-level design activity.

5.9 UNIT AND FUNCTION TEST

The unit test is the first time that the code is executed. Unit testing is usually performed by the same person who designed and coded the module to be tested. The unit test primarily refers to the isolated testing of each logic flowpath of code within each module. The function test is the testing of each of the product's functions through one or more modules. In both cases, artificial testing environments may be necessary since other modules of the product may not be sufficiently far enough along in their development to be included in the testing.

Since there is no requirement to finish all coding before unit testing can begin, an overlap is shown (Figure 5.1) between the coding activity and the unit and function test activity. That is, once a module has been coded, it can begin to be unit tested. Once all the modules required to test a function have been unit tested, they can begin to be function tested. The relative time period for unit and function testing shown in

Figure 5.1 represents the period when testing occurs. The test cases to be used must, of course, be defined and written before this test period begins, or at least before those test cases are required.

5.10   COMPONENT TEST

The component test is the first test of a product in which all or some of the components are tested together. Typically, no artificial testing environment is required. This independent, or formal, test is best performed by people other than those who developed the code.

When a product is tested by an independent test group, the objectivity of the test increases. All the product's externals should be tested. The tests are developed primarily by studying the product specifications. Occasionally, the design documentation is also studied to gain more insight into areas to be tested. The component test is typically the first time that all of the product's modules are placed under change control. This term refers to a method designed to restrict further changes to a module. Change control is managed by a group that did not develop the code.

Figure 5.1 shows that component testing does not begin until all of the unit and function tests have been completed successfully. Some project managers may choose to integrate unit- or function-tested code into the component test in preplanned drops, or stages. The relative time period for component testing shown in Figure 5.1 represents the period when testing occurs. All the test cases to be exercised during component testing should be defined and written prior to the start of the component test, or at least before those test cases are required to be exercised.

5.11   PUBLICATIONS DRAFT ONE

Publications draft one is the first draft of the product's publications that is available for review by groups within the project. The product's publications are primarily the documentation that the user will receive with the product and are also called user documentation. However, the product's publications can also include technical manuals that explain how to solve problems discovered by the user. The publications draft one should be available at, or near, the start of component testing — both for review by the project's personnel and for use by the testing organization. It should be essentially complete and accurate. Comments should be returned to the writers by the midpoint of the component test. This will help ensure that updates are available for the final draft at the start of system testing. The duration shown in Figure 5.1 covers only the period when the first draft can begin once the publication specifications have been completed.

5.12   SYSTEM TEST

The system test is an independent, or formal, test performed by programmers who did not develop the code. It is also performed by test subjects who represent typical users for the product. A system test generally tests the major functions of the product and some error situations. This testing is performed strictly by exercising the externals defined at a user level in the product specifications. Functions and interfaces internal to the product are not directly tested. These internals are only directly tested by exercising the externally documented functions.

During system testing, the product is also tested in a total systems environment with other software and hardware product combinations that are supported by the product. For example, if the product being developed is an application that must run on several different display screens and printers, then it is advisable to test the new product with all of the stated hardware. Sometimes, however, a reasonable subset may be acceptable. This applies similarly to software products. That is, if the new product must also operate in harmony with other applications, or even with different release levels of an operating system, then these product combinations would also be tested during the system test.

System testing does not begin until the component test has been completed. The product is expected to be approaching a customer-delivery quality level when this test begins. However, some project managers may choose to integrate component-tested code into the system test in preplanned drops, or stages. The relative time for system testing shown in Figure 5.1 represents the period when testing occurs. All the test cases to be exercised during system testing should be defined and written prior to the start of the system test, or at least before those test cases are required for testing.

5.13   PUBLICATIONS DRAFT TWO

Publications draft two is the second draft of the publications. As with the first draft, the duration shown in Figure 5.1 covers only the period when the draft is distributed for review. The activities associated with the second draft actually begin immediately after the comments are available from reviewers of the first draft, and end when the final publications are ready for the final print. For most products, the second draft will be the final draft that is distributed for review. It should be available at the beginning of the system test — both for review and for use in the final testing of the product. Comments should be returned to the writers by the midpoint of system testing so that final changes can be made before the publications are printed. The final print of the publications should not be initiated, however, until all product testing has been completed. If product testing continues, a strong possibility exists that a problem will surface, requiring a change to the publications as part of the problem resolution.

5.14 REGRESSION TEST

The regression test is the final test of the product. This test typically is comprised of a carefully selected set of test cases that are run against the final level of code and supported hardware. These test cases are run as final verification that the product's code is indeed functioning as it should. Regression testing should not begin until the system test has been completed. The test cases for regression testing typically consist of selected cases from both the component and the systems test. If a problem is found during regression testing, the problem is corrected and, with few exceptions, the entire set of regression test cases are rerun. Restarting the regression test from the beginning provides verification that the problem did indeed get fixed and that the fix did not cause a new problem.

5.15 PACKAGE

Packaging involves collecting the pieces of the product for delivery to a customer. Once all testing and publications changes have been completed, the code and publications are ready to be packaged in their final form. The product's programs are placed on media, and the product's publications are formally printed. Then the pieces are packaged in their final wrap and readied for delivery.

5.16 DELIVERY

Delivery is the point at which the packaged product is ready for distribution to the customer. The customer may be the product's user, a distributor, or a third party that will repackage the product in some fashion for eventual sale.

Part II

APPLICATIONS DEVELOPMENT

6

THE APPLICATION
DEVELOPMENT PROCESS

6.1 INTRODUCTION

This chapter discusses the Application Development Process (AD/Cycle) with specific emphasis being placed on the traditional life cycle of application development and maintenance, the five general phases, and the activities AD/Cycle tools intend to support related to those phases.

The basic approach to application development is based on the important relationship between an enterprise's business strategy and requirements and the applications that support then. The approach also includes the concept of interactive application development. Figure 6.1 illustrates these concepts.

This approach will support the following activities:

- Modeling the enterprise to reflect the enterprise strategy and its data processing requirements. This activity is important in building a data processing strategy that is aligned with the enterprise's goals.
- Validating the enterprise model to ensure the correctness of the requirements.
- Analyzing the requirements and designing the applications to meet those requirements based on information in the enterprise model.
- Prototyping the design information to revalidate the requirements and to ensure the quality and usability of the resulting applications.
- Producing the applications from the design information with the technology that best meets the application and business needs.
- Maintaining the application based on business requirements or design changes, and reflecting those changes in the enterprise and design information maintained in the AD/Cycle.

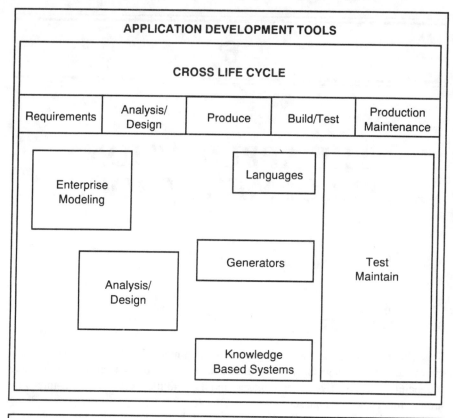

Figure 6.1   AD/Cycle framework

6.2 ENTERPRISE MODELING

Enterprises are dynamic. Their processes and information requirements are ever-changing. As assistance to you in defining accurate, up-to-date application requirements that reflect this changing environment, AD/Cycle will support an enterprise model in its repository and tools for keeping it current. These tools also include facilities for validating and prototyping the information in the enterprise model.

From an application development perspective, the motivation behind modeling all or selected portions of an enterprise is this: The data processing organization needs to understand the enterprise strategy, processes, and data flows, and where these are related, to develop accurate requirements for integrated application systems and the databases that support them.

Many activities take place before you make a decision to support a business process with an application system and databases. Important aspects of selecting a process for data processing support include economic justification, the determination of priorities, and the allocation of resources.

Assuming you have defined an enterprise strategy and a data processing strategy to support it, the next task is to perform an enterprise or business modeling study. In general, business modeling involves analyzing the processes that the business performs; the information that these processes use; and the business rules, policies, and practices that control these processes.

Most analysis use a top-down, structured approach in refining enterprise models. They start with the overall processes and high-level data each process uses, such as payroll processing with time cards coming in and checks going out. Then they interview business experts and end users to refine these high-level descriptions to finer and finer detail, until the processes, data views, and individual data elements are understood and documented.

AD/Cycle enterprise modeling tools will allow the analyst, the business expert, and the application user to perform this refinement process together, thus reducing the possibility of error or misunderstanding. The resulting information will be stored in AD/Cycle's repository.

When refinement is complete for a business process and its data requirements, tools, such as CASE tools, will provide validation of the model by prototyping the process. This will assist in identifying and resolving any misunderstanding and in identifying requirements that have changed since the analysis began.

6.3 ANALYZING AND DESIGNING THE APPLICATION

Using the requirements defined during the enterprise modeling activities, AD/Cycle analysis and design tools will assist in developing the application design specification that supports these requirements.

Because there are many accepted methods for designing applications, AD/Cycle will support the integration of CASE tools that are consistent with today's software engineering and information engineering principles. These tools will support such techniques as decomposition diagrams, data-flow diagrams, E-R diagrams, and data structure diagrams.

There are often two kinds of design activities: functional design and data design. This is especially true when the application systems being designed use integrated databases.

Functional design activities take the business requirements and analyze them to determine the application functions necessary to satisfy the requirements, including the business rules, policies, and practices that apply. The initial screens and reports required by these application functions are also defined.

In data design, the data views for all the application functions are gathered together and analyzed to group common data elements. A logical data model for the application system is defined, using the groups of data elements to identify the basic database or file records needed to support the application.

CASE tools that support the design activities will provide prototyping of the application system before going to formal implementation. Prototyping accomplishes two things: It revalidates the user's requirements and validates as much of the design as is prototyped. Prototyping can be as basic as displaying panels and sample reports to the end user, or as sophisticated as running a sample application using detailed design specification fed to an application generator.

6.4 PRODUCING THE APPLICATION

To facilitate application production, AD/Cycle and some CASE tools will support traditional third-generation languages such as COBOL, application generators, and emerging technologies for knowledge-based applications.

6.4.1 Languages

The programming languages such as COBOL, FORTRAN, PL/1, and procedure languages form the base for AD/Cycle and CASE tool's support. Over time, these language products plan to provide facilities to integrate with front-end tools, language-sensitive editors, and interactive debugging aids.

6.4.2 Application Generators

Support for application generators is an integral part of AD/Cycle and CASE tools. Generators typically provide greater productivity for application development because they require less detailed specifications than procedural languages, allowing less skilled programmers to produce quality applications.

6.4.3 Knowledge-Based Systems

Knowledge-based application-enabling products are fast becoming an integral part of today's data processing strategy. Over time, these products will be integrated into the AD/Cycle framework, using CASE tools and services to support the development of applications. These applications will be able to mix knowledge-based and high-level language or generator components. Knowledge-based system application components will be stored in the data dictionary (repository) and shared throughout the life cycle.

Along with the development of end-user applications, knowledge-based systems also have the potential of creating application development tools, which could have a significant impact on the development process, and on the productivity and quality of application development.

In summary, AD/Cycle and CASE tools will assist program developers in the following ways:

- The framework will employ workstation-based editors with language-sensitive capability.
- Program development tools will move from the HOST environment to a cooperative workstation environment, and be tightly coupled with editors and debugging tools that support unit testing from the workstation.
- Data structure definitions will be generated from data structure design information in the repository for inclusion into source programs and generator specifications.
- Database and file definitions needed in the operational environment will be generated from design information in the repository.
- Panel specification and generation tools will be provided to assist in the creation of interactive applications.
- Information about the application components created by developers will be stored in the repository. This information will aid in impact analysis and reuse activities.

6.5 TESTING, BUILDING, AND MAINTAINING APPLICATIONS

Application testing is often separated into two activities. If the application system is large, programmers are usually responsible for testing the major logic paths of their programs. They may write code to simulate inputs and capture outputs. Depending on the completeness of their set of modules, they may run in a test execution environment or run in a simulated environment. This is commonly referred to as unit test. CASE tools will support unit test from workstations whenever possible.

As application units are combined for component and final system test, AD/Cycle tools will assist in the development of test cases, capture test case information, and report on the results of testing.

Test tools for interactive applications will capture the activity of test sessions, allowing the same tests to be rerun for retesting of new applications and regression testing following maintenance activities. CASE tools will also provide test coverage measurement and analysis, including an animated display of test execution.

6.5.1 Building the Application

Most applications are composed of many components. Library systems have evolved to support the management of these application components. Many organizations recompile or regenerate all the application programs and other application components, using a library management system to place them into production libraries with controlled access.

AD/Cycle will include services that allow a library administrator to define library organizations and to establish levels of user authorization to these libraries. Other services will be provided to allow authorized users to request a component, such as the source code of a program, and get the latest version, to move components from one level of process status to another, such as from test to production, and to build a new version of an application system by compiling and link editing only those components that have changed.

6.5.2 Maintenance

Maintenance of applications developed by CASE tools and within the AD/Cycle framework is greatly simplified. These tools support maintenance by allowing designers and developers to use the information in the repository to perform impact analysis, and then use the same tools used for a new application to apply changes to existing application components, typically creating new version or modification levels.

Maintenance of existing applications will be supported at source code level by most CASE tools. If you use a data dictionary, facilities are provided to assist you in moving dictionary information, thus enhancing your control over the maintenance of both applications and their databases.

Several CASE tools now support restructuring and reverse engineering of some existing application components, allowing design-level information about them to be captured. This greatly enhances the maintenance of older applications.

6.6 CROSS LIFE CYCLE ACTIVITIES

Several CASE tools support cross life cycle activities across many or all of the life cycle phases. As shown in Figure 6.2, these activities include process management, project management, impact analysis, documentation, and reuse.

6.6.1 Process Management

AD/Cycle provides two ways to manage the application development process: user-initiated and process model-initiated. The user-initiated method allows you to assign work items to developers, that is, you define the application components on which developers can work but leave the sequence of activities to the developer.

The process model–initiated approach enables you to define a process model that describes the components, the work activities related to those components, and the sequence for performing those activities for a specified project. The process model then guides developers through the application development methodology according to the activities defined in the model. This model provides a greater degree of

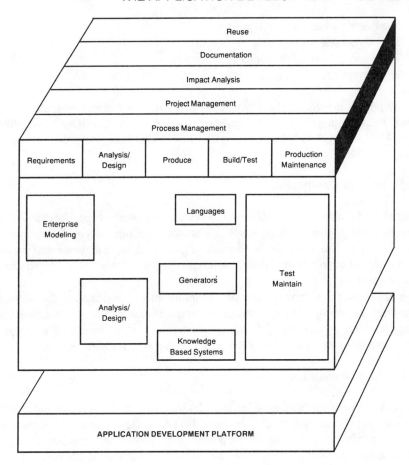

Figure 6.2   AD/Cycle cross life cycle tools

consistency in the development process and can enhance the overall quality of application systems.

6.6.2 Project Management

Most organizations maintain information about the status of their application development projects. This information includes:

- The people assigned to a project
- The work items for which they are responsible

- The overall schedule for the project
- The current status of the project schedule
- The projected cost of the project
- The current cost of the project

Many project management systems, most of them workstation-based, are tied to resource tracking information and spreadsheet programs. Many CASE tools, including CA-PLANMACS, CA-ESTIMACS, and EXCELERATOR, support project management.

6.6.3   Impact Analysis

Impact analysis information enables you to evaluate the effect of specific changes to the components of your application systems before the changes occur. For example, if you wanted to change the size or format of a given data element, you could use an impact analysis tool to help you identify which panels and code units would be affected by that change.

The application development component information maintained in CASE tool repositories, including relationships among these components, provides a base for creating impact analysis tools. These tools have the potential for dramatically improving your change-management capability and reducing your maintenance costs.

6.6.4   Documentation

The development of applications often includes design, specification, and procedure documentation. CASE tools provide facilities that enable the production of documentation using existing application development information where appropriate. This support includes the ability to create documents that can be produced in hardcopy form or displayed at the workstation.

6.6.5   Reuse and Reengineering

There are significant productivity gains inherent in the reuse of application components. A long-term goal of CASE tools is to support an inventory of reusable application components, using information maintained in the data dictionary or repository. This reuse capability will eventually guide developers in creating applications from this inventory and other components created specifically for the application.

A critical aspect of establishing this inventory of reusable components will be the design and development of modular, component-oriented applications.

6.7   APPLICATION DEVELOPMENT PLATFORM

The application development platform is the integrating framework for CASE tools. The platform should provide common services for tools and tool users, and facilities and guidelines for the integration of application development tools. The application development platform will provide the following services and specifications:

- User interface services and specifications
- Workstation services
- Data dictionary (repository) services
- Information model specifications
- Tool services

6.7.1 User Interface

Most CASE tools, including AD/Cycle workstation-based tools, will conform to IBM's SAA Common User Access (CUA). This means that users will access and use these tools across the life cycle through the same graphic-oriented interface.

Application development platform services that provide user access to tool selection, profile establishment, library administration, and other platform services will also adhere to CUA.

6.7.2 Workstation Services

Several CASE tools are now based on a cooperative processing approach in which a PS/2 workstation, operating under OS/2, serves as the primary window into the environment. This cooperative approach combines the advantages of a highly interactive graphical workstation with the multi-user support, shared resources, and capacity of a host system. This approach is essential to the support of multiple, concurrent application development activities at the user's workstation.

Some application development tools run at the PS/2, others operate at the host, and still others run cooperatively between the two. In general, CASE tools associated with the front end of the life cycle are workstation-based to take advantage of the PS/2's powerful graphics capability for modeling and diagramming. As an application progresses through the development process to the production environment, development activities become more host-based to support application system testing and the building and distribution of the application system to the production environment.

6.7.3 Data Dictionary Services

The major weakness of CASE tools was the lack of adequate data dictionary services. However, with the announcement of the IBM Repository and the ANSI X3/H4 IRDS dictionary, this weakness is steadily being overcome.

A key concept of CASE tools and the AD/Cycle framework is the repository, a storage facility for information about application development and other business and data processing activities. The repository is now the CASE tool information base — the single point of control for the administration, definition, storage, and retrieval of all application development information. It is also the primary vehicle for the sharing of application development information among tools.

There are typically two kinds of information involved with developing applications information: information about application development activities and components, and the components themselves. For example, analyzing the impact of changing the size of a data element requires information about what panels, databases, and programs use that data element, whereas modifying a program or panel to apply that change requires access to the component source statements.

The data dictionary provides facilities for defining, controlling, and manipulating data described in an entity-relationship (E-R) format, and for the specification and enforcement of constraints related to the use of that data.

The repository also provides services for controlled access to application development objects. In this age of object-oriented database design, the data dictionary provides information about objects — collections of information and the operations associated with these objects.

6.7.4   The Entity-Relationship Concept

The structure of information in the repository is based on an entity-relationship (E-R) modeling technique. This technique provides for the definition of entities, the relationships among them, and constraints on the information described by these entities and relationships.

The E-R modeling technique is well suited for modeling business processes and business data and information about application design and implementation components, such as data structures, panels, databases and programs, and their relationships. It allows very discrete descriptions of information to be related to, and thus shared with, other information. For example, a single data element description can be related to the descriptions of the files and panels that contain and display the data elements.

The entity-relationship concept was discussed in some detail in Chapter 4.

6.7.5   The Object-Oriented Concept

Objects permit tools and tool users to access both information stored in the repository and information contained in other data stores. Objects provide a high-level view of data independent of its storage format. They also provide a high-level view of operations on the data independent of the implementation of these operations.

Objects are conceptually divided into two parts:

- Object data
- Methods (functions)

Object data are collections of information such as source code files, the description of business process, or a relational table design construct. Object data may be stored in the repository, conforming to the E-R model, or in some other file or database in the CASE tool or AD/Cycle environment.

Methods are reusable functions that can be performed against object data. Examples of methods include traditional library functions and operations, such as edit, copy, delete, and store. Methods use repository services to manipulate object data stored in E-R format and use other access techniques to manipulate object data in other forms.

Objects are classified according to the form and structure of their object data, and the methods that can operate on that data. A set of objects that uses the same methods is called an object type.

The object concept provides the base for the AD/Cycle information model and for many of the application development platform tool services. Objects provide the means for representing both the information the AD/Cycle tools share and the functions that tools can perform against that information.

Object services reduce the complexity of tool logic by providing common operations that can be used by many CASE tools.

6.8 INFORMATION MODEL

CASE tools support an architected information interface between the tools and the application development information managed by the data dictionary. This information interface is called the application development (AD) information model. It consists of both the object and E-R representation of application development data.

By using the object services of the repository, the application development information model will provide a high-level view of application development-related information stored in AD/Cycle environment. Much of this information will be stored in the repository, as described by its E-R model. Some information, such as program source code, object code, and large documents, may be stored in other data stores. No matter where the information physically resides, the way in which it will be presented to a tool will be consistent with its description in the AD information model.

By using the E-R services of the repository, the AD information model will provide a detailed view of application development-related information stored in the repository. Using this view, CASE tools and methods can directly process information in its E-R format.

The AD information model will describe application development objects, the methods that operate against these objects, the format and structure of the information returned to a tool that uses these methods, and the underlying E-R format of information in the data dictionary.

6.9 APPLICATION DEVELOPMENT PLATFORM TOOL SERVICES

A key aspect of the application development platform will be the services it provides for application development tools. Methods designed to support the objects described by the AD information model will provide many of these services.

Some methods will be general to most objects, performing functions such as copying, deleting, or moving object data to and from the workstation, or retrieving object data from or storing it into the repository. Some will allow tools to easily perform administrative functions such as getting user profile information, obtaining and replacing descriptive information about objects for review or modification by the tool user, or creating relationships between objects.

Other methods may be specific to only certain types of objects, such as adding a new business process description to a business model or validating that a general data structure description contains sufficient information to generate equivalent language source statements for the data structure.

Another set of application development platform tool services will provide the library management services mentioned earlier. The application development platform will also provide facilities that assist with the invocation of tools.

6.10   ESTABLISHING A DEVELOPMENT METHODOLOGY

It is the consensus of many CASE tool vendors that before an enterprise considers purchasing a tool, it should have established a development methodology.

The AD/Cycle concept of an open framework is specifically intended to allow you to select participating tools that match your development methodologies, particularly in the early part of the development cycle. You will be able to use AD/Cycle most effectively if you adopt a formal application development approach and train your development staff accordingly.

Assessing the following areas will help you decide on a methodology best suited to your development needs and resources:

- On a project-by-project basis, develop a high-level outline of the activities used to create some of your more recent applications. Identify the projects that were more successful in terms of time, cost, effective communications, and resulting application design and implementation.
- Pay particular attention to the front end of the development cycle. Business modeling, requirements gathering and analysis, and high-level application data design are where many current application development approaches are less rigorous, and where many errors are introduced.
- If you use manual modeling and design techniques, note the types of design documentation involved: data-flow diagrams, entity-relationship diagrams, and structure charts. You will probably find common elements among the best projects. Use these elements as the basis for your methodology, but be flexible enough to change as new methodology, tools, or developer skills warrant a change. Establishing a methodology for application development is not a trivial task, but once established it can have a significant and positive effect on

application development productivity, application quality, and communication among developers, analysts, and end users.

6.11   MANAGING THE INFORMATION RESOURCE

In order to provide centralized sharing and management of application development information, there must be a means of acquiring and maintaining information about information: who creates the information, who owns it, who uses it, who stores it, and what it looks like.

The task of performing these activities is often called data administration or information resource management. Regardless of its name or the organization responsible for it, the function is extremely important to application development and to the enterprise as a whole. Once you have this information and the facilities to store it, maintain it, query it, and create reports from it, you are starting to manage the information resource. Although we typically think of this resource in terms of business data or information, the concept applies equally to application development–related information. Application development is a business process, much like manufacturing or distribution.

If the concept of a single source of information is to become a reality, naming conventions must be established for business entities, business data panels, databases, data structures, and many other objects related to application development.

Standards and conventions should be established for controlling multiple versions of application components and authorizing access to them.

The rules and constraints associated with the information elements of the business must be understood, documented, and maintained as business conditions cause them to change.

The original source and ownership of the elements of business information should be determined and described, as well as the attributes of those elements: size, format, edit rules, primary storage location, and definition.

6.12   INVENTORY OF APPLICATION DEVELOPMENT ASSETS

Application development information exists in many forms: written documentation, libraries, dictionaries, data flow diagrams, and others. An inventory of such information is invaluable, not only for locating information that may be eventually moved to the data dictionary, but also to assist you in change management and component reuse activities.

The time spent in taking an inventory is worth the effort. Early preparation for CASE tools should include identifying as much of this application development–related information as possible. The activities of a data administration group and business modeling task force will uncover a lot of this information. You should plan to capture this information as it is identified.

Simple entity-relationship diagrams can be constructed relating the major components of each application system to each other. A short description of each component can be included identifying the major functions, data elements used, and current versions of the components.

During inventory, take note of design, specification, and procedure documents, especially data flow charts, and other documents that no one can ever seem to find when they are needed.

Once the basic inventory is completed, establish a procedure for keeping it up to date. You may want to store this information in a dictionary or repository.

6.13 SUMMARY

This chapter outlines an application development (AD) life cycle and the CASE tools that are used by the enterprise to develop systems in compliance with each phase of the life cycle.

The chapter emphasizes the IBM AD/Cycle, an IBM application development environment for commercial systems. Several CASE tool vendors are now making their product compliant, not only with AD/Cycle, but also with Systems Application Architecture (SAA).

The CASE tool industry is attempting to provide solutions and not products. The era of cooperative processing and platform-to-platform compatibility is now fully entrenched.

7

THE CASE TOOL
ENVIRONMENT

7.1 SOME INTRODUCTORY REMARKS

Computer-aided software engineering (CASE) has been promoted as the panacea for curing an organization's backlog problems in meeting development schedules, coordinating design efforts, and maintaining its systems. It has also been touted as the tool to increase programmer and systems designer productivity as much as 2- to 10-fold.

This chapter will introduce CASE tools as a design and development aid. It will discuss some selection criteria for deciding on the tool that will best suit a particular environment. Finally, it will list some vendors of CASE tools and the contacts within each vendor.

7.2 SEVERAL DEFINITIONS OF CASE

CASE, although now widely accepted as an acronym, does not yet have a single, widely accepted definition. Perhaps a more appropriate acronym would be CASD (computer-aided systems development), which could be defined as "computers applied to aid in any aspect of systems development."

Because CASE can encompass so many aspects of systems development, the question "When is CASE the right choice?" must be addressed separately for each of three types of CASE tools:

1. Programmer/Project Productivity Tools — provide support for designers and programmers of software, but only at the back end of the systems development life cycle. These may include tools for natural language programming, project management, and documentation.
2. Systems Development Methodology Tools — most systems development methodologies are collections of techniques, combined in structures made to minimize redundant effort and maximize coordination between tasks. These methodology tools provide support for and enforce a systems development methodology at any or all stages of the life cycle. They may include any of the systems development support tools as appropriate for the methodology. In addition, they enforce methodology rules and thus provide systems development expertise to the users.
3. Systems Development Support Tools — provide support for techniques and tasks of systems development at any or all stages of the life cycle, but do not necessarily enforce a systems development methodology. These may include diagramming tools, data dictionaries and analysis tools, or any of the productivity tools.

7.3 CATEGORIES OF CASE TOOLS

An individual CASE tool automates one small, focused step in the life-cycle process. Individual tools fall into these general categories:

- Diagramming tools for pictorially representing system specifications.
- Screen and report painters for creating system specifications and for simple prototyping.
- Dictionaries, information management systems, and facilities to store, report, and query technical and project-management system information.
- Specification — checking tools to detect incomplete, syntactically incorrect, and inconsistent system specifications.
- Code generators to be able to generate executable code from pictorial system specifications.
- Documentation generators to produce technical and user documentation required by structured methodologies.

CASE "toolkits" provide integrated tools for developers seeking to automate only one phase of the life cycle process, while "workbenches" provide integrated tools for automating the entire development process. "Frameworks" integrate CASE tools and/or link them with non-CASE software development tools, as "methodology companions" support a particular structured methodology and automatically guide developers through the development steps.

7.3.1   Well-equipped Toolkits

Toolkits can focus on the design of real-time, information, or project management systems. They also can be classified by the hardware and operating system on which they run; by the ease with which they can be integrated into a family of compatible CASE tools; by their architecture − open, so that it can be used with products from other vendors, or closed, by the structured methodology or methodologies they support − and by development languages, such as, ADA, COBOL, FORTRAN, C, and PL/1.

Many CASE toolkits run on an IBM PC or are compatible under DOS. Some run on the Apple Macintosh, Wang PC, or Texas Instruments Professional PC. Others run only on 32-bit workstations, such as Sun, Apollo, or Digital Equipment Corporation (DEC) Vax Station II; on an IBM or Data General mainframe, or across the DEC Vax family. Many open-architecture products are not limited to one specific hardware, operating system, target programming language, or structured methodology.

The analysis toolkit has four basic components: structured diagramming tools, prototyping tools, a repository, and a specification checker.

7.3.2   Structured Diagramming Tools

Structured diagramming tools are computerized tools for drawing, manipulating, and storing structured diagrams such as data-flow and entity-relationship diagrams, which are required documentation for various structured methodologies.

Diagramming tools often reside on PCs or workstations that support graphics manipulation; at the minimum, they draw, update, and store data-flow and entity-relationship diagrams.

7.3.3   Prototyping Tools

Prototyping tools help determine system requirements and predict performance beforehand. Essential to prototyping are user-interface painters − screen painters, report painters, and menu builders − that prototype the user interface to give users an advance view of how the system will look and to identify and correct problem areas. Screen dialog and navigation with data entry and edits can be simulated with or without compiles; source code for record, file, screen, and report description can be generated automatically.

Also essential are executable specification languages. These are the most sophisticated prototyping tools. They involve specifying system requirements and executing specifications iteratively to refine, correct, and ensure completeness of the system to meet user requirements.

7.3.4   The CASE Repository

The CASE repository is a design dictionary for storing and organizing all software system data, diagrams, and documentation related to planning, analysis, design, implementation, and project management. Information entered once can be maintained and made available to whoever needs it.

The repository stores more types of systems information, relationships among various information components, and rules for using or processing components than a standard data dictionary used in data management systems. The repository usually has many reporting capabilities that gauge the impact of proposed changes on the system, identify redundant or unneeded data elements, and resolve discrepancies. System diagrams and dictionary, and some CASE tools provide automated means of verifying entities for completeness and correctness.

7.3.5   Data Design Toolkits

These support the logical and physical design of databases and files: logical data modeling, automatic conversion of data models to third-normal form, automatic generation of database schemes for particular database management systems, and automatic generation of program-code level file descriptioins.

7.3.6   Programming Toolkits

Supported tools include hierarchical tree-structured diagramming tools with a syntax and consistency checker; procedural logic diagrammer and on-line editor; CASE repository with information manager; code generation; test data generator; file comparer; and performance monitor.

A code-generating tool is especially useful because it automatically produces codes from a program design. CASE code generators can generate compiled, structured codes in languages such as COBOL, PL/1, FORTRAN, C, or ADA, manage program specification and design information, generate documentation, and support prototyping.

7.3.7   Maintenance Toolkits

The most useful maintenance tools include documentation analyzers — to read source code from existing systems and produce documentation, program analyzers, to evaluate execution paths and performance, reverse engineering — to identify the model upon which a system is based, and restructures — to enforce structured programming and documentation standards.

7.3.8   Project Management Toolkits

Automated project management tools can help project managers better track, control, and report on software projects, thus improving software development and maintenance. To be most effective, these tools should be able to access the CASE repository in the toolkit or workbench. Besides storing technical system information, the repository should be the central location for current status, estimation, budget and quality-assurance information.

Some of these toolkits include tools for word processing; interfacing to electronic mail; spreadsheets; project-management forms; configuration management for change, version, and access control; project plans; a calendar and task assignment system; and estimation of time tables and scheduling.

7.4   DEMONSTRATED USE OF CASE TOOLS IN THE SDLC

CASE tools have demonstrated their usefulness in all three components of the CASE environment: planning, systems design, and systems development.

7.4.1   CASE in the Planning Environment

CASE tools can be used to gather information about user problems and requirements, setting goals and criteria, and generating alternative solutions.

They assist in budget determinations, project duration and scheduling, manpower planning and scheduling, cost and time estimates, and project control.

7.4.2   CASE in the Systems Design Environment

CASE tools detail the design for a selected solution, including diagrams relating all programs, subroutines, and data flow. They can generate data modeling nad relationship diagrams and functional models.

The functional modeling and data modeling processes have tools to construct the appropriate types of design diagrams such as data-flow diagrams, program structure charts, and entity-relationship diagrams.

More detailed tables and text contain the necessary concept descriptions, testable requirements, and data element definitions.

7.4.3   CASE in the Systems Development Environment

CASE tools develop a construct of database information about the physical database scheme and the requirements for building, testing, and checking databases. They produce language codes from definitions of data and processes stored in the data dictionary.

7.4.4   Samples of Deliverables from CASE Tools

The next several pages illustrate the deliverables from the three components of the CASE environment.

The deliverables illustrated below were produced from the following sample problem (see Figures 7.1 and 7.2).

Sample Problem: Our sample problem concerns a video rental store with the following conditions:

- Customer rents tapes and makes rental payments
- Customer returns tapes and may pay late charge of $1 per day
- Time to notify overdue borrowers
- Store submits new tape
- Store submits rate changes in some movie titles
- Customer changes address
- Customer requests particular movie title

Other Details: The standard time period for a rental is two days after the borrowed tape is rented. If the customer fails to return the tape in time, then it is time to send a tape overdue notice to the customer address with the title and copy number and past due return date.

A tape is a cassette of videotapes with a prerecorded movie that can be rented. Each tape has a movie title and copy number. All copies of a single movie have the same rental rate. Not all movies have the same rental rate.

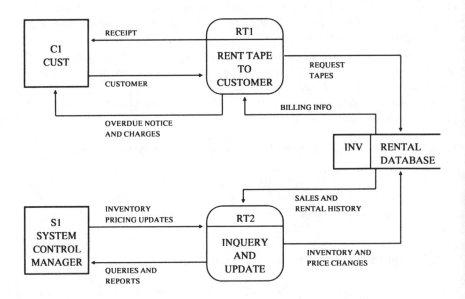

Figure 7.1 Excelerator produced data-flow diagram

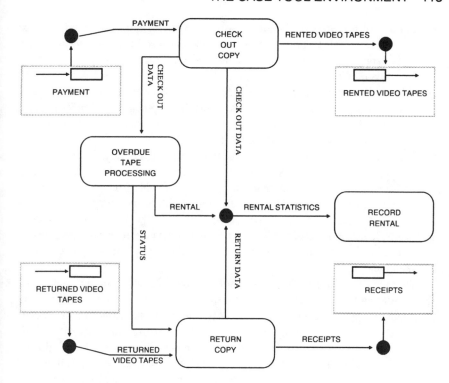

Figure 7.2   Knowledgeable Produced Data-Flow Diagram

A rental is the lending of a tape to a person in exchange for cash. A rental has a check-out date, a return date, and a rental charge. If a tape is late, there is a standard $1-per-day late charge paid upon return. A customer can rent more than one tape at a time.

A tape can be rented, on the shelf waiting to be rented, or overdue. This video store has no membership plan and doesn't take American Express. All transactions are cash on the spot, and no deposits are accepted.

7.5   SELECTION CRITERIA FOR CASE TOOLS

The ever-growing array of CASE tools makes it very difficult to decide which tool is best suited for a particular environment. This section attempts to ease that uncertainty by setting down a list of questions for which the buyer should seek to get answers before buying a tool.

- Is the tool a DBMS or dictionary software system? Dictionary and database management systems provide greater integration capabilities. As a result, CASE tools with these underlying structures have a greater capacity for sharing specifications across functions.
- What is the future direction and functionality of the tools? When evaluating CASE tools, remember that CASE systems development is still in its infancy, so don't reject a tool with valuable attributes just because it currently does not have the full capabilities that you want.
- Does the tool's manufacturer have an open architecture philosophy? A manufacturer's willingness to share file formats with all viable, noncompeting CASE manufacturers means that you can move smoothly from planning through to systems development because you will be able to integrate specifications across CASE components. Moreover, you will have a healthy variety of options for CASE software configurations. CASE manufacturers entering into exclusive hierarchical integration agreements with other noncompeting CASE tool manufacturers ultimately limits choice.
- Does the CASE tool produce utility software that will read procedure and source libraries and create CASE component specifications for existing systems? The acquisition of CASE tools in a non-CASE environment creates a potential for inconsistencies in maintenance activities. Design and development specifications for systems designed and implemented before the installation of CASE components will not be consistent with those created after installation of CASE tools. Thus, a multiplicity of maintenance activities will be necessary. Certain CASE tools offer utility software that will ready procedure and source libraries and create development specifications for existing systems, thereby mitigating the difference between pre-CASE and post-CASE systems documentation.
- Does the tool have an effective interface to other CASE design tools already purchased or under evaluation? Often, several methodologies are used to design a system, so it is important that a CASE tool provide a healthy array of methodological techniques to use in the process. The dictionary entries must be capable of being shared across these methodologies, so the dictionary should be strong and versatile.
- Does the tool have graphical methodologies capable of "exploding" design diagrams and dictionary specifications to a reasonable depth? Most of the CASE design tools provide graphical methodologies for representing proposed systems design. The graphical diagrams and the dictionary entries behind the components of the graphical diagrams must be capable of exploding to a reasonable number of lower, more specific levels.
- Will the tool be capable of executing with windowing capabilities? An advantage of the windowing capability is that multiple portions of the design can be displayed simultaneously and can therefore compensate for weaknesses in embedded explosion capabilities. As a result, the levels of explosion will not be

restrictive, and the comprehensiveness and integration of CASE design and development specifications should improve.

- Does the planning model in the CASE planning component provide comprehensive coverage of corporate and functional unit strategic planning and systems planning? The planning component contains a model for representing the corporation and for use in determining the direction of the corporation and systems development. The strength of the CASE top-level components lies in the comprehensiveness of this planning model.

- Does the tool provide a thorough means of prototyping? CASE development tools, rather than CASE design tools, provide the strongest prototyping methods. While it is not necessary that both types provide strong prototyping capabilities, at least one must provide this capability.

- Will the tool be able to generate automatically first-cut physical design specifications from logical design specifications? The conversion of logical design diagrams into initial physical design diagrams should be automatic because it involves simply the exchange and addition of graphical display table entries. While most CASE design tools currently do not offer this feature, ask your CASE vendor if the tool will offer it in the future.

- Does the CASE design tool provide analysis support for design documentation? This concerns the capacity of the CASE tool to analyze design documentation and determine if the specifications entered by the analyst conform to prescribed methodological rules. The analysis should also indicate where design dictionary entries are incomplete. For example, a DFD diagram with a freestanding block should be highlighted as violating one of the rules of structured methodology. In addition, blocks on a DFD not having a corresponding dictionary entry should be highlighted.

- Does the tool have the capacity to generate design specification reports automatically? The specifications created during logical and physical design activities serve as a source of documentation for the system. While they are permanently stored on disk devices, it is often advisable to get hardcopy printouts of the design specifications for reference. Many CASE tools provide various report formats for this purpose, including the capability of indicating design flaws.

- Does the lower-level CASE development component provide methods for convenient and comprehensive customization of the generated system? The CASE development component can already generate the major portions of the code. Systems development activity using CASE involves customization of the generic code to fit the system. The custom specifications must provide comprehensive coverage of the system requirements. The generated programs must also be able to call on existing routines to prevent the system from "reinventing the wheel."

- Does the tool permit distribution of design/development responsibilities? CASE design and development tools must provide a serviceable means of segregating job responsibilities and interfacing the individual efforts into a single system project.

- Do the CASE design and development tools have the capacity to export portions of the design and development dictionary specifications? This is important, as design and development specifications for one system may be reusable in the design and development of other systems. "Reusable design" will join "reusable code" as a result of this capability.

- Can the tool interface design and development specifications to the functional DBMS be used to maintain the company's data? It is rare to develop systems that are not affected by the database environment, and the development of systems using CASE tools is no exception. Therefore, it is important that the CASE tools be able to interface design and development specifications of application systems to mainframe DBMSs and database creation or modification.

- Does the tool have word processing capabilities? In addition to built-in word processing capabilities, the tool should have an effective interface with standard word processing systems. An added feature of some tools is the ability to pass documentation to a desktop publishing software system for more professional representation.

- Does the tool enhance project management? The use of CASE tools does not preclude the need for effective project management. In fact, their use can enhance such management. Specifications that are entered using a planning component provide a boundary for design and development activities. This boundary provides a built-in means of determining when design and development activities diverge from originally planned specifications. Some CASE design and development tools can generate reports on the progress of individual project assignments and some can interface to existing project management software systems. Currently, this interface is a temporary exit from the CASE tool into the project management system, but the interface will become much stronger in the future and provide more automatic updating of the project schedule.

- Is it possible to modify the CASE design and development tools relative to your firm's internal or existing methodology? CASE tools are prepackaged systems and may need modifications to make them more suitable for individual installations. Thus, it is important that the system has the ability to add or delete menu options or to modify the style of graphical or dictionary entry screens.

- Can the tool automatically generate design, operations, and end-user documentation? As systems are designed and developed with CASE tools, documentation concerning components and users of the system are entered into the dictionary. Thus, the majority of design, operations, and user documentation required for documentation manuals is available from these dictionary entries. CASE systems should provide this documentation in either on-line or hardcopy form, with little additional work required from the project development team.

- Does the tool have facilities for maintaining design as well as systems? When conditions in business warrant changes in the information systems function, the people responsible for maintenance should be able to effect the required system changes in the system's design specifications automatically. Or, once those changes are made, the development tool should be able to designate where the current systems need changing, as well as indicate which users need to be notified of the changes and what they need to be told. Some development systems already provide some of these capabilities. As the interface between CASE design and development software systems becomes stronger, modifications to design specifications entered into the design software will be able to modify development specifications and, utimately, the entire system. Since the planning component was the last to emerge, the interface between it and the design component is weak. Subsequently, as the interface between it and the design strengthens, it should have the same effect on those activities as the strengthening of the interface between design and development did.

* Can the tool generate programs that span a range of systems? The hardware and software to create a transparent micro, mini, and mainframe environment are not far off. Consequently, the programs that the CASE tool generates must be able to provide the same execution services on a desktop micro as on a mighty mainframe. Some of today's CASE development systems already offer this.

It goes without saying that the CASE tool manufacturer should be willing to provide a list of installations using its software and grant permission to contact them. This major criterion should govern the purchase of any software system. Should a software vendor refuse to supply this information, you have reason to doubt the validity and comprehensiveness of its product.

7.5.1   Analysis of Selection Criteria

A subset of the above questions were sent to about a dozen vendors of CASE tools. Their responses are recorded in Appendix B.

7.6   VENDORS OF CASE TOOLS

This section lists some of the major vendors of CASE tools and gives a brief summary of their products.

7.6.1   Vendor List

ADPAC COMPUTING LANGUAGES CORP.   Adpac Computing Languages Corporation develops, markets, and services technology support tools for the IBM mainframe operating under MVS. Adpac's CASE tools (DPDP and DESIGN) provide a front-end CAD/CAM diagramming technique that asists analysts in drawing any type of diagram and design analysis with the capability of verifying the contents of diagrams.

AGS MANAGEMENT SYSTEMS INC.   AGS/MS is recognized as the world's leader in systems development methodologies and project management system. MULTI/CAM, the micro-mainframe CASE system created by AGS/MS, integrates software development tools, software design and production models, project management and any other user-selected CASE tools into a unified, automated work environment.

AMERICAN MANAGEMENT SYSTEMS   AMS is a major computer services firm specializing in applications development. AMS's Life-cycle Productivity System (LPS) integrates productivity tools from AMS and other vendors for strategic system planning, design, development, maintenance, and project management. LPS produces all deliverable work products required by most methodologies. Major portions of LPS operate on PCs. Implementation, configuration control, and foundation software modules operate on IBM mainframe.

ANALYSTS INTERNATIONAL CORP.   Analysts International Corporation, a professional data processing software and services company and a leader in the computer industry for over 22 years, introduces CORVET. CORVET is a graphics-oriented, PC-based, interactive CASE design and development product that generates stand-alone COBOL programs and comprehensive documentation for IBM mainframe environments.

ARTHUR ANDERSEN & CO.   FOUNDATION is a computer-integrated environment for software engineering developed by our consulting practice. Covering the entire systems development life cycle, FOUNDATION consists of METHOD/1, a PC LAN-based tool for planning and design, and INSTALL/1, and IBM mainframe-based environment for implementation and support of DB2 applications.

ARTHUR YOUNG & CO.   Arthur Young is an international accounting, tax, and management consulting firm which is working with KnowledgeWare to develop the Information Engineering Workbench (AY/IEW), markets KnowledgeWare products internationally, and uses the AY/IEW for systems building. Arthur Young will present its experience-building systems using the AY/IEW and Information Engineering techniques.

ASYST TECHNOLOGIES, INC.   The DEVELOPER provides multi-user, automated support for the systems development process, through its repository located either at the PC, at the mainframe (using DB2), or at both sites. The DEVELOPER and its CUSTOMIZER module allow the use of any methodology at all levels of compliance and rigor. Repository integrity is maintained through a menu-driven SQL query language and built-in ASYSTants capabilities.

BACHMAN INFORMATION SYSTEMS, INC.   Bachman Information Systems, Inc. is exhibiting The Bachman Product Set which supports the development of new applications while supporting existing applications. It provides the powerful maintenance, enhancement, and migration capabilities MIS departments need to control the largest component of their workload.

CATALYST   CATALYST, an information technology firm of Peat Marwick, will present PATHVU, RETROFIT, ReACT, and DataTEC. PATHVU provides analysis and detailed reporting of program logic and structure. RETROFIT restructures COBOL code. ReACT translates Assembler programs to structured COBOL. Data-TEC provides data element analysis, standardization, and migration capabilities. These products make up the reengineering baseline necessary to migrate existing systems to advanced technical environments.

CGI SYSTEMS, INC.   PACBASE is a full-cycle CASE product. It integrates Mainframe and PC-based analysis and design workstations for the development and maintenance of application specifications. This is done through active prototypes, a centralized enterprisewide dictionary that controls and manages all business specifications directly into complete COBOL applications, including all code and documentation.

CHEN & ASSOCIATES, INC.   Chen & Associates provides products, training, and consulting in data-oriented system development. Products (PC-based) are: ER-Designer, which defines information requirements in entity-relationship diagrams; SCHEMAGEN, which generates schemas for your database systems (from micro-based to mainframe based); Normalizer, which normalizes data or words.

COMPUTER SCIENCES CORP.   The Technology Activity's Design Generator is an object-oriented, expert system that automatically selects a central transform from a data flow diagram and generates an initial design represented in structure chart notation. The graphic-intensive user interface features intelligent pop-up menus and multipane browsers.

CORTEX CORP.   CorVision is an application development system that automates the entire software development cycle for the DEC VAX/VMS environment using a technique called Picture Programming. Picture Programming allows DP professionals to visualize an application by diagramming the design and then automatically generating a production-ready application directly from the pictures.

DIGITAL EQUIPMENT CORPORATION   As a leading manufacturer, Digital provides a range of integrated Application Development tools for solutions to business and engineering problems. The offerings are workstation based and address all aspects of the Applications Development Life Cycle. They are integrated into the VAX hardware, software, and network architecture to provide enterprisewide solutions.

ETECH ALGORITHMS AND SYSTEMS, INC. ETECH SOFTROBOT is an intelligent workbench built on PSDDL (Problem Statement and Diagram Description Language). ETECH-D is a fully automatic diagramming toolkit without screen editing. ETECH-M intelligent project manager is driven by Project-Makefile, ETECH-R reusing language and ETECH-G language-independent code generator based on reusability. It meets many professionals' goals.

HOLLAND SYSTEMS CORP./DELOITTE HASKINS AND SELLS Deloitte Haskins & Sells and Holland Systems Corp. have pooled their proven consulting and software product expertise in the IRM area. The result is a line of products that address the entire information resource management process from business modeling to database design and analysis to application development and implementation. The companies will feature the 4Front Family of IRM products.

I-LOGIX, INC. I-Logix, Inc. pioneers system design automation with STATE-MATE, the only available tool that models the dynamic behavior of real-time systems as well as system functions and architecture. With STATEMATE, users produce a specification that is compiled allowing its execution to be viewed on screen. STATE-MATE includes three graphic languages for modeling, execution, and simulation capability; rapid prototyping in Ada; and 2167A documentation.

INDEX TECHNOLOGY Index Technology markets the Excelerator family of products that automate systems development. Products include PC PRism for systems planning, Excelerator/RTS support a variety of techniques and methodologies and can be tailored for each organization's needs.

INFODYNE INTERNATIONAL, INC. InfoDyne, Inc. markets and distributes MASTER, a PC-based CASE tool and methodology, based on the E-R (entity-relationship) approach to systems planning and design. MASTER accommodates numerous approaches to the problem of analysis, design, and documentation of all design activities relating to the conceptual, logical, and physical model of data and international processes in an information system.

INFOREM PLC Inforem's Professional Application Generation Environment (PAGE) is a unique CASE offering. A multi-user product, it combines on-screen graphics with a systems encyclopedia and uses a relational database on networked PCs. PAGE is based on the Inforem Method, which provides a seamless transition right from analysis to program code both for PC and mainframe systems.

INTEGRATED SYSTEMS, INC. AutoCode focuses on the needs of Real-Time Software Engineers and addresses all steps from analysis to design, stimulation, and code generation. The graphical specification environment features engineering block-diagrams, data flow/control flow, state transition, and process descriptions. Ward-Mellor real-time software methodology with Boeing-Hatley extensions are included in an environment where simulation and analysis can be performed for design verification; and real-time code in C, Ada, or Fortran can be generated automatically.

INTERACTIVE DEVELOPMENT ENVIRONMENT (IDE)   IDE's product, Software through Pictures, is a set of integrated graphical editors and error-checking tools supporting structured analysis and design methods. The editors are linked to a data dictionary supporting definition of names, types, constants, and associated text. Users can generate Ada declarations and define process and module templates to generate specifications.

JAMES MARTIN ASSOCIATES   James Martin Associates, an international consulting firm established by James Martin, is considered the leader in creating systems development methods and CASE tools to support those methods. With more than 250 professionals throughout the world, JMA's teams provide commercial and government clients with technical and management services.

KNOWLEDGEWARE, INC.   Knowledgeware, Inc. provides a complete Integrated Computer-Aided Software Engineering (I-CASE) environment for the planning, analysis, design, construction, and maintenance of computer-based information systems. The Information Engineering Workbench (IEW) provides enterprise modeling, data modeling, process modeling, systems design, and code generation experts. The "Knowledge-Coordinator/Encyclopedia" team uses state-of-the-art artificial intelligence technology.

LANGUAGE TECHNOLOGY   Language Technology provides CASE products to the IBM mainframe market. The company's flagship product RECODER is the leading COBOL structuring tool. RECODER automatically transforms difficult-to-maintain, unstructured COBOL into structured COBOL. Language Technology's INSPECTOR is the only quality assurance tool based on scientific measurement of COBOL quality and maintainability.

AGEMENT SYSTEMS, INC.   LBMS will present its PC-based tools, SUPER-MATE and AUTOMATE PLUS. SUPER-MATE provides a powerful set of automated facilities for strategic planning, including business area/activity analysis, analysis of competitive strategies, the prioritization of applications, and the development of the strategic plan. Results of this plan may be passed to AUTO-MATE PLUS, which provides full support for systems analysis, logical design, and automatic generation of physical designs and data dictionary syntax for ADABAS, DB2, and other DBMS.

MANAGER SOFTWARE PRODUCTS (MSP)   The MANAGER Family of Products (PC and Mainframe) is dedicated to automating all phases of the systems life cycle, from strategic information planning to the generation of enabled code. MSP will present managerVIEW, the intelligent workstation-based graphical information engineering tool driven by the central knowledge base resident on the corporate dictionary. ManagerVIEW is integrated with the mainframe corporate dictionary and also runs on the IBM PC family and PS/2.

MICHAEL JACKSON SYSTEMS, LTD.   Jackson CASE tools automate the widely acclaimed Michael Jackson methods of system development and program design. SPEED-BUILDER supports the analysis phases of development through powerful graphical and text facilities and automates documentation production. The cooperating Program Development Facility (PDF) generates complete, well-structured program code from Jackson structure charts.

MICRO FOCUS   Micro Focus COBOL/2 Workbench puts a mainframe programming and testing environment on a PC platform under MS-DOS or OS/2. It is used by developers of COBOL, CICS DL/I, and IMS DB/DC applications to improve productivity and cut applications development backlogs. Micro Focus COBOL compilers and CASE tools are the choice of IBM, AT&T, Sun Microsystems, Microsoft, and others.

NASTEC CORP.   Nastec Corporation develops tools for commercial, government, and engineering software developers. CASE 2000 DesignAid is based upon an interactive, multi-user database with features for process modeling, real-time system modeling and documentation. Operating in the IBM PC and Digital VAX environment, CASE 2000 also includes tools for requirements management, project management and control, and consulting and training in CASE technology.

NETRON INC.   The NETRON/CAP Devlopment Center is a CASE system for building custom, portable COBOL software using a frame-based software engineering process called Bassett Frame Technology. NETRON/CAP unifies the prototyping/development/maintenance life cycle into an automated specification procedure. The open design architecture allows unlimited automation of additional application functionality for IBM mainframes and PCs, VAX systems, and Wang VS minis.

OPTIMA, INC. (formerly Ken Orr & Associates)   Optima, Inc. integrates the use of tools and technology with the experience of people. DSSD (Data Structured Systems Development) the flagship product, is a life cycle methodology that serves as the base of the product offering. CASE tool products which automate the methodology are Brackets, for the diagramming process, and Design-Machine, for requirements definition and logical database design.

ON-LINE SOFTWARE INTERNATIONAL   On-Line Software International presents CasePac-Automated Software Development with a powerful DB2 data dictionary. As the foundation for On-Line Software's CASE platform, CasePac provides a complete, fully active central repository, software engineering facilities including a graphics front end, change management, and maintenance facilities.

PANSOPHIC SYSTEMS, INC.   Pansophic Systems, Inc. presents TELON. The TELON application development system captures design specifications to generate COBOL or DL/I applications. TELON assists the transition from analysis to design by providing interfaces to leading front-end analysis tools. TELON components include directory, data administration, screen/report painters, prototyping, specification facilities, automated documentation, generator, and test facility.

POLYTRON CORP.   POLYTRON offers the leading configuration management system for MS/DOS PC and VAX/VMS software development. PVCS maintains versions and revisions of software systems. PolyMake automatically rebuilds any desired version of the system. PolyLibrarian maintains libraries of reusable object modules. The tools work together or independently with any language and your existing tools.

POPKIN SOFTWARE & SYSTEMS INC.   Popkin Software & Systems offers SYSTEM ARCHITECT, a PC-based CASE tool running under Microsoft Windows. Its set of process and data-driven methologies for structured analysis and design include DeMarco/Yourdon, Gane and Sarson, Ward & Mellor (real-time), structure charts, and entity-relationship diagrams. SYSTEM ARCHITECT's Data Dictionary-Encyclopedia utilizes dBase II file format.

READY SYSTEMS   Ready Systems will present CARDTools, which supports automatic DoD 2167 documentation generation, specific Ada requirements, including object-oriented design, packages, information hiding, and rendezvous. CARDTools offers real-time performance deadline analysis on multitasking architectures, and hardware/software interface specification, including intertasking synchronization and communication designs, allowing for design analysis verification prior to actual implementation.

SAGE SOFTWARE, INC.   Sage Software, Inc. develops, markets, and supports a family of CASE tools for developers of IBM-based information systems. The company's product family (known as the APS Development Center) encompasses the software development cycle and supports the physical design, interactive prototyping, coding, testing, and maintenance of COBOL-based applications software.

SOFTLAB, INC.   Softlab, Inc. will present MAESTRO, the integrated Software Engineering Environment. MAESTRO organizes, manages the software cycle through real-time project management, time accounting, and your standards. MAESTRO integrates customizable tools for design — coding, testing, documentation, and maintenance — is language independent, and fits in numerous hardware and software environments.

TEKTRONIX   TekCASE is a family of automated software development tools that help software engineers and project managers analyze, design, document, manage, and maintain complex real-time systems. Because they support Digital's complete VAX line and integrate with VAXset software, TekCASE products are flexible, extensible, and especially well suited for large projects.

TEXAS INSTRUMENTS   Texas Instruments' integrated CASE product, The Information Engineering Facility, is designed to automate the complete systems development life cycle. It consists of a powerful mainframe encyclopedia and PC-based, graphical toolsets to support analysis and design. T1 can demonstrate today the major components of this product, including strategic planning, analysis, design, COBOL code, and database generation.

THE CADWARE GROUP, LTD.   The CADWARE Group, Ltd. designs, produces, and markets rule-based frameworks and modeling tools for development of complex systems. Managers, planners, systems analysts, and designers use these tools to help manage the complexity of defining and evaluating mission-critical business, industrial, and technical systems.

TRANSFORM LOGIC CORP.   Transform addresses the development and maintenance of the entire application life cycle. Using expert system technology, complete COBOL applications are produced for IBM mainframe DBMSs DL/I and DB2. The concepts behind automated development, data-driven design architecture, prototyping, and maintenance are reviewed with examples of user accomplishments.

VISUAL SOFTWARE, INC.   Visual Software, Inc. markets personal CASE tools for workstations, LAN, and mainframe design environments. The base package, vsDesigner, is a methodology-independent workbench supporting shared access to LAN-based information repositories. Several default design syntaxes come with the product, including those for real-time design. Extensive analysis is supported and an optional SQL interface to the design data is available.

YOURDON INC.   The YOURDON Analyst/Designer Toolkit supports both the traditional and real-time YOURDON Techniques and allows for the creation of all the diagrams associated with the techniques. The diagramming facilities of the Toolkit are integrated with a powerful project dictionary which features dBase III compatibility. The Toolkit provides error checking to ensure the accuracy of diagrams and dictionary entries.

7.7   GETTING CASE IN PLACE

There are three basic steps for implementing CASE technology in a software development organization:

Determine methodology and automation support requirements
Select a CASE product
Implement the CASE product

This is a lengthy process involving numerous people, so do not expect major results for a couple of years. Even then, the biggest and longest-term benefits may come in application maintenance. CASE tools make it much easier to maintain specifications.

7.7.1   Determine the Methodology

Following agreement on the organization methodology, whether data-flow or entity-relationship diagrams, your next step is deciding what you need most in automation support. For a larger organization, with complex applications, you may want some of the following capabilities:

- Interactive drawing of analysis diagrams
- Automatic data normalization
- Consistency checking
- Initialization of physical design from requirements
- Prototyping tools
- Directory of reusable code modules
- Interface with application development environment

A second key decision is whether you want a single integrated environment or a CASE front-end to a more classical development environment.

7.7.2   Select a CASE Product

Once you have determined your methodology and decided which CASE capabilities will be useful, you need to select a product. You may do this on the basis of:

- Environment — PC or mainframe
- What application(s) the tools support — some tools support a specific database; e.g., DB2, or language; e.g., Ada
- Does the tool support your methodology
- Is the vendor financially secure? You may want to talk to people who have experience using the vendor's CASE tool

7.7.3   Implement the CASE Product

An aggressive strategy for CASE implementation in smaller organizations is to automate many software engineering techniques simultaneously on a small trial project. The basic steps are as follows:

- Select a new development project to be used for the CASE trial situation
- Staff the trial project with your best requirements and design analysts
- Assign a full-time CASE administrator to learn the tool, make detailed methodology decisions, enter information, run analysis reports and generate specifications

A large organization with thousands of users nationwide must take a different approach. Most such organizations find it physically impossible to decide on a complete automated methodology and then get hundreds of people trained on it in a short time period.

In this circumstance, a method of support groups acts as change agent, introducing a few techniques at a time and supporting them with automation.

7.8 CONCLUSION

This chapter introduced a tool that has literally "taken the software development world by storm." CASE tools are making a big impact on software development and will continue to do so for years to come.

The chapter introduced CASE tools and showed how they could be selected and used in small or large organizations.

Finally, I would like to refer my readers to Appendix B, where a number of unedited responses from CASE tool vendors are presented.

8

PROTOTYPING WITH CASE TOOLS

8.1 INTRODUCTORY REMARKS

Prototyping tools play an important part in automating the early life-cycle phases. They are used to determine system requirements and answer questions about the behavior of the emerging system. The following are some CASE tools used to prototype various aspects of a software system:

- Screen painters
- Report generators
- Menu builders
- Fourth-generation languages
- Executable specification languages

Screen generators, report generators, and menu builders are used mainly to prototype the user interface as a quick, friendly way of clarifying the user requirements. The prototype provides the user with a concrete model of how the systems will look from the user's experience and perspective. At this level of prototyping, screen dialogue and navigation with data entry and edits can be simulated with or without compiles. Also, source code for record, file, screen, and report descriptions can be generated automatically. This is an effective method for identifying and correcting misunderstandings about user expectations for the system.

Fourth-generation languages can be used to develop a more complete model of the system. In this case, the prototype includes the major functions of the system, but does not check for exceptions or invalid input data and does not worry about execution performance. The purpose is to give the user experience with the system by using a fairly complete model. Sometimes the model is found to be adequate enough to serve as the actual system.

Executable specification languages are the most sophisticated prototyping tools. They change system development into an interactive process where the system is specified and the specifications are executed to determine if the system is complete and correct. Then, based on the experience of using this prototype, the specifications are refined and then reexecuted. The interactive process continues until the system is able to perform in a manner that meets all the user requirements.

8.1.1   Simulation

Certain types of software systems are embedded within other systems. These systems, called real-time/embedded systems, must interact with their outside environment through signals and controls.

For real-time/embedded systems it is valuable to simulate as well as prototype the system at the analysis/design stage of development. Where a prototype is a model of the software system, the simulation is a model of the environment to which the software system must respond and control. The simulation enables a review of how the software system will behave in its actual real-world environment. Realistic real-world inputs from the environment must be provided to verify the correctness and completeness of the system design model. With the aid of CASE simulation tools, the designer can find design errors before even beginning the coding phase of development.

8.1.2   Code Generation

At the other end of the software life cycle from prototyping is code generation. A CASE workbench automates the program implementation step by generating code from the program design specification. Either a skeleton or a full program generation, code for the database, file, screen, and report descriptions, plus commented outline automatically. Additional program logic must be hand-coded to complete the program.

In the case of full program generation, the complete program is generated automatically from the design specification. This includes:

- Executable code
- JCL
- Database/file access; e.g., screens
- Help screens
- Error messages
- User and program documentation
- Test cases

All of these components of the completed programs are linked together and stored in the CASE repository for easy access, synchronized updating, and maintenance.

Generated code is either object code or source code. Many developers prefer source code because, if necessary, it can be understood and supported by human programmers. Also, it is more portable and may be more compatible with existing software systems. Widely used languages such as COBOL, PL/1, C, Ada, Fortran, or proprietary vendor-supplied languages are generated by CASE workbench generators.

The code is generated for operating environments such as MVS, CICS, IMS/DC, DB2, DL1, VSAM, VM/CMS, ISO, IDMS, ADABAS, and OS/1100. The ability to generate code for various target environments is an important part of the CASE workbench code generator's capability.

Object code offers the advantage of greater efficiency and probably will become more widely accepted by CASE workbench users in the future as they are assured of the reliability and efficiency of automatically generated code. Also, as CASE workbench's capability to maintain systems at design specification level improves, object code generated will be seen as more practical than source code.

8.2   CLASSIFICATION OF PROTOTYPES

There are many ways to classify prototypes. One classification labels prototypes as: (1) explorative, (2) evolutionary, and (3) experimental, and gives the following definitions:

- Explorative prototyping is used to arrive at a functional definition of what the user wants from the system. The prototype is constructed to model areas of uncertainty or important features of the system. It helps in deciding among alternative solutions. This type of prototype is generally considered a throwaway.
- Evolutionary prototyping is done with the express purpose of evolving into the final production system. These prototypes are characterized by incremental releases (versions) and progressively the inclusion of more functionality. It can be argued that the evolutionary model is not a prototype at all, but rather what has classically been called "version one" of the production system.
- Experimental prototyping is used to assist in determining feasibility of a proposed solution prior to large investments in developing the system. This type of prototype is undertaken during the feasibility and requirements definition stages of the SDLC. This type of prototype may be considered throw-away or may evolve into the final system.

Another view of prototyping concentrated on the logical and physical aspects of the system. These prototypes are known as mock-ups, functional prototypes, and simulations. The primary target for mock-ups is usually the user interface of a system. The user interface is much more than a format of screens — it is a model of the entire interaction between the user and the system. Functional prototypes focus on the specific features and functions that are required in the delivery system. A functional prototype is used to help refine a new system's requirement and resolve uncertainty. Simulations are used to estimate matrix and other performance characteristics of the production system. Simulations are generally performed after mock-up and functional prototypes have been developed.

8.3 ASSUMPTION UNDERLYING PROTOTYPING

The major assumption underlying the introduction of prototyping is that software development is an interactive design process. Effective design is achieved only as a result of feedback between designer and user. A process that exposes the user to lifelike scenarios of the first application allows a wide consideration of design alternatives early in the developmental process. The prototype is designed with the expectation of change. Requests for changes to the system design are accepted and regarded as a regular part of the development process. The system design is accepted and regarded as a regular part of the development process. The system design is never "frozen" for long, making systems designers unable to react to newly identified requirements or changes in the user's environment.

Prototypes are most effective when:

- Users do not know their specific requirements
- There is a need to move forward quickly
- New concepts need to gain acceptance
- A dynamic business model is needed

Prototyping is a development strategy used to determine requirements and clarify user needs. Once determined, the requirements are then developed by building a working model of the system rapidly and in context. Prototyping is a technique that recognizes that system development is an interactive process. Prototyping accepts the inevitability of change and the need for continual revision.

8.4 DESIGN AND THE PROTOTYPING SDLC

Prototyping often conjures up negative stereotypes and unrealistic expectations. With no clear goals defined and laid out for the prototype stage, the project's real objectives eventually get lost. This lack of discipline results in an expensive, tenuous, and often time-consuming prototyping process, which is uncontrollable. But prototyping can be a viable productivity tool when managed like any other aspect of systems development. Prototyping should be viewed in the larger context as an important methodology which encourages interactive software development; it is not an end to itself, nor a solution to all design problems.

The benefits of an interactive approach are strongly supported by the technique of prototyping. An architecture-based methodology considers three specific levels of interaction. The first set of interactions makes use exclusively of scenarios developed by the system developer or analyst. These scenarios table the form of fixed-information display screens. User and analyst iterate on the screen design until a first-cut representation of the system is achieved.

When details of data-dependent calculations need to be developed, a second "demo" level of interactions is required. In this interaction, actual database interactions and application computations using sample data occur. Often a third level of interaction needs to take place because many aspects of the system will not have been addressed.

A final series of interactions then may take place. It is at this point that a "prototype" of the system is produced.

What makes prototyping different from other techniques employed is the user's perception and view of the process. From the user's view, a flexible, familiar, workable medium is being created. In order to obtain efficient development, the prototyper, like any other application builder, needs guidelines.

As engineering practice, it offers both practical design guidelines and evolution methodologies. The focus is on human concerns such as ease of use, simplicity in learning, improved reliability, and enhanced user satisfaction while balancing them against machine efficiency. The application of this perspective to computer system design is a relatively new development.

8.5 THE USER INTERFACE

A system's user interface allows the user to communicate with the computer. It enables the user to enter, store, manipulate, retrieve data, and initiate commands. The interface provides the user impressions which influence his judgments regarding overall system quality. A well-designed user interface allows the user relatively easy access to the power of the system. Conversely, a poorly designed user interface can make even the best system unnecessarily complicated, thereby rendering it virtually unusable. User Interface Management Systems (UIMS) are packages which allow designers to rapidly prototype interface design. The user interface of an application system is the means by which the system communicates to the end user and therefore is important for prototyping.

8.6 PROTOTYPING AND HUMAN FACTORS/USER INTERFACE

Use of a prototype in human interfaces system development has at least six key advantages:

- Ease of use is not always obvious
- Actual experience can be observed before building
- One demonstration is better than two volumes of specifications

- Temporal aspects of system behavior can be experienced
- Prototypes allow incremental evaluations
- Prototypes make it easier to run controlled experiments

A prototype is something tangible, something people can see and touch. Prototypes allow users to evaluate and suggest changes to the final product while changes are still possible. The introduction of prototyping into human factors engineering and the development of the user interface will allow more thorough evaluation during the requirements and design phases of the life cycle.

8.7 PROTOTYPING AND THE SDLC

Developments in software design requirements such as "groupware" and the advent of new software technologies will require a fundamental shift in the way software is produced. This shift will be characterized by the increased use of prototyping as a design tool, incorporation of human factors in all phases of the software development life cycle (SDLC) and use the interactive development concept.

The methodology described here has been devised in an attempt to bring together the critical elements of prespecification methods, prototyping, and human factors engineering in an integrated methodology that takes advantage of all three approaches. Prototyping and human factors can be used in conjunction with the traditional SDLC to enhance the user's participation in an understanding of the requirements, conceptual design, and detailed design stages.

Figure 8.1 illustrates a view of a revised systems development life cycle. This revised life cycle is composed of the original traditional systems development life cycle plus a separate prototype development cycle with human factors stages incorporated. The specifics of each step have been illustrated in Figure 8.1. Two points of interest must be discussed here:

- The inclusion of a prototype decision point after the feasibility study stage of the SDLC. This allows for an evaluation as to whether prototyping, prespecification, or a combination of the two techniques should be followed. This decision should be based upon the nature of the system to be built. If a system has a low risk in the development of the user interface or in meeting performance requirements, and if it has a high risk in budget and schedule predictability and control, then the decision would fall toward prespecification and the traditional SDLC. However, if a system has a low risk of budget and schedule control and high risk in understanding requirements or getting the user interface wrong, then the decision should be made to enter the prototyping life cycle.
- In Figure 8.1, the multiple paths that lead from the PDLC back to the SDLC indicate that a decision point is included, which, based upon the goals and objectives set at the beginning of the prototyping life cycle, can lead to multiple paths as follows:

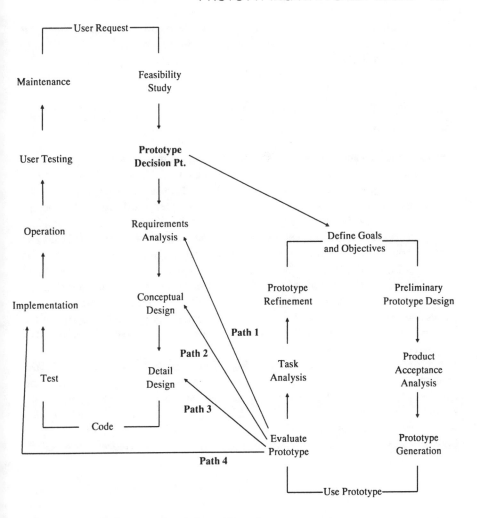

Figure 8.1   Revised systems development life cycle

— Path 1 leads back to the requirements analysis stage in the SDLC. The prototype is used to discover only certain aspects of the system's requirements.
— Path 2 leads back to the conceptual design stage of the SDLC where a formal physical design is constructed.
— Path 3 leads back to the final detailed design stage of the SDLC where only external design considerations are made.
— If, however, the prototype meets all the user's requirements and has been developed on the target machine with the appropriate software, then Path 4

could be taken, which would lead to implementation. In this instance, the stages of the life cycle would be collapsed into a prototyping life cycle and a system could be developed very quickly.

8.8 PROTOTYPING AND ORGANIZATIONAL IMPLICATIONS

The incorporation and integration of prototyping and human factors into the systems development life cycle will undoubtedly lead to a change for not only the analysis, but for entire software development departments. In the past, these departments have separated analysts, application programmers, and other technical support functions.

The distinction between analyst and programmer has created an artificial boundary during systems development. Rather than create an incentive to cross boundaries and develop both skills and informal communication links, the opposite is true and walls are put up. Formal communication channels are then established, which led to an unproductive proliferation of paperwork. With prototyping and human factors incorporated and the development of support tools, the focus is on communications with the user along with analysis and design of the system. No longer will programmers or analysts narrowly focus on their specific area of the system, but rather a new breed of computer design specialist will emerge.

No longer will communication flow from user to analyst to developer, with the analyst the barrier to communication. There will be a synchronous communication flow between the user and the system professional. As prototyping and a human factor perspective become integrated into the SDLC, a dedication of resources will be needed to encourage the more productive development process. These resources include not only people, but workspace, software, and hardware and new management styles.

9

PRODUCTIVITY CASE
TOOLS FOR DEVELOPMENT

9.1 INTRODUCTORY REMARKS

Productivity CASE tools are defined as those tools that provide support for designers
and programmers of software, but only at the back end of the system's development
life cycle. These include tools for natural language programming, project management, and documentation.

This chapter discusses CASE tools marketed by vendors and represent the classifi-
cations listed above.

9.2 MEASUREMENT OF APPLICATION PRODUCTS

CASE tools offer an unprecedented opportunity to measure the sizes of products
developed using them. The sizes of CASE application products are required for the
measurement of the productivity of CASE technologies themselves and of developers
using those technologies. A series of development phase sizes of a CASE application
product are needed, from the initial size of the job to be done, through various
specification and design phase sizes, down to the size of the code ultimately generated.
Several partial sizes may also be useful, for example, the size of the data model alone.

In this section, we examine issues concerned with the dependence of size metrics
on the instrumented CASE tools that measure them and the search for a technology-
independent measure of job size. Candidate units of size measure are examined, and
it is suggested that dictionary token counts and function point-like metrics are the most
promising. Also, we discuss an attempt to measure one of two main types of productivity, namely:

promising. Also, we discuss an attempt to measure one of two main types of productivity, namely:

- Technology productivity — how good is a specific CASE technology at getting the job done
- Developer productivity — how good is Joe or Jane at getting the job done with a specific CASE tool

In both of the above cases, we are concerned with the size of the particular job to be done. Productivity in this context will typically be measured in cost, effort, or time per unit size of the job to be done.

9.3 CASE APPLICATION PRODUCT SIZES

It is the claim of many CASE tool suppliers that their products will fit many different life-cycle models. However, regardless of the life-cycle model used in any particular environment, there will be a sequence, or more precisely a network, of sizes of interest during development of a CASE application product (CAP). The particular sizes of interest will depend on the application category to which the CAP belongs, among other factors. In order to be specific, let us consider a particular application category, that of data-centered business systems. Applications in this category can be characterized briefly as consisting of a database, together with a set of relatively simple transactions which update, and report on, the database contents. It must be emphasized that this application category has only been chosen as an example and that the principles described here are of much more general applicability.

The sizes of interest in the development of a data-centered business system may include some or all of the following, as illustrated in Figure 9.1.

- A general data model size — this is an early measure of the size of the data model, or of a subview of interest, say, in entity-relationship terms. It should contain all entities and relationships of concern to the application. However, at this general level, entities and relationships are merely named and the cardinalities of the latter identified, their attributes not listed.
- A general data flow model size — this is an early measure of the size of the data flow diagram exploded several levels to an agreed level of process and/or data flow detail. The flows and processes are merely named and their attributes are not identified. There are, of course, potential problems with such a general measure, mostly related to determining and maintaining a consistent level of generality. Guidelines for a general data flow diagram, at other than the trivial top level, may be difficult to establish.
- An outline system size combining both examples above. Such an outline system model size is likely to be the earliest size obtainable from the analysis level of a CASE environment, which can give some basis for an overall estimate of the size of the job to be done.

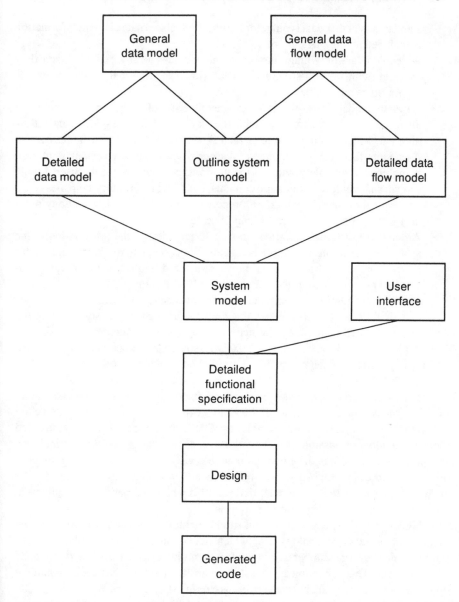

Figure 9.1 CASE application product components whose sizes may be of interest — a data-centered application category example

- A detailed data model size — revised as necessary due to new information becoming available as development proceeds, together with all named attributes of all entities and relationships. It is a matter of availability, choice, and local standards, whether data typing, formatting, and related data element information is included at this stage or not.

- A detailed data flow diagram size — this includes a fully exploded data flow diagram, with the full structure of each flow specified and all data elements within flows named, though not necessarily typed.
- A system model size — this is a measure of the size of the data model, including all named attributes, together with the size of the fully exploded data flow diagram, with the full structure of each flow specified and all attributes named.
- A user interface size — this takes a "black box" view of the subsystem of interest, being concerned solely with its inputs from, and outputs to, the user. Menu, screen, and window formats and contents, including all prompts, help messages, and error messages, together with report formats and contents, and any other user interactions are included in complete detail.
- A detailed functional specification size — includes all the information in the system and user interface models together with complete dictionary entries for all data elements, structures and flows, structured English, action diagrams or similar, process descriptions, access controls, accounting requirements, and other system administration functions of relevance to the user.
- One or more design sizes, depending on the structure of the design process and the design method used; e.g., structured design or data structure-driven design.
- A generated code size, say, of the COBOL source code generated, if the CASE environment used generates this, or possibly of machine-level code.

The sizes referred to above may be measured for subsystems or increments, rather than for whole systems. Because all the elements making up any particular size are automatically countable, or measurable, by CASE tools themselves, or associated tools, the number of possible sizes is very large, depending on just what is included in a particular size. Since development practices vary; there is a strong argument to allow users to define their own size requirements, in addition to building specific sizing tools for measuring some well-defined sizes which emerge as commonly used sizes of importance for comparative purposes.

A higher-level CASE planning tool might include business characteristics and parameters, or sizing-by-analogy data, which enables an even earlier ballpark size to be obtained. The large number of potential sizes might raise the question, do we need all these sizes? This is not an easy question to answer until one has actually had the opportunity to use them all, but we can discuss the question a priori. We certainly need an early size, or sizes, as a basis for estimates on which to make go/no-go or resource allocation and scheduling decisions as soon as possibly in a project. We also need a sequence of sizes corresponding to development phases or milestones in order to monitor progress, and reschedule resources during development. It would also be useful to be able to look separately at different component sizes, or size aspects, of a system. In the data-centered business applications category we have chosen as an example, these aspects could include:

- The data dimension — an examination of the data model alone can give us some measure of the amount and complexity of the application data.
- The transformation — an examination of the data flow diagram, exploded to some convenient level, can enable us to assess functional aspects of a system in terms of the numbers and types of transformations required to derive output flows from input flows and also which inputs particular outputs depend on.
- The user interface dimension — a separate examination of the size and complexity of the user interactions with a system, perhaps in relation to their degree of friendliness.

If, as seems likely, all these sizes are of interest to someone in some aspect of project management, then, given tools which can produce them automatically, the answer to our question above is, yes, all of these sizes, and perhaps even others also, serve some purpose in the management of CASE developments.

9.4   UNITS OF SIZE MEASURE FOR CASE

Having established that a number of sizes are needed for the effective development of CAPs, we now need to look at ways of measuring these different CAP sizes. The first issue is what unit or units of measure to use.

CASE tools are concerned with a wide variety of object types; e.g., entities, relationships, data types, data flows, processes, and many others, which are represented in several different ways, including:

- Graphically
- As user entries in screen forms
- As dictionary entries
- As items in reports

A few objects may be represented in all these different forms. There are clearly problems in measuring the size of a diagram, as a diagram, and combining it with the size of a number of user entries in a screen form. It is not the purpose of this section to ask, or answer, philosophical questions about the nature of size itself. There are, however, fundamental problems in determining the size of any software product or representation that consists of a large number of different objects.

Traditionally, these problems have been solved in one of two ways:

- By finding a common measure for all objects — traditionally, this common measure for software has been lines of code.
- By constructing a composite measure that assigns different weights to different objects appropriate for the purpose at hand and then adds the weighed object counts or measure together.

To these we must add another approach that has recently emerged, namely the use of a vector of size metrics rather than a single size value. This approach recognizes the fact that systems are made up of different kinds of objects which are, in some senses at least, incommensurate. Thus a vector of counts or measures of several key software object classes may be more useful for some purposes than a single common or composite measure.

9.4.1 Common Units of Size

Traditionally, the most popular common unit of software size measure has been lines of code, often also equated with delivered source instructions. In most CASE developments, however, lines of code are quite uncommon. For example, in data-centered business CAPs, lines of codes as such may only occur in parts of process descriptions, process module code and the final generated code itself. The final generated code may be source code for some compiler, or it may be machine code. Other objects are either graphical, or entries in screen forms. It would seem to be unnatural to look for line of code equivalents, except perhaps for the purpose of comparison with earlier conventional developments.

All objects, however, are entered into a dictionary as tokens or fields. The tokens in the dictionary description of the objects of interest for a particular CAP size can be counted and added together and a total size in dictionary tokens obtained. As with lines of code, there are advantages and disadvantages in the token approach. The advantages include:

- Tokens are simple, universal and easily counted.
- It can be argued, as it has been for lines of code, that, although all tokens are not equal, on average they can provide a useful common measure comparable across many CASE tools, language and other software representations.
- Each token can be thought of as a kind of atomic decision that the developer must make concerning the CAP under development.

The disadvantages include:

- Possible alternative dictionary representations use different number tokens for the same objects; for example, an arithmetic expression may be stored in the dictionary in either parenthesized or parenthesis-free notation.
- The correspondence between tokens and developer decisions may not be one-to-one and may depend on the CASE interface; for example, a screen position may be represented in the dictionary as two coordinates, whereas a user with a mouse may regard choosing a position as a single decision.
- Some important objects, such as entities, may be represented by relatively few tokens, whereas some less important objects, such as data types, may require rather more tokens to describe them completely.
- CAP token counts are dependent on the CASE technology employed.

- Questions arise as to whether all tokens within the CASE dictionary files should be counted, including those in developer notes, comment text, etc., or whether some should be omitted — which, and why? In some situations, some comments may in fact contain meaningful code, such as calls to nonstandard software products.
- There are potential difficulties, at least initially, in assigning a meaning to a size in tokens, or thousands of tokens, and relating it to existing size measures in lines of code and function points.

The advantages and disadvantages are not dissimilar to those usually adduced for lines of code. Indeed, the advantages seem rather greater and the disadvantages rather less than those for lines of code.

9.4.2   Size Metric Vectors for CASE

The metric vector approach recognizes that a concept such as size has more than one dimension and therefore cannot be embodied completely in a single value. Just as two different people may weigh the same, although one is tall and thin and the other is short and fat, so two systems may have the same token or function point count, but one may be better described by weight, height and growth, as it were, than by weight alone. Figure 9.1 indicates an implicit recognition of this fact by its isolation of three different size aspects of a data-centered business system, namely, the data model, data flow diagram, and user interface, each of which can readily be sized separately in a CASE environment.

CAPS involve so many different types of objects that several levels of metric vectors may be of interest. For example, for data-centered systems the following may be useful:

- Data model size, data flow diagram size, user interface size, functional specification size, where sizes are measured in tokens and the fourth entry in the vector is the sum of the other three.
- Entities, relationships, attributes, data model token count, where the first three entries are counts of the respective data model components.
- Data flows, processes, data stores, external entities, data flow diagrams token count.
- Menus, windows, reports, user interface token count.

It must be emphasized that the above are only examples and that experience with the descriptive power of metric vectors will, undoubtedly, suggest other metric vectors and metric vector components.

As databases of completed systems are built up, metric vectors can also be used to match the characteristics of an outline system model with completed systems for prediction by analogy.

Size metric vectors do not replace common or composite size metrics. They complement them, adding extra dimensions and filling out the sizing picture.

9.4.3 Composite Units of Size Measure

Composite units of size measure can be regarded as functions of metric vectors. The most common composite measures are function points, which are a complex function of module type; e.g., file, input, output, inquiry, or external interface and the counts of files, record types, and data elements for each module, summed over modules. There are several variants of function points including extensions for real-time and scientific systems.

Several questions arise as a result of considering these or other component size measures in a CASE environment:

- Are function points natural CASE measures?
- What do function points actually measure in a CASE environment?
- What do these composite metrics mean in a CASE environment?
- How can they be used?
- Does this shed light on their meaning in general?

In terms of Figure 9.1, for data-centered business application category, Function Point Analysis (FPA) provides a measure of the parts of the detailed data flow model which have flows to or from external entities, together with a measure of the detailed data model in terms of files, record types, and data elements, depending on a suitable mapping of these to the data model components.

The composite measures all give early size measure, based on a parallel system model. Thus, for partial purposes, composite metrics should be better estimators because the weights they give to different component types and object counts can be tailored to the purposes in hand. For general purposes and for objective target sizes, tokens are suitable.

9.4.4 Calibration

Calibration is necessary to achieve some comparability between tokens and function points, and also between these and traditional lines of code. In order to do this, it is necessary to have a sample of a sufficient number of common systems that can be measured in each of the desired ways. Once this has been done, there is no difficulty in obtaining calibration ratios of tokens/function point, or whatever, for the particular application class represented by the chosen sample of systems and for the technologies on which the metrics are implicitly or explicitly dependent. It is important to realize, however, that these are merely overall system-level equivalences in most cases and are not necessarily applicable to individual components. For example, the distribution of tokens between FPA component types may not be uniform due to the different weights applied to different FPA component types. Calibration is also necessary for establishing comparability of similar FP-like metrics, using different component partitions and weights, across different CASE technologies.

9.4.5   Technology Dependence and Productivity

In order to compare the productivity of two different technologies, we need some measure of the size of the job to be done which is independent of both technologies. Ideally, we would like an abstract size of the job to be done independent of any software technology or methodology. However, there is no canonical measurable description or specification language available for this purpose. The best we can hope for is some common measurable model or other descriptive basis which will fit both of two CASE technologies that we wish to compare.

The nature of technology dependence or independence depending on one's point of view, is illustrated in CASE tools in Figure 9.2. Any particular CASE tool uses particular models and notations and tends to be associated with one or more preferred families of software development methodologies. At the top level, only the models are important. These models, such as data flow diagrams and entity-relationship models, are both fundamental and general, but not universal. For example, a tool based on Jackson Structured Design would not use data flow diagrams and a tool based on another methodology would use them. Tools based on object-oriented concepts may use quite different models, based on hierarchies of objects and messages which pass between them. As CASE tool use moves from analysis to design to implementation, more specific methods are used, and the process, and hence the developing product, becomes progressively more technology-dependent. Eventually, expressed in generated source or machine code, the product and its size are very dependent on the target methodology.

Even the common measurable descriptive basis, if such exists, which can be mapped onto the technologies of both CASE tools A and B of Figure 9.2, will not be completely independent of any software technology; it is merely more independent than any of the lower-level aspects in the figure.

9.5   CONCLUDING REMARKS

Many studies have been done of the effects of information system (IS) productivity tools, and these show major improvements in some organizations but low improvements in others using the same tools. To achieve productivity, it is necessary not only to select the best tools, but also to adapt IS organization and methods to take full advantage of these tools.

The simplest CASE tools are little more than diagramming aids. They might be thought of as word processors for diagrams. These tools enable diagrams to be drawn more quickly and kept tidy. They have a productivity effort comparable to the introduction of word processors into a lawyer's office. Lawyers' word processors often

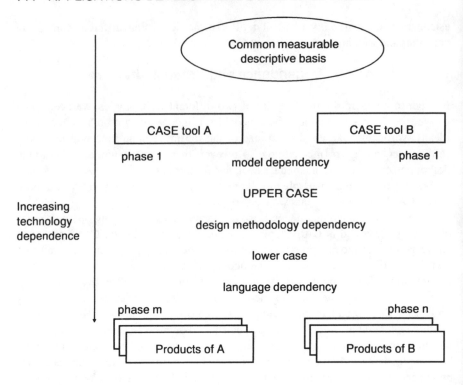

Figure 9.2 Technology dependence and technology productivity

result in far more text being created; diagramming tools often result in far more diagrams being created.

A more valuable effect of good CASE tools is the removal of errors and inconsistencies at the design stage. The designs are of higher quality, leading to fewer problems and less time taken in removal of errors from code.

Code generators enable implementers to produce a working program quickly. However, if the generator is not linked to a data dictionary, data model, or design tools, the programs generated may be incompatible fragments, ill designed, and not linking together. To achieve high productivity, the tools for design need to be tightly coupled to the code generator. The design tools should employ a data model and should enable design to be represented in a powerful, visual, easy-to-modify form from which code is generated directly. The programs should be quickly executable so that the designer can observe what they do, adjust or add to the design, rerun the programs, enhance the design, and so on, until a comprehensive system is created. The need for manual coding should be removed to the maximum extent.

The generator first produces structured code, which relates to the design screens. This code may be used for prototyping and debugging. Structured code does not give optional machine performance, so, for heavy-duty applications, the code may be fed into an optimizer, which creates code with optional machine performance. This code will never be touched by maintenance programmers.

The designer-generator tool should facilitate prototypes being built and modified quickly. It should generate test data and provide testing tools. It should generate database code and job control code, so that the program can be quickly executed when design changes are made. With powerful prototyping tools, an iterative development life cycle is used. The implementer designs something on the screen of an I-CASE tool, generates code, executes the code and tests it, then modifies or adds to the design, regenerates code, and so on. The faster the cycle of design-generate can be, the more productive the implementer is likely to be. Powerful design tools with interpretive generators are needed, which make the cycle as fast as possible.

Part III

CASE TOOLS MANAGEMENT ISSUES

10

ENVIRONMENT ARCHITECTURE AND CASE TOOL INTERFACES

10.1 INTRODUCTORY REMARKS

The environment architecture in which CASE tools are promoted may be defined as the software development environment, the hardware platforms, and the user/human factors that exist during the introduction of the tools.

The software development environment has been discussed at great length throughout this book. The user/human factors have ramifications still not understood by the CASE industry and they will not be discussed here. This leaves the hardware platforms.

Information engineering and CASE tools have been greatly enhanced by two introductions by IBM over the last few years: Systems Application Architecture (SAA) and AD/Cycle. The bulk of this chapter is devoted to the discussion of these two items.

10.2 SYSTEMS APPLICATION ARCHITECTURE

Systems Application Architecture is a collection of selected software interfaces, conventions, and protocols that form the framework for developing consistent, integrated applications across the future offerings of the major IBM computing environment.

The interfaces, conventions, and protocols of SAA are designed to provide an enhanced level of consistency and connectivity in the following areas:

- Programming interface — the languages and services that application developers use in building their software
- User access — the design and use of screen panels and user interaction techniques
- Communications support — the connectivity of systems and programs
- Applications — the software built and supplied by vendors

Systems Application Architecture facilitates an increased level of consistency and connectivity across participating systems. As a result, the development and use of applications should be less expensive and more timely, and optimal use can be made of enterprise resources.

Consistency provides several advantages. Those users who need access to data on one system today and another tomorrow can benefit. The program they run will be similar, and the actions they perform while running these programs will be more uniform. Panels, keyboards, and procedures will often be the same in appearance and behavior. With less relearning, users have faster and easier access to data, and business efficiency increases.

Programmers, too, benefit from this increased consistency. Skills learned in one environment are transferable to others, and there is less need for retraining or for Systems Specialists. A programmer familiar with one environment can readily move to another and soon be productive.

Consistency means portability, and building applications for multisystem solutions becomes faster and easier. It is the source for a program built on one system and implemented more smoothly on another. Effort expended in creating general data processing solutions is therefore lessened, along with development time.

Connectivity allows programmers to create applications that span systems and run partly in one environment and partly in another. Distributing an application in this manner permits its various functions to be processed where most desirable. This allows maximum leverage of existing capabilities, utilizing the unique strengths of an enterprise's various systems.

A particularly advantageous arrangement is the use of intelligent workstations with a host. The host system gives powerful processing and fast access to large databases. The intelligent workstation offers attractive graylines and convenient menus and conversations for the user. Using SAA's connectivity features, an application can be split so that its logic and data access run efficiently on the host, while its human interaction takes place on the user-friendly PC.

10.3 SAA SUPPORTED ENVIRONMENTS

Several combinations of hardware and software have been selected as SAA environments. These are environments in which IBM will manage the conformance to specification and the availability of support for all applicable SAA elements. These environments are:

- TSO/E in the current version of MVS operating system
- CMS in the current version of VM/SP and VM/XA
- CICS/MVS in the version of MVS operating system
- IMS/VS Data Communication in the current version of MVS operating system
- System/3X
- OS/2 Extended Version

10.4 COMMON PROGRAMMING INTERFACE

One important part of SAA is a common programming interface which consists of the language commands and the calls that the programmers supply. The components of the interface fall into two general categories:

- Languages

  - Application Generators
  - C
  - COBOL
  - Fortran
  - Procedures Languages

- Services

  - Communication Interface
  - Database Interface
  - Dialog Interface
  - Presentation Interface
  - Query Interface

10.5 COMMON USER ACCESS

The Common User Access defines the rules for dialog between the human and the computer. It establishes how information appears on a display screen and how people respond to that information. It includes definitions of interface elements and rules for interaction techniques. Those include panel appearance, procedures for moving from one panel to another, choice selection, color and emphasis, messages, help, and terminology.

The Common User Access consolidates the latest technology in the interface elements and techniques. Based on a foundation of fundamental concepts and designed from the top down, its principles will apply across the SAA range because the Common User Access is consistent across participating systems and it has the benefits of familiarity. Users moving from application to application or from system to system need less time to adapt. And the programmers who create and maintain these applications should also do so more quickly and easily.

10.5.1 Elements of the Interface

An interface between user and computer has three main components:

- The way the machine communicates with the user
- The way the user communicates with the machine
- What the user understands about the interface

The first aspect is what the user perceives, what face the program and the hardware show to the person at the workstation, how the instruction and data are presented. The user has to recognize this information, understand it, and come up with an appropriate response. This response, consisting of established actions such as key selection, is the second aspect of the interface.

The third aspect, how users understand this entire process, is really part of the first two. Users' expectations — their "conceptual models" — are influenced by their previous experience.

An interface can be consistent with respect to three broad categories of dimensions: physical, syntactical, and semantical.

10.6 COMMON COMMUNICATIONS SUPPORT

Common Communications Support is used to connect applications, systems, network, and devices. This will be achieved by the consistent implementation of designated communication architectures in each of the SAA environments.

Included in the Common Communications Support at this time are data streams, application services, network, session services, and data link controls.

10.7 COMMON APPLICATIONS

These common applications will offer consistency in how business functions are implemented, how panels are laid out, and how the use navigates within the application in all supported environments. Thus, an application initially developed for one environment and subsequently ported to another will appear consistent to the application user.

Users of mainframe terminals and intelligent workstations will have a consistent set of defined functions, and where applicable, the intelligent workstation user may have additional defined functions available for the application. Hosts controlling the mainframe terminal will provide the user access functions. These functions will, within the limits of technology, have a reasonable consistency with the intelligent workstations user access.

10.8 APPLICATION DEVELOPMENT (AD)/CYCLE

AD/Cycle is an integration architecture or framework for a full life-cycle CASE environment. It comprises several layers addressing presentation, data, and control integration. AD/cycle includes a repository, tool integration services, vertical tools, horizontal tools, and a common user interface.

In the AD/Cycle environment, system planning is supported by IBM's Developmate, Index Technology PC Prism, and Knowledgeware Planning workbench. Systems analysis and design tasks are aided by Bachman's Data analyst, Index's Excelerator, and Knowledgeware's Analysis/Design workbench. IBM provides the standard complement of source code editors, debuggers, and compilers for the common languages including SAA-compliant versions of COBOL, Fortran, PL/1, RPG, and INSPECT.

Central to the AD/Cycle strategy and the SAA strategy is the Cross Systems Product (CSP) code generator. In fact, according to IBM's plan, all front-end CASE tools will target their output to be compatible with CSP, initially through the external Source Format (ESF) data transfer interface, and eventually the AD/Cycle Repository. Because CSP will eventually support all strategic SAA platforms, in a sense it will act not only as a code generator, but also as a switch allowing developers to target application specifications to any desired platform. For the testing phase, IBM has two tools of its own. The software Analysis Test Tool is a test coverage analyzer that helps a developer evaluate how well a test data set exercises the code. The tool provides a graphical representation of program structure and measures the complexity of each module so the developer can focus on modules that have a higher probability of containing defects. It also determines what percentage of paths have been exercised by a particular test sequence. The Workstation Interactive Test Tool is a regression testing aid that mimics a user exercising the application under test and detects any errors in the application by comparing the actual output with a predefined pattern.

In the AD/Cycle diagram (Figure 10.1), the horizontal layer above the phase-oriented tools depicts cross-life-cycle or horizontal tools; that is, tools that are used throughout the software development process. On top of the horizontal tool layer is the common presentation interface employed by all tools to interact with the user.

Other tools to round out the environment include the Dictionary Model Transformer for transferring information from the primary dictionary to Repository Manager.

All the tools sit on top of the AD/Cycle platform, which provides tool integration services and library management services. Also included in the platform is the Repository Manager, which manages the data created by CASE tools, and an information model, defined using Repository Manager entity-relationship (E-R) facilities, by which the tools can interpret the meaning of each other's data.

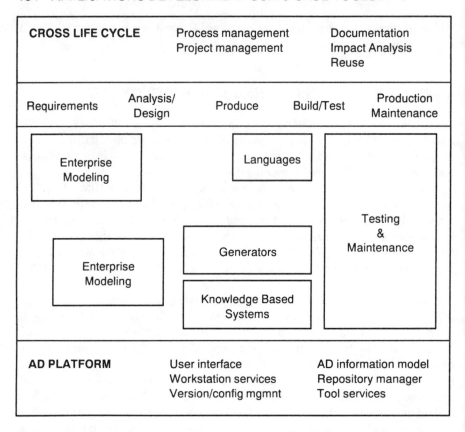

Figure 10.1 AD/Cycle is an integration architecture or framework for a full life cycle CASE environment. It comprises several layers addressing presentation, data and control integration. AD/Cycle includes a repository, tool integration services, vertical tools, horizontal tools and a common user interface.

10.8.1 The Repository Manager

As a major element of AD/Cycle, the Repository Manager provides the means to manage design information created for application development, systems management, and business modeling. It includes interactive and program-callable services to support a repository of enterprise-wide information allowing users to:

- Model the enterprise and application specific information in the entity relationship format
- Describe the view of that information that a particular tool can access

- Define controls and constraints on the use of repository information, globally or specific tool
- Read, write, and update the repository contents
- Perform utility and service functions

10.8.2   Hardware and Software Requirements

AD/Cycle operates on a cooperative processing model; i.e., a host and programmable workstation. Currently, the AD/Cycle host is a System 370 mainframe running MVS. The AD/Cycle framework, including the Repository Manager, CSP compilers, and testing tools, operates on the host. The front-end tools operate under Presentation Manager on a PS/2 running OS/2 Extended Edition.

10.9   SUMMARY

This chapter discussed environment architecture having tremendous impact on Information Engineering and CASE tools. Compliance to these environments has been swift for both SAA and AD/Cycle. In most cases, vendors are planning to evolve their tools to be compatible with both environments.

Index Technology is converting Exceleration to run under OS/2 and Common User Access. Another version of Bachman Information System's Bachman/Re-engineering Product Set for data analysts and administrators is being developed to run under OS/2EE and Presentation Manager.

Knowledgeware announced a new OS/2-based version of its product line called Application Development Workbench, which will be divided into four tool sets addressing separate phases of the life cycle. A vendor response to these environments is shown in Figure 10.2.

Vendor	Product	AD/Cycle Support
Adpac	PM/SS	
Aion	Aion Development System	
American Management Systems	Life Cycle Productivity System	SAA-compatible version of CORE Foundation Software. Intent to make LPS operate within AD/Cycle framework.
American Software		
Andersen Consulting	Foundation	Commitment to SAA compliance. Support for CSP through ESF. Look forward to adopting IBM Repository once it becomes viable for large-scale development.
Applied Business Technology	Project Workbench	
Asyst	The Developer, The Integrater	Will maintain AD/Cycle compatibility across different IBM and non-IBM hardware platforms.
Business Software Technology	Endeavor	Will employ Repository Manager/MVS as a central location for all its software management information in three phases.
Cadware	Modeling Platform	
Caseworks	CASE:PM	
CGI-Informatique	Pacbase	
Computer Command & Control Co.	Model	
D. Appleton Co.	Leverage	
FB Technologies	High Productivity Systems	
Gamma International	ESPACF MEGA	
Information Builders	Focus, PM/Focus, Fact, Level 5	
Integral Systems		

Figure 10.2   Vendors' compliance with AD/Cycle

Vendor	Product	AD/Cycle Support
Learmonth & Burchett	System Planner, Systems Engineer	
Management Science America	Information Expert	
Manager Software Products	Manager family	Support the coexistence of Manager products and IBM Repository manager by 1) using both repository systems and synchronizing via DICTIONARY MANAGER or 2) migrating all data to IBM Repository while continuing to use Manager products to provide value added in key areas.
McCormack & Dodge	Millenium	
McDonnell Douglas	ProKit Workbench	
Micro Focus	COBOL/2 Workbench, compiler, Dialog System	Intend to support AD/Cycle and SAA in all products.
Nastec/Transform Logic	DesignAid/Transform	Intends to support Repository Manager and CSP through ESF. Will provide SAA-compliant user interface for DesignAid.
Netron	Netron/CAP	SAA code and standards reflected in frame library
Pansophic Systems	Telon, Panapt, Panvalet	
Policy Management Systems Corp.		
Sage Software	APS	Committed to use AD/Cycle as the integration framework for its family of workstation and maniframe-based development tools. Application Domain data model will serve as an extension to AD/Cycle's information model.
SAS Institute	SAS System	
Softlab	Maestro	

Figure 10.2 Vendors' compliance with AD/Cycle *(continued)*

Vendor	Product	AD/Cycle Support
Softool	Change and Configuration Control	Endorses AD/Cycle initiative. Currently offer relational versiona of CCC using DB2 and SQL/DS. Supports ISPF/PDF and will integrate with Repository Manager.
Sterling Software	Presentation/Answer, Mark IX	
Synon	Synon/2E	
Systematica	Virtual Software Factory	
Texas Instruments	Information Engineering Facility	Future releases will comply with AD/Cycle framework. Current interface to CSP through ESF.
Viasoft	VIA/Center	Fully compatible with IBM's AD/Cycle direction and repository service.

Figure 10.2   Vendors' compliance with AD/Cycle (*continued*)

11

QUALITY AND PRODUCTIVITY BENEFITS OF CASE TOOLS

11.1 INTRODUCTORY REMARKS

The CASE tool vendor has been making noises about substantial increases in productivity and quality once a tool has been introduced into the data processing organization. Some claims of 100% increase in productivity have been made. This chapter discusses the two aspects of quality and productivity and seeks to establish metrics by which each can be measured.

11.2 THE BENEFITS OF CASE TOOLS

For many software development organizations, the qualitative benefits of CASE tools outweigh the quantitative benefits. Design and development times will almost always be reduced by using CASE tools, but perhaps their most satisfying benefit comes in the form of insurance, or peace of mind, that the job is being done properly, on schedule, and to the user's specification. CASE tools yield a tremendous benefit in revealing many requirements before the implementation begins.

11.2.1 Complete Requirements Specifications

Most software engineers have witnessed the failure of a software application out in the field because what they build was not what the end users wanted. Encouraging the software designer to completely specify the system's requirements is the goal of requirements analysis and specification CASE tools. Most specification methodologies enforce end-user involvement because it is impossible to complete the specification without developing a model of the end user's process or business functions. Although the risk of creating an Edsel still exists, despite the best efforts of all involved, the probability of doing so is greatly diminished with complete, detailed, and accurate requirements specifications.

11.2.2   Accurate Design Specifications

There is nothing more frightening for a novice software engineer to face than the task of maintaining a large software system with incomplete, inaccurate, or nonexistent design documentation. Rarely is in-line software documentation sufficient to communicate the system's architectural design without embroiling the reader in unnecessary detail. Furthermore, we have all seen designs that violate sound design practices: designs that expose unnecessary detail, encourage "spaghetti code," and ignore the "separation of concerns" doctrine.

Often, development teams say "we'll write design specifications after the code has stabilized." As a software engineer, you should never let a software development team write the code first and then draw up the design specifications unless the project is considered a throwaway prototype aimed at uncovering new end-user requirements.

11.2.3   Current Design Specifications

Perhaps worse than incomplete design specifications are inaccurate design specifications that have not been kept up to date, relative to modifications made to the source code base. Many futile hours can be wasted trying to understand a system's architecture from pouring over the design specification but not being able to reconcile it against the actual implementation.

CASE design tools can help maintain synchronization with the code implementation. Many of these tools actually attach the code to the specification, so that as the specification changes, so does the underlying code. Other CASE tools, most notably user interface design tools, automatically generate code. There is no need to maintain synchronization because you never touch the underlying code; only the design is edited.

11.2.4   Reduced Development Time

Completely specifying the software architecture substantially reduces, if not eliminates, waste from unnecessary or throwaway code. Reducing such waste translates directly into reduced implementation time. Many software professionals feel most productive when they are sitting in front of a screen actually writing codes. The constant gratification of a compile and run cycle is tremendously appealing to most of us, a trait which most likely stems from our homework assignments in overburdened undergraduate programming courses, where good program design skills are rarely emphasized. The immediacy of homework project deadlines compels junior programmers to start writing code without considering its design. Software professionals must feel they are being as productive in the requirements analysis and design specification phases as they feel when writing code during the implementation phase. Because of the highly interactive, graphical orientation of most CASE tools, using a CASE tool seduces many software engineers into believing they are writing codes when, in fact, they are really designing software architectures. Time spent designing is repaid many times over during implementation, testing, and release phases.

11.2.5 Highly Maintainable Code

Any successful software project will never really be finished. End users will either demand functional improvements or will identify bugs in the software's operation, mandating some form of continuing development or maintenance work on the software. This becomes particularly acute when the software application is an actual product for sale to end users. It is much easier to develop a design specification when embarking on a new software project or a major rewrite of an existing system; it is much more difficult to keep the design specification synchronized with evolutionary maintenance and enhancement work.

Although each minor enhancement or bug fix may not warrant an update to the design specification, the aggregation of several modifications will. It is difficult to enforce the discipline of making periodic design specification updates under these conditions, especially when the maintenance has been left to a skeleton crew.

It is difficult even for CASE tools to provide assistance in maintaining design specifications if the software built from the specifications is handwritten. But those CASE tools that automatically generate software from design specifications are not encumbered by this problem. In fact, this trend predominates in areas where software can be automatically generated, such as user interface design and database access design.

11.3 INCREASING SOFTWARE PRODUCTIVITY

The key to productivity is automation. This applies to software development as well as to other types of product manufacturing. Computer-aided software engineering is the automation of many of the tasks in the software life cycle. The CASE technology is the focus of productivity improvements in the late 1980s.

The proof that CASE works is already coming from many companies for which dramatic software productivity increases are being reported. Although very different, these companies share their successful use of CASE tools for increasing productivity. In each case, they have chosen tools that help automate structured methodologies.

Structured methodologies, many of which were developed in the 1970s, provide a proven way of producing high-quality, reliable software systems. The drawback of

	EXCELERATOR	IE WORKBENCH	FACTORY
Type	Analysis Toolkit	CASE Workbench	Case generator workbench
Primary Use	System analysis and documentation	System analysis and design	System development and maintenance
Productivity Gains	Factor of 2 to 10 times	Factor of 2 to 4 times	Factor of 2 to 20 times

Figure 11.1   Case productivity statistics

structured methodologies, however, has been the time-consuming manual effort they require. Automated tools solve this problem by taking over many of the burdensome details and paperwork of applying these methodologies. This frees the software developer to concentrate on the creative part of the software development process. The result is a very significant increase in each individual developer's ability to produce more and better-quality software systems.

The basic idea behind CASE is to support each phase of the life cycle with a set of labor-saving tools. Some CASE tools concentrate on supporting the early phases of the life cycle. They give automated assistance in the form of automated diagram drawing, screen painting, and correctness checking. Others focus on the implementation phases of the life cycle. They include automated code and test case generators.

In some cases, these tools are used in conjunction with third- and fourth-generation languages. In other cases, they replace them by allowing the developer to create high-level program specifications from which program code can be generated. In Figure 11.1, we report some productivity gains across the various phases of the life cycle.

11.3.1   EXCELERATOR Productivity Experiences

EXCELERATOR, from Index Technology Co., is a productivity tool aimed at designing and documenting information systems and real-time systems. It is a PC-based tool to be used by a professional systems analyst and designer.

EXCELERATOR has four basic facilities:

- An automated diagramming tool for drawing structured diagrams, like data flow diagrams, structure charts, data models, control flow diagrams, and finite-state diagrams.
- Screen and report painters for specifying and prototyping the user interface of an information system.

- An integrated repository for storing and cross-checking all systems analysis and design information.
- An automated analysis tool for checking and reporting the syntactic correctness, completeness, and consistency of structured diagrams.

EXCELERATOR is best described as an analysis toolkit because it provides an integrated set of tools for automating systems analysis and design tasks.

EXCELERATOR provides its user with three major benefits. First, it makes structured methodologies such as DeMarco structured analysis and Yourdon structured design practical to use. Automated drawing and redrawing of structured diagrams, capturing of design information in the automated repository, and automated tracking and maintaining of all design details allow the analyst to concentrate on the design problem rather than on paperwork.

Second, EXCELERATOR improves overall system design quality. Keeping all design information on the computer and then checking its consistency and completeness automatically assures the highest-quality design information.

Third, EXCELERATOR speeds up the design process. With EXCELERATOR's automated assistance, major design modifications can be made in seconds, work can be checked at the same time that the design is being developed, and the designs can be reused by retrieving them from EXCELERATOR's repository.

Recent case studies from 12 organizations using EXCELERATOR in systems analysis and design work cited productivity increases ranging from a factor of 2 to a factor of 10 times. The 12 organizations have a similar development environment:

- IBM mainframe shop using VM and/or MVS
- Installed database management systems such as IMS and DB2
- Use of fourth-generation tools such as FOCUS, DATA DICTIONARY, and DATA MANAGER
- Use of COBOL for large mainframe-based applications

At each organization, EXCELERATOR was used mainly in new system development efforts as a tool for automating currently used structured methods. The primary user was a system analyst and the primary use was for a system requirements specification. EXCELERATOR users reported an average of 8 to 30 hours to become proficient users of the tool. They were already trained in structured methods.

11.3.2 U.S. Government EXCELERATOR Experiences

One of 12 case studies came from a U.S. government organization, which reported that with the aid of EXCELERATOR, it could reduce the length of the development cycle to a point where a system could be implemented before it became obsolete. Analysts completed system specifications in four months instead of the estimated two years.

11.3.3 ARCO EXCELERATOR Experiences

Another EXCELERATOR case study came from ARCO. At ARCO, most software development for mainframe applications is done using COBOL and the SDM structured development methodology. ARCO chose EXCELERATOR because they were looking for a tool to automate the data modeling process. They needed a way to enhance the productivity of software developers since, due to a restructuring in business, their development staff size had been greatly reduced. ARCO began using EXCELERATOR in 1984. By mid-1986, ARCO had 23 copies of EXCELERATOR installed.

On a major production redevelopment project, ARCO reported that systems analysts using EXCELERATOR prepared logical data models of information systems with a 10-to-1 gain in productivity over doing it manually.

ARCO enhanced EXCELERATOR's import/export capability by writing its own software that enables importing and exporting of information from EXCELERATOR's dictionary to and from IBM's Data Dictionary. From a data administration viewpoint, this means that data can be better controlled. To ARCO, this is just as important as performing software tasks faster.

11.3.4 Touche Ross EXCELERATOR Experiences

Touche Ross was one of the first users of EXCELERATOR because EXCELERATOR supports Yourdon structured methodology. Touche Ross has EXCELERATOR to design many different types of applications, such as order entry, inventory control, criminal justice, and bidding systems. The primary user of EXCELERATOR is a systems analyst trained in Yourdon structured techniques. There are four personal computers each with a copy of EXCELERATOR at Touche Ross. One personal computer is assigned to a project where one person is responsible for entering and updating all system information in the EXCELERATOR dictionary.

They reported that EXCELERATOR dramatically changes the way they do systems analysis. They use EXCELERATOR down to a system design level. System specification quality is greatly improved, user involvement quality is greatly improved, user involvement is made practical, and automated drawing of diagrams make changes easy to make. Although the primary use of EXCELERATOR is for system requirements specification, Touche Ross has also used EXCELERATOR to describe all sorts of systems for the purpose of better understanding and streamlining the systems, rather than with the intention of eventually automating the systems.

Touche Ross feels that a major productivity advantage of using EXCELERATOR is that it is easy to review system requirements because it is easy to revise automated diagrams with EXCELERATOR. Another advantage is the consistency of the output it produces.

The consensus among EXCELERATOR users is that the key to productivity success is good management, a solid understanding of structured analysis and design, and powerful automated tools.

11.4 APPLICATION FACTORY PRODUCTIVITY

The Application Factory from Cortex Corporation is a productivity tool for generating on-line, multi-user information systems. The core of the FACTORY is its automatic code generator. The FACTORY runs on DEC VAX computers.

The APPLICATION FACTORY includes five basic facilities:

- Screen and report painters for specifying and prototyping the system's user interface
- A repository for storing all information about a system
- Automated checking for completeness and consistency of program specifications
- A code generator capable of automatic generation of 95% of the program code from program specifications
- Automated program documentation generator

The APPLICATION FACTORY is used by systems analysts and programmers to develop and maintain medium-sized to large information systems. The FACTORY is appropriate for building medium-sized to large production systems in high-volume transaction environments interfacing to real-time devices.

Users noted three major benefits. First, developers are more productive with the APPLICATION FACTORY than programming in third-generation languages such as COBOL and Fortran. Also, developers are more productive with the APPLICATION FACTORY than programming in fourth-generation languages. The FACTORY generates highly efficient code and has the power to handle large as well as small application systems. Unlike fourth-generation languages, the FACTORY has been used successfully to build high-volume transaction systems. With the FACTORY, the bigger, the better in terms of application size. The FACTORY has been used to build systems with 2,500 function points handling 15,000 transactions daily and 300 users.

Second, the APPLICATION FACTORY makes rapid, iterative prototyping a practical way of building systems to meet user requirements. A series of prototype models of the systems are built as a way of more clearly identifying user requirements. The final system eventually evolves from the prototypes. The APPLICATION FACTORY makes this process quick and easy by generating code automatically from prototype specification.

Third, the APPLICATION FACTORY greatly simplifies program maintenance because the program specification, not the code, is maintained. When there is a need to change a system, its specification is changed, and then the code and its documentation are regenerated automatically from the system specification. In this way, documentation is a by-product of development and maintenance and is always kept up to date.

CASE studies of system development with the APPLICATION FACTORY reported an average productivity increase of a factor of 13 times with FACTORY over COBOL. The case studies included the development of 26 application systems at 22 separate locations. Productivity increases were measured with function points by comparing the estimated COBOL effort to the actual FACTORY effort. System size ranged from 78 to 2,418 function points, which is approximately the size range of 8,300- to 253,000-line COBOL programs. In addition, the case studies showed that the FACTORY productivity relative to COBOL increases as application size and complexity increases. Experiences show that project size and developer experience significantly affected productivity, and that developer experience had the greater effect of the two.

11.4.1   Deere & Co. IEW Experiences

At Deere & Co., there are 39 decentralized systems development groups and no overall company standards. Because the farm industry has been depressed, there has been a hiring freeze at Deere & Co. since 1979. During this period, the addition of multiple database management systems such as DB2, ORACLE, and dBASEIII has meant growing complexity for the development organizations, which previously supported only IMS. Also, during this period, Deere & Co. has developed its own system development methodology based on the information engineering methodology.

The character of Deere & Co.'s System Planning and Data Administration Department is to:

- Perform early requirements analysis for projects involving shared corporate data.
- Improve data administration and its integration with system development.
- Position the entire organization to improve system development by supporting the Deere methodology with automated tools.

The major productivity issue at Deere & Co. is to achieve a 30% software development productivity increase. They want fewer people to do more work in less time. They want to do a better job of specifying system requirements. They want to move analysis more easily from project to project. Finally, they want to reduce their maintenance effort.

Deere & Co. chose INFORMATION ENGINEERING WORKBENCH (IEW) to help them achieve their productivity goals. Since 1985, there have been 10 copies of the IEW installed at Deere & Co. This is an average of one personal computer per analyst. The total cost of hardware and software is $15,000 per CASE workstation. It was a two-week effort to integrate IEW use with the Deere methodology. The primary user of the IEW is the systems analyst. The primary use is to design new systems. The time to become proficient with the tool averaged two days, assuming that the user was already familiar with structured analysis techniques.

Deere & Co. plans eventually to have one IEW PC-based CASE workstation for each of its 300 programmer and analysts. Currently, five medium-sized system development projects are using IEW. Productivity gains of a factor of 2 have been reported for requirements analysis and data analysis tasks using the IEW rather than doing it manually. One system under development is the Track Project Development

Cycle System. Ninety data flow diagrams and 50 entity-relationship diagrams were used to describe its 430 business functions. Automatic diagramming tools make diagrams a practical analysis tool and help improve communications with the users. In addition, Deere & Co. reported that automated checking for design errors in the structured diagrams was the most important factor in increasing productivity. Getting errors out early in the development process simplified the job down the line in the later development phases.

The Deere philosophy and advice is to have the development methodology in place first. Tools do not provide the methodology, only the automated assistance for the methodology.

12

DATA DICTIONARIES AND CASE TOOLS

12.1 INTRODUCTION

The role of the data dictionary in the design, implementation, and maintenance of database systems has been well documented in the current literature.

The growing awareness of data as a corporate resource, resulting in data-driven, rather then process-driven systems, has led to recognition of the impact of data on departments outside of data processing. In this way, the system development life cycle has developed from a point where the focus of concern was on highly localized data processing problems. It is now recognized that the efficiency of a given system usually depends upon its end-user orientation and how well it represents and serves the organization as a whole. Current methodologies are becoming less process-oriented and more data-oriented.

It is because of this new awareness that the data dictionary can play a significant part in supporting the SDLC. It provides a wealth of detail on which early research work can be based and is then an invaluable communication tool between the different departments that are involved in the SDLC.

It is for these reasons that the succeeding sections discuss the role of the data dictionary in the SDLC.

12.2 WHAT IS A DATA DICTIONARY?

The data dictionary can be defined as an organized reference to the data content of an organization's programs, systems, databases, collections of all files, or manual records. It may be maintained manually or by computer. Sometimes the term "data dictionary" refers specifically to a software product that is utilized to maintain a dictionary database. The data dictionary will contain names, descriptions, and definitions of the organization's data resources.

12.3   THE CONCEPT OF METADATA

In the broadest sense, a data dictionary is *any* organized collection of information about data.

In the real world, any information system, whether or not it is computerized, exists to store and process data about objects (entities). We then create data records to represent occurrences of these entities. We define specific record types to represent specific entity types. Frequently, we also assign keys or identifiers, such as customer names and invoice numbers, to differentiate one record occurrence from another. A data dictionary can then be designed that contains data about those customer and invoice record types.

The customer and invoice records in the database contain ordinary data. The record in the data dictionary contains metadata, or data about the data. For example, the record in the data dictionary may contain the name, the record length, the data characteristics, and the recording mode of the record in the database.

12.4   ACTIVE VERSUS PASSIVE DATA DICTIONARIES

Data dictionaries are often categorized as active or passive. This refers to the extent of their integration with the database management system. If the data dictionary and the DBMS are integrated to the extent that the DBMS uses the definitions in the dictionary at run time, the dictionary is active. If the dictionary is freestanding or independent of the DBMS, it is passive.

An active dictionary must contain an accurate, up-to-date description of the physical database in order for the database management system to access the data.

In a passive dictionary environment, more effort is required to keep two copies of the same data, and great care must be taken to ensure that the two copies are actually identical.

12.5   THE ROLE OF THE DATA DICTIONARY IN THE SDLC

The role of the data dictionary in the system development life cycle is best exemplified in Figure 12.1.

Any analysis of Figure 12.1 will show that the data dictionary is the core of the systems design and development. The metadata collected in the dictionary about the

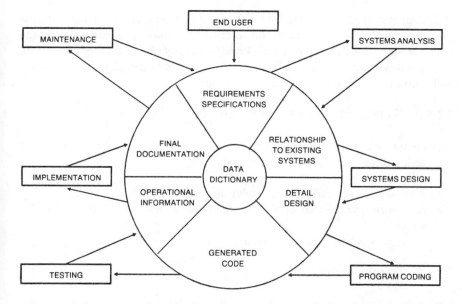

Figure 12.1   The SDLC Showing the Data Dictionary as a Communication and Documentation Tool

different phases of the SDLC are demonstrated in the second layer of the diagram. The third layer depicts the various interfaces to the different phases of the SDLC. The directions of the arrows indicate that the interfaces act as input to the phases and also extract design information from the phases.

As we move in a clockwise direction around the second layer, we notice, starting with the input from the end users, that the following types of metadata are collected:

- Requirements specifications
- Relationships to existing systems
- Detail design
- Generated code
- Operational information
- Final documentation

12.5.1   Requirements Specifications

As indicated in Chapter 1, the systems analyst or the data analyst collects data from the end user on the entities in which he has a particular interest. He may collect definitions and descriptions about the entities, data characteristics, security requirements, attribute content, and the processes involved in moving the data across interfaces and manipulating that data.

The analyst synthesizes this data and then enters as much of it into the data dictionary as the constructs of the dictionary allow. For example, in the DATAMANAGER data dictionary marketed by Manager Software Products (MSP), the analyst can enter data about the system, file, groups of data, and data items that will constitute a solution to the user's requirements.

12.5.2   Relationship to Existing Systems

In arriving at what may be the optimum solution to the user's requirements, the analyst must seek to determine from the dictionary if:

- A system already exists that can solve the problem.
- No system exists, what portions of the existing systems can be used in his solution.
- Alternate solutions can be obtained.

12.5.3   Detail Design

During detail system design, the analyst will enter data about the data models, the process flows, the programming specifications, the file layouts, and report formats. If the current design has any relationship to designs already existing in the data dictionary, the analyst can extract that portion and implement it with the new metadata.

12.5.4   Generated Code

The data dictionary may contain copy books (source statements) and source statements or pointers to source statement libraries that may be extracted to use for program testing.

It is now possible to generate code from process definitions and programming specifications stored in the data dictionary. Current CASE tools can generate this code for several languages and several different platforms; e.g., PC or mainframe.

12.5.5   Operational Information

The data dictionary may contain information which will enable the data processing staff to execute the programs. This information may include run instructions, job control language (JCL) setup, distribution information, test plans and requirements, and processing exceptions.

12.5.6   Final Documentation

The final documentation information stored in the data dictionary may include user-manual instructions, impact analysis information, acceptance testing and sign-off information, change control information, and job control language information.

12.6   DATA DICTIONARY INTERFACES

Interfaces with the data dictionary are many and varied. They act in two directions: those that provide the deliverables to the dictionary and those that extract information from the dictionary. These interfaces include:

- End user
- Systems analysis
- Systems design
- Program coding
- Testing
- Implementation
- Maintenance

12.6.1   The End User

The end user is the primary source of input to the requirements specifications phase of systems development. It is during this phase that data is collected on the objectives and scope of the project, the data and processing requirements, the operating environment, alternative processing, data security, and the input and output formats.

The advent of database management systems, structured design methodologies, and new development tools has signaled a larger role for the end user in systems development. The end user is as much a part of the systems development team as the data analyst or systems analyst. The success or failure of the system depends to a large degree on the quality of the data collected on the user requirements.

12.6.2   The Systems Analysis Phase

During the systems analysis phase, data is obtained from the end user and the user requirements specifications and is fed into the systems design phase. The relationship to existing systems data is stored in the data dictionary.

During this phase, the data and systems analyst will iteratively extract data from the requirements specifications already stored in the data dictionary, augment it with that from the end user and any obtained from existing systems to come up with data process models that form the primary deliverables of the systems design phase.

If during the systems analysis phase no data is found in the data dictionary that connects the current system with other systems, the analyst enters any existing relationships into the data dictionary.

12.6.3   The Systems Design Phase

During the systems design phase, the data analyst extracts information from the analysis phase and relationship to existing systems stored in the data dictionary and develops a data model. This model is, in turn, stored in the data dictionary as detail design metadata. Meanwhile, the systems (process) analyst develops a process model with information from the data dictionary and the systems analysis phase. The data collected during this phase is stored in the detail design section of the data dictionary and used as input, through programming specifications, to the program coding phase.

12.6.4   The Program Coding Phase

During the program coding phase, the programmer/analyst takes specifications from the systems design phase and couples it with metadata from the detail design information stored in the data dictionary to produce program code for the testing phase and to be stored as metadata and sometimes source data in the data dictionary.

12.6.5   The Testing Phase

During this phase, the analysts take program code from the program coding phase and generated code stored in the data dictionary and test it to obtain operational metadata to be stored in the data dictionary and program code for the implementation phase.

12.6.6   The Implementation Phase

During this phase, operational information metadata stored in the data dictionary is coupled with the tested program code to produce implementable systems. The results from the phase are stored in the data dictionary as a final document and are used as input to the maintenance phase.

12.6.7   The Maintenance Phase

During this phase, metadata from the final document stored in the data dictionary and input from the implementation phase are used to maintain the production systems.

This phase also encompasses the updating of requirements specifications stored in the data dictionary and the constant reporting to the user of the results of these changes.

12.7   THE DATA DICTIONARY AS A DOCUMENTATION TOOL

As was mentioned earlier, the data dictionary plays a significant role in the systems development life cycle. One major role is documenting the results of each phase of the SDLC. This section describes some of the entries that are documented in the data dictionary for the major phases of the SDLC.

12.7.1   Documenting the System Design Phase

The data dictionary can offer substantial assistance to the designer during the system design phase by providing the source and storage for the inputs and outputs of the design step.

The inputs to data design are full descriptions of the business processes and the data required by these processes. The outputs are the logical views and the logical database (also known as logical schemas). A logical database refers to a structuring of entities and relations between entities supporting the business processes of the application.

There are many different methods of transforming the business processes and their required data into a logical database. One is a top-down data design method identifying entities and the relationships between the entities before defining the attributes of each entity.

Alternatively, there are bottom-up data design techniques, which encourage the description of entities and the attributes identifying the entities, before identifying relationships between entities.

There are five basic steps in top-down data design:

- Identifying the business functions of the application.
- Identifying the data required by each function and the procedure by which data is collected.
- Identifying the entities of the application.
- Defining the relationships between the entities.
- Ascribing attributes to their entities.

Nowhere is the importance of the data dictionary more obvious than in the building of the function's logical model. As the keeper of the "who," and "how" of the organizational information system, the data dictionary provides full descriptions of:

- The business functions
- The data generated by and used by the business functions
- The application entities
- The relationships of the application's entities to one another
- The attributes of the entities

Frequently, data itself goes through an evolutionary process, its definition becoming more and more refined until it can finally be set. Data also can be perceived simultaneously from several user points of view. A data dictionary that has facilities for multiple logical dictionaries can document the history of a data item or process as well as hold these varied points of view. This can be a most valuable aid during the design stage.

12.7.2 Documenting the Detailed Design Phase

In a Business System Plan (BSP) the design phase is comprised of two levels, the general design and the detailed design, in which business activities, data, entities, relationships and attributes are described, not just on the application level, but from a higher level providing a corporate, transfunctional perspective. In BSP, the methodology is the same as with SDLC; it is simply engineered on a higher plane. Once these elements are plugged in, they remain in documented form on the data dictionary and can be accessed for future systems development as well. Another feature of the data dictionary that can be most useful at this point in the SDLC is its facility for providing implicit as well as explicit relationships. The systems designer, who might otherwise overlook these implicit relationships, is spared one more trap to fall into.

12.7.3 Documenting the Physical Design Phase

The details of physical design depend very much on the characteristics of the DBMS chosen for the database design.

In an IMS environment, the physical design includes the following selections:

- Physical databases and types of logical relationships, whether unidirectionally or bidirectionally physically paired.
- Access methods, whether HISAM, HIDAM, or HDAM.
- Segments and hierarchical structures and data representation, including type and size.
- Secondary indices.
- Types of pointers in relationships.

The data dictionary is a very useful tool to document these selections. In addition, volume and usage statistics necessary for the ordering of database segments and for determination of storage estimates can be documented in the data dictionary.

12.7.4 Documenting the Implementation Phase

The implementation phase is very often not considered a part of the SDLC because by that point, the system has been installed and consequently has entered a separate, operational period. It is a stage that has enormous impact on not just the system, but the entire organization as well. Maintenance is also a task which is especially well served by the data dictionary, which can provide:

- Complete up-to-date documentation of the system.
- An historical and multi-user perspective view of the development of the definitions of the systems entities, process entities, and the relationships among them.
- Enforcement of the use of definitions in a logical manner.

- Security of the integrity of these definitions.
- The means of assessing the impact of system changes.

Consequently, the maintenance staff is provided with a comprehensive and logically consistent picture of the system, its functions, processes, and data components. They are thus properly prepared to respond to ways which will minimize error and save time, money, and frustration.

The maintenance stage is also the point at which the use of the data dictionary as a systems development tool is most easily validated. Systems founded upon data dictionary resources are the most likely to be spared the unnecessary and yet most typical function of maintenance — rectification of bad systems planning and specifications. Consequently, they are the ones most likely to free the maintenance stage for its proper function of adapting the system to the organization's changing environment. Obviously, this frees up the staff for the development of new systems and reduces many of the external pressures otherwise imposed on all systems.

12.7.5   Documenting the Structured Maintenance Phase

Structured maintenance deals with the procedures and guidelines to achieve system change or evolution through the definition of data structure change to accommodate the requirements of system change. The inputs to structured maintenance are user change requests and the current system, including database design and systems design. These are included in the data dictionary. The output from structured maintenance is, ideally, a system reflecting the user change request.

There are five steps in structured maintenance:

- The identification of the changes to the data structures required to accommodate the user request.
- The identification of the program functions which currently process the data structures. These program functions are reviewed and systems changes are identified.
- The determination of the cost of the change. One of the benefits of this method is that it quickly indicates significant costly changes, seen when the data structures required to accommodate the change are very different from the current data structures.
- Perform the implementation — if the cost is acceptable.
- Test the results.

Structured maintenance thus goes through all of the steps of the structured system development methodology as defined here.

This is an effective way to minimize the need to have to recover from past mistakes of the system, whether they are the result of unstructured or structured methodologies.

A system development life cycle is used to produce the means by which the organizational data is to be manipulated. Before it can be manipulated, however, it must be managed, and that is the function of the data dictionary.

12.8 THE DATA DICTIONARY AND DATA SECURITY

The data dictionary can be used in the database environment to protect the organization's data. Entries in the data dictionary can be used to indicate who has access rights to what data and who can update or alter that data. It can also be used to indicate who has responsibility for creating and changing definitions.

Current data dictionaries utilize several different protection mechanisms to effect data security in an environment. Also, data dictionaries can have pointers in an "AUTHORIZATION" section to various data security software packages. Some of these are:

- Access management
- Privacy transformations
- Cryptographic controls
- Security kernels
- Access matrix

Due to space constraints, I will not discuss all of these mechanisms at length, but will instead refer you to some of the current literature on data security. However, here is brief discussion on some of them.

12.8.1 Access Management

These techniques are aimed at preventing unauthorized users from obtaining services from the system or gaining access to its files. The procedures involved are authorization, identification, and authentication. Authorization is given for certain users to enter the database and request certain types of information. Users attempting to enter the system must first identify themselves and their locations, and then authenticate the identification.

12.8.2 Privacy Transformations

Privacy transformations are techniques for concealing information by coding the data in user-processor communications or in files. Privacy transformations consist of sets of logical operations on the individual characters of the data. Privacy transformations break down into two general types: irreversible and reversible. Irreversible privacy transformations include aggregation and random modification. In this case, valid statistics can be obtained from such data, but individual values cannot be obtained.

Reversible privacy transformations are as follows:

- Coding — Replacement of a group of words in one language by a word in another language.
- Compression — Removal of redundancies and blanks from transmitted data.
- Substitution — Replacement of letters in one or more items.
- Transposition — Distortion of the sequence of letters in the ciphered text; all letters in the original text are retained in this technique.
- Composite Transformation — Combinations of the above methods.

12.8.3   Cryptographic Controls

Cryptographic transformations were recognized long ago as an effective protection mechanism in communication systems. In the past, they were used mainly to protect information transferred through communication lines.

There is still debate about the cost/benefit ratio of encrypting large databases. My experience with encryption indicates that the cost of producing clear text from large encrypted databases is prohibitive.

12.8.4   Security Kernels

Security kernels, as the name suggests, are extra layers of protection surrounding operating systems. The kernels are usually software programs which are used to test for authenticity and to either authorize or deny all user requests to the operating system.

A request to the operating system to execute a task or retrieve data from the database is routed to the security kernel, where the request is examined to determine if the user is authorized to access the requested data. If all checks are passed, the request is transmitted to the operating system, which then executes the request.

12.9   DATA DICTIONARY STANDARDS

There are two types of data-related standards for data dictionaries: data definition standards and data format conformance.

"Data definition" refers to a standard way of describing data. One example is the naming of data. The naming standard may be in the form of rigid rules or established conventions for assigning names to data entities.

All user areas within the enterprise will know that, for instance, the data element "customer name" — used in files, programs, and reports — means the same throughout the enterprise.

"Data format conformance" is content-related. It means that a data element, in addition to having the same name throughout the enterprise, must also conform to a common set of format rules for the data element to retain the same meaning. For example, all data elements involving "date" should have the same format throughout the enterprise — and only that format should be assigned. Similarly, if codes are to be used throughout the enterprise, these must be uniform. If an acceptable "state" code is two letters, that must be the universally accepted code in the enterprise, and no other code, whether one, three, or four letters, should be used.

12.9.1   Standard Formats for Data Dictionary Entries

Standards are required for the format and content used in defining and describing meta-entities of the data dictionary. This means setting standards for the type of information that must be collected for each entry type and, most important, for the conventions that must be observed in defining these attributes. In effect, this amounts to defining a set of standards for methods of preparing attribute, entity, and relationship descriptions.

There are a number of general guidelines for establishing a standard. Several standard entries are available in commercially produced dictionaries. However, a typical standard entry for a data element is illustrated in Figure 12.2. A data element may be described in terms of the attributes in the figure.

12.9.2   Standards for Programs Interfacing with a Data Dictionary

Data dictionary standards for programming interfaces basically fall into the area of the structure of the "call" statement from the programming language to the dictionary package.

Other standards in this area will indicate how high-level languages will use the data dictionary to build file structures and record layouts from "COPY" books. They will also indicate how these languages will access the dictionary itself.

12.9.3   Security Standards

Standards for access rules and controls will indicate who can access the dictionary, how the dictionary will be accessed, and whether the contents will be accessed in their original form or as copies.

Standards in the area of security will cover the use of the data dictionary as a protection mechanism and the entries that must be made in the data dictionary to achieve those standards.

12.10   THE REPOSITORY

The repository is defined as a place for storing information about items and activities of importance to your enterprise — an organized, shared collection of information which supports business and data processing kinds of activities.

Data Element	Definition
Identification number	A 7-character unique identifier beginning with ELXXXXX.
Designator	A short name composed of the keywords of the DESCRIPTION.
Programming name	An abbreviated form of the DESIGNATOR using only approved abbreviations. Example: LEGL-CUST-NAME.
Description	A narrative explanation of the data element; the first sentence must identify the real-world entity being described. The second sentence may expand on usage characteristics. Example: The name of a customer, which is the legal name. It may not be the commonly used name. It is usually derived from legal papers.

Figure 12.2   Sample standard for data element description

The repository is clearly more than a data dictionary and more than a project management database; in effect, a complete repository combines the functions of a project database, a data dictionary, and a process dictionary. It stores the deliverables of the software development process, as well as information about those deliverables.

The repository concept also encompasses the common notion of an encyclopedia, which is a database that includes all design information for an integrated CASE toolkit in an abstract, internally consistent form that is independent of any particular tool or representational style.

12.10.1   Repository Data Management and Protection

A repository provides services to help manage the large amount of design data generated by a full CASE environment. It provides operations to input, organize, and select data, to produce reports, to manage multiple versions, and to recover in the event of system failures. While most interaction with the repository will be via specific CASE tools, a direct repository user interface is also a useful facility for making ad hoc queries.

12.10.2   Data Integrity

A repository provides facilities to validate data on input and to ensure consistency among related data elements. This includes mechanisms to check data types and value ranges, to flag incomplete objects, to automatically initiate cascading deletes when required, and to perform specific tests specified by the repository administrator.

12.10.3 Information Sharing

The repository makes it much easier to share information among developers. It provides standardized, multi-user access controls and keeps track of synchronization requirements and change dependencies.

12.10.4 Tool Integration

The repository provides a set of data manipulation services and a semantic model to enable individual CASE tools to share information. This becomes particularly important for environments supporting the full life cycle, since tool-to-tool "pipes" become very wieldy over many development phases, especially when prototyping and other interactive approaches are used. In addition, code generation typically requires input from multiple tools, and it is much easier if the task of synchronizing the input is left to the repository. The repository also acts as a place to store information about existing programs generated by reverse engineering tools.

12.10.5 Methodology Enforcement

Besides ensuring that the design data is valid, the repository plays a role in helping developers follow the organization's methodology. The repository can store a blueprint of the system development process and compare this to the actual status of the project, since it also has knowledge about the specific deliverables for an application.

12.10.6 Extensibility

In some integrated CASE workbenches, the methodology is "hardwired" into the tools and their accompanying dictionary. The repository provides an opportunity to extend the definition of representations, design rules, and process tasks and deliverables, allowing the user to define a methodology unique to the organization.

12.10.7 Documentation Standardization

The repository defines a standard schema for design information and provides mechanisms to generate reports in standardized formats. If a repository is used across the development organization, the documentation of each project and application will be more complete and understandable to anyone having to interface with a new system.

12.10.8   Consolidation of an Information Architecture

Once an organization has come to grips with the need to understand and optimize its own information architecture, it needs a secure place to store the definition of that architecture and to maintain it over time. The repository not only provides such a storage facility, but provides the lineage to the system development architecture which builds applications that operate against the information architecture.

13

APPLICATIONS
MAINTENANCE USING
CASE TOOLS

13.1 INTRODUCTION

Maintenance is an ever-increasing part of the cost of a data processing department. If we take the accepted definition of the maintenance cycle as any change to a program that occurs after it has been developed, it is found that 80% of the cost of the total cost of a program is the maintenance cycle. The reason for this lies in the competitive edge that revitalizing such software gives to a company; it is not enough to do something, it must be done better, faster, cheaper, and more effectively than the competition. The winds of change blow increasingly through the business community, new markets, repacking of existing services, new technology, better methods, new laws — the list is endless.

So, given that change is inevitable, how do we go about designing our systems for maintenance, and what do we do with the legacy of previous generations?

There are a whole host of methodologies and tools to help us with new development: analyst workbenches, fourth-generation languages, structured analysis techniques, and many others. Ninety percent of the CASE tools available deal with designing new systems and development. Yet, as we have seen, this represents a very small part of the problem.

Why has all the effort gone into the production of tools to help with designing and writing new systems? There are several answers to this.

First, it is always easier to draw a picture on a clean slate. It is glamorous and it is glitzy and the tool designers can really let themselves go. Maintenance has always carried slight connotations of "slopping-out" after somebody else has made the mess. We are talking about monochrome mainframes and a mono-culture here.

Second, there is very little understanding of how to improve maintenance performance. Many managers pay lip service to "structured programming" without a real appreciation of the concepts involved. There is always a tendency to "bend the rules to suit the reason" and it is a fact that it is not always easiest at the development stage to use structured methods. Many managers, who are under fire from the slippage of a development project, cut corners and consequently standards slip.

Last, the effects of bad programming may not make themselves felt for many months following development. Faulty logic may remain buried for years. Usually, the first signs that all is not well manifest themselves when maintenance is attempted. Since the logic is twisted, changes to one part of a program produce strange effects in another. The program becomes a danger zone — only the most experienced programmers can touch it, and they spend most of their time testing. In the most extreme cases, the program becomes a "no go" area, and it falls to the MIS manager to explain to the Board why the brilliant new incentive scheme will take much longer to implement.

13.2   RESTRUCTURING OF COBOL PROGRAMS

The major portion of application maintenance using CASE tools is concentrated on the restructuring of COBOL programs.

A structured program is divided into blocks. Each block performs a unique function, and the execution of each block is controlled at the highest level of program.

This approach is sometimes called top-down programming because the logic flow is hierarchically down from the control. Its great advantage is that separate blocks are procedurally independent; that is, code within each block may be considered self-contained. Of course, the data may be related inasmuch as if a value is changed in one block, its use in subsequent blocks is affected.

Each statement within a block is executed in sequence, so there are no control transfers out of or into a block. Blocks can be repeated a number of times or iterated by specifying the appropriate logic in the control paragraph. However, the number of times each statement in a block is executed is common to all statements in that block.

This is the essence of structured programming. In order to create the blocks in COBOL, the simplest unit of a paragraph is taken. A paragraph is a set of statements executed in order. The utility paragraphs are controlled by simple PERFORM statements located in a control paragraph. Iteration is controlled by the PERFORM-VARYING UNTIL construction.

If a program is written in this way, it truly reflects the block structure of the design. The control paragraph represents an abstract of the program logic. Moreover, any changes that preserve the block structure do not degrade the maintainability by obscuring the logical structure.

13.2.1   Styles of Structured Implementation

Two styles of structured implementation are in common use. The first relies on PERFORMED SECTIONS and the second on PERFORM THRU paragraphs. Each block consists of two paragraphs: one action and one exit. These can be used in exactly the same manner as simple PERFORM, but they are subject to misuse. If a paragraph contains a test which identifies that an early exit is desirable, there is a temptation to jump straight to the exit paragraph using explicit control; e.g., GO TO. This should be avoided because it degrades the block structure and removes the rule that each statement of a paragraph be performed in sequence.

Another shortcut is to combine control logic with the utility paragraph. Since controlling an iteration from outside may necessitate an extra switch variable, programmers commonly create the loop from inside using a local looping GO TO, provided this transfers control back to the paragraph label of iteration. It does not obscure the logic of a block, but it does mean that less of the control logic is abstracted in the control paragraph.

The correlation between low maintenance and good structure is so obvious that one is tempted to ask why unstructured programs are even written. There are several reasons for this. One reason is poor design, leading to incremental or evolutionary programming. The original function of the program vanishes beneath a plethora of "good ideas" or "patches" when the program is in production. Old programs which have been patched or amended repeatedly seldom show a clear block structure.

Another reason is flowcharting. Because of the sequential nature of program execution, designers assume that the best way to construct a program is sequentially.

13.2.2   Example of Restructuring of COBOL Programs

Algorithms for procedural restructuring were developed in the 1960s as a logical development from the work of Bohn and Jacopini on process flow. To put this into an "intelligent" form that rebuilt process logic took further research, and it was not until the late 1970s that RETROFIT appeared. RETROFIT works on the procedural code of a program, reconstructing it into a logically equivalent structured form.

To demonstrate the effectiveness of procedural restructuring, I have applied RETROFIT to the modified payroll program. The before and after results are shown in Figures 13.1 and 13.2

13.3   SOFTWARE REUSABILITY

Software reusability is defined as an approach that takes software parts, modifies them, and puts them together to form a new system.

```
000100 IDENTIFICATION DIVISION
000200***********************
000300 PROGRAM-ID. TAPREAD2.
000400***********************
000500* THIS PROGRAM READS TAPE FILES AND WRITES THEM TO
000600* AN OUTPUT FILE - ONE FILE MAY SPAN SEVERAL BLOCKS


004300*****************
004400 PROCEDURE DIVISION.
004500*****************
004600 A-OPEN.
004700      OPEN INPUT FILE.
004800
004900 A-READ.
005000      READ INFILE
005100         AT END STOP RUN.
005200      MOVE ZEROS   TO BLK-COUNT
005300                EOB-SW.
005400      IF EOF GO TO C-WRITE-RECORD.
005500
005600 A-OPENFILE.
005700      ADD 1 TO FIL-NAME-SUFFIX.
005800      OPEN OUTPUT OUTFILE.
005900      ADD FIL-COUNT TO BLK-COUNT.
006000      MOVE ZEROS   TO FIL-COUNT
006100                EOF-SW.
006200 B-PROCESS.
006300      IF FIL-COUNT = FIL-SIZE
006400         MOVE 1  TO EOF-SW.
006500      IF FIL-COUNT = BLK-SIZE
006600         MOVE 1  TO EOB-SW.
006700      IF EOF
006800         PERFORM C-CLOSE
006900         GO TO A-READ.
007000      IF EOB
007100         GO TO A-READ.
007200      ADD 1 TO FIL-COUNT.
007300      MOVE FIL-REC(FIL-COUNT)   TO OUT-REC.
007400
```

Figure 13.1   Modified payroll program

```
007500 C-WRITE-RECORD
007600      WRITE OUT-REC.
007700      GO TO B-PROCESS.
007800
007900 C-CLOSE.
008000      CLOSE OUTFILE.
008100      IF NOT EOB
008200          GO TO A-OPENFILE.
```

Figure 13.1   Modified payroll program *(continued)*

```
000010*
000020 IDENTIFICATION DIVISION.
000030*********************
000040*
000050 PROGRAM-ID
000060    TAPREAD2.
000070*********************
000080* THIS PROGRAM READS TAPE FILES AND WRITES THEM TO
000090* AN OUTPUT FILE - ONE FILE MAY SPAN SEVERAL BLOCKS
000100* RESTRUCTURED BY RETROFIT - THE CATALYST GROUP


001020/
001030 PROCEDURE DIVISION.
001040*********************
001050*
001060 A0000-MAINLINE-SECTION SECTION.
001070*
001080 A0010-MAINLINE.
001090      OPEN INPUT INFILE.
001100      PERFORM B0010-A-READ
001110          UNTIL SR-LOOP-FINISHED.
001140    STOP RUN.
001150*
001160/
001170 B0000-UTILITY-PARAGRAPHS-SECTION.
001180*
```

Figure 13.2   Restructured payroll program

```
001190 B0010-A-READ.
001200    PERFORM Z9010-READ-INFILE.
001210    IF    SR-10-STATUS-ON
001220          MOVE SR-FINISHED-FLAG    TO SR-LOOP-SW
001230    ELSE
001240          MOVE ZERO                TO BLK-COUNT
001250                                      EOB-SW
001260       IF EOF
001270          PERFORM Z9020-WRITE-OUT-REC
001280          PERFORM B0020-B-PROCESS
001290             UNTIL SR-LOOP-FINISHED
001300          MOVE SR-CONTINUE-FLAG
001310                                   TO SR-LOOP-SW
001320       ELSE
001330          PERFORM B0050-A-OPENFILE
001340          PERFORM B0020-B-PROCESS
001350             UNTIL SR-LOOP-FINISHED
001360          MOVE SR-CONTINUE-FLAG
001370                                   TO SR-LOOP-SW.
001380*
001390 B0020-B-PROCESS.
001400    PERFORM B0030-B-PROCESS.
001410    IF    EOF
001420          CLOSE OUTFILE
001430          PERFORM B0040-C-CLOSE
001440          IF SR-PRV-001
001450             MOVE ZERO             TO SR-PRV-SW
001460             PERFORM B0050-A-OPENFILE
001470          ELSE
001480             MOVE SR-FINISHED-FLAG
001490                                   TO SR-LOOP-SW
001500    ELSE
001510    IF    EOB
001520          MOVE SR-FINISHED-FLAG    TO SR-LOOP-SW
001530    ELSE
001540          ADD 1                    TO SR-LOOP-SW
001550          MOVE FIL-REC (FIL-COUNT)
001560                                   TO OUT-REC
001570          PERFORM Z9020-WRITE-OUT-REC.
001580*
001590 B0030-B-PROCESS.
```

Figure 13.2   Restructured payroll program *(continued)*

```
001600    IF    FIL-COUNT = FIL-SIZE
001610          MOVE 1
001620    IF    FIL-COUNT = BLK-SIZE
001630          MOVE 1
001640*
001650 B0040-C-CLOSE.
001660          IF NOT EOB
001670             MOVE 001            TO SR-PRV-SW.
001680*
001690 B0050-A-OPENFILE.
001700          ADD 1                  TO FIL-NAME-SUFFIX.
001710          OPEN OUTPUT OUTFILE.
001720          ADD FIL-COUNT          TO BLK-COUNT.
001730          MOVE ZERO              TO FIL-COUNT
001740                                    EOF-SW.
001750*
001760/
001770 Z9000-INPUT-OUTPUT-PARAGRAPHS SECTION.
001780*
001790 Z9010-READ-INFILE.
001800             READ INFILE
001810             AT END
001820                MOVE HIGH-VALUES  TO SR-10-STATUS-SW.
001830*
001840 Z9020-WRITE-OUT-REC.
001850             WRITE OUT-REC.
```

Figure 13.2 Restructured payroll program *(continued)*

Reusing software components is the key to dramatic software productivity increases. Reusability can cut development schedules by months or even years. The CASE repository, in which reusable software components can be stored, makes reusability practical. Not only does CASE enable the reuse and sharing of source code, but better yet, the reuse of project plans, prototype models, data models, and design specifications.

By reusing software components and software development experience to the greatest extent possible, reusability can significantly:

- Streamline and simplify software development
- Improve software reliability
- Reduce software costs

Reusability of software development experience is the primary means of reusing software. The methodology driver is an expert system that captures the expertise of experienced software developers and enables all developers to have access to this knowledge.

13.4   FORMS OF SOFTWARE REUSABILITY

The application of the concept of software reuse can be taken in the forms shown below:

- Reusable prototypes
- Reusable data
- Reusable system and program architectures
- Reusable program and data structure designs
- Reusable program code
- Reusable software packages

13.5   PROBLEMS WITH SOFTWARE REUSABILITY

Although recognized as a great productivity idea, software reusability has had only limited success in practice. Why? The first reason is that reusability requires planning for reusability when a component is originally defined and implemented. The second reason is that it is difficult to represent a software component in a way that it can easily be classified, described, understood, and reused without causing unforeseen side effects.

The solution to the software reusability practicality problem is threefold:

- Choose an appropriate formalism for representing a reusable software component
- Provide tools to support a reusable development approach
- Provide a library of reusable parts

13.6   LIMITATIONS OF CODE REUSE

At the code level, software reuse is very limited. Code reuse is language dependent, operating-system dependent, application dependent, and at the discretion of the individual programmers. Also, no development methodology provides for code-level reuse between dissimilar application systems or for classifying and selecting modules to be reused.

However, the major problem with code reuse is that the code often must be changed before it can be reused. With change comes the risk of introducing errors and other unforeseen side effects. The difficulty of changing code has been a major deterrent to considering software reusability as a feasible development technique.

13.6.1 ICASE and Code Reuse

It has been demonstrated in this chapter how CASE tools have tackled the code reuse issue. It should be added here that any CASE approach to reusing code must include a CASE repository and CASE change impact analysis tools.

13.7 HIGHER-LEVEL SOFTWARE REUSE

A higher form of software reuse is needed to overcome the limitation of code reuse. The closer we get to code level, the less feasible software reuse becomes. Therefore, we should think in terms of reusing program specifications instead of program code. At the specification level, the problems arising from programming language specifications, operating system dependencies, and inefficiencies of reusable code disappear. The CASE technology and, in particular, the CASE repository make program specification reuse practical.

13.8 SPECIFICATION REUSE

Specification reuse with the support of CASE works as follows. The system developer selects from the CASE repository the program specification design that is similar to the program to be built. He or she locates the candidate designs by searching the CASE repository directory for systems that perform the same or similar function as the system that he or she is currently designing. The specification design is in the form of a family of related structured diagrams that represent the program architectural structure, procedural components, data structures, data entities, and attributes. The CASE repository automatically links together all related systems diagrams. CASE code generator tools are used for automatic generation of the program code and database definitions from this high-level specification.

However, the design probably cannot be used as is. It may be too general or, on the other hand, address only a subset of the functions. Therefore, the existing design must be modified to meet all the requirements for this new program. It is important to note that the changes will be made at the design specification level, not at the code level. Since the CASE repository stores all system information and the relationship between system components and automatically tracks and controls all changes, reuse of program design specifications is practical. With the use of CASE analysis tools, the developer can adjust the design to meet the requirements of the new system.

Adjusting an existing design, rather than designing from scratch, should substantially reduce analysis and design effort. Generating code from the adjusted design rather than manually coding the system should substantially reduce implementation time.

13.9 REUSABILITY INCREASES PRODUCTIVITY

The whole approach not only dramatically changes software development but also reaches into the maintenance phase of the life cycle. When the whole approach is used, techniques needed for developing a program become much more similar to techniques needed for maintaining a program. The line that has always existed between software development and software maintenance disappears. This is the reason why reusability has the potential to substantially improve overall software productivity. It is also the reason why reusability revolutionizes the software development process.

14

APPLICATIONS DEVELOPMENT STANDARDS AND CASE TOOLS

14.1 INTRODUCTORY REMARKS

There are two major failings of the CASE tool industry that threaten to severely limit the usefulness of these tools. First, there is the long delay in introducing an adequate data dictionary or repository. Second, there is the lack of consistent standards or the reluctance of the vendors to come to an agreement on an adequate set of standards.

I would have liked to discuss some standards that should exist in the CASE tool industry that will go a long way toward increasing the usage of CASE tools once they are purchased by organizations. However, the establishment of standards can only be done once there are provable and accepted metrics on which those standards are based. One knows better than the vendors themselves that claims of 10-fold increases in productivity are meaningless across the CASE industry since there is no standard and accepted definition of productivity. Therefore, instead of my original intent for this chapter, I will discuss a set of metrics that may be used in establishing standards for both information engineering in general and the CASE tool industry in particular. However, before that discussion I will list some major improvements that are needed for CASE tools that would increase their usage in the industry.

14.2 CURRENT FEATURES OF CASE TOOLS

The toolkits available in the marketplace today have focused on supporting a variety of analysis and design techniques. These include variants on information engineering, entity-relationship modeling, structured analysis, structured design, and data structured design. Many toolkits support several of these techniques. Each technique provides us with a different view of the same information system.

The toolkits supporting these techniques usually include these features:

- A graphic facility for drawing diagrams appropriate to the technique
- A textual facility for naming and describing objects and relationships used in the graphics
- A facility for assigning attributes and properties to objects and relationships
- A screen and report prototyper
- A consistency analyzer to enforce, either interactively or in listings, the syntax rules for objects drawn, named, and described
- A facility to list the objects and relationships and their specifications
- A facility to produce formatted interfaces for generation of schemas and/or program skeletons

These features are implemented with varying degrees of usefulness. For example, the E-R oriented tools describe entities with lists of attributes, but seem to ignore the real-world fact that entities frequently have substructures prior to normalization; data-flow-oriented tools describe the dynamics of flow, changing states and triggers, but don't provide checks on the use of attributes in process descriptions; information engineering tools provide facilities for describing and organizing existing ways of doing business but don't support abstraction from current implementations. These problems will eventually be ironed out, we hope, as the various techniques become merged into a unified software engineering discipline.

In contrast, the following features are badly needed and are not provided in the typical commercial CASE product:

- Topological repartitioning
- Interphase/intermodel transformation
- Extensible properties
- Formal specification
- Software metrics

14.2.1 Topological Repartitioning

Models of information systems can often be simplified by "topological repartitioning;" i.e., encapsulating sets of lower-level objects into a higher level. For example, encapsulating sets of transforms bounded by external entities and data stores on a dataflow model often yields the simplest subsystem structure because all functions inside the partition are related by time. Topological repartitioning is also referred to as "recomposition." It is a primary tool of architectural design.

Recomposition is important in developing an abstract model. We can use a high-level partition as the basis for deriving a non-procedural model of a system. Or we can simplify complex sets of objects which proliferate at the "primitive" level. Or we can use an object-oriented partition in isolated data abstractions and design decisions and minimize coupling between major components of the model. Or we can "package" components when designing work assignments, memory overlays, or job streams. Partitioning with minimal connectivity between processes is a major goal of software engineering. It results in a high degree of simplicity and reduction of the "ripple" effect which leads to costly maintenance.

14.2.2 Interphase and Intermodel Transformation

Verification of specification is the ability to trace each specification back to its predecessor. Requirements specifications must be traced back to needs statements, design specifications back to requirements. There should be a way of tracing each specification back to the need that it meets. Very few CASE tools actually support this form of verification. Usually, each transformation of a specification must be manually entered. For example, if a relationship between entities is specified in an E-R model, then the user must reenter the specifications for the dataflow engineered by that relationship in a dataflow model.

CASE toolmakers should, therefore, provide facilities for automatically carrying specifications forward from phase to phase and model to model, not just at a data dictionary or textural level, but also at the object level. Also, they should provide a facility for tracing specifications backwards from phase to phase, model to model, object to object, and even from version to version.

14.2.3 Extensible Properties

A systems analyst collects a large amount of information about a user's needs, environment, and problems. This information is frequently nonfunctional in nature. We call this type of information a "property," as opposed to an "attribute," which represents the domain of values that functional data can have. For example, we need to understand how much a process costs, how many times an entity is accessed per day, whom to contact in an external entity department or with what frequency a dataflow occurs. CASE tools have very little facility for capturing this information, and even less for reporting it. This information can be predefined or user defined. Both forms should be incorporated in CASE models.

14.2.4 Software Metrics

The CASE toolmakers are claiming significant increases in productivity, but when asked to prove their claims, they cannot. This is true for over 60 vendors. In software engineering, it is not good enough to make qualitative claims. It is time to measure things quantitatively. The toolmakers keep saying "there are no measures." This is simply not true. We have many good measures for software, and the CASE tools should support us by counting, calculating, collecting, and reporting the results of various measures. The measures which should be collected, at a minimum, deal with size, complexity, completeness, and defects.

- Size-function points should be counted. This simple metric, which is becoming widely used, is a nondimensional metric based on a count of the input inquiries, outputs, and files used by the proposed system.
- Complexity — *cyclomatic complexity* is a well-established and useful metric developed more than a decade ago. It can be computed from flowcharts and pseudo-code. A module complexity of more than 10 is considered high, since a module is very likely to contain defects. A design can be evaluated by counting the coupling. This is total number of invocations, the total number of modules, and the total number of tokens (attributes) passed between component transforms or modules. The rates of tokens per module and tokens per invocation should be minimized. *Cohesion* is a measure of the degree to which the different actions performed by a module that has contributed to a unified function can also be measured. This is a simple discriminated metric which classified modules on a scale of 0 to 1. The more cohesive a model, the easier it is to maintain. *Fan-out* is the ratio of total invocations to the number of modules which invoke other modules. It should be less than or equal to 9. *Fan-in* is the ratio of total invocations to the total number of modules minus 1. It should be greater than 1.
- Completeness can be determined from the ratio of objects completely specified to the total number of objects. A completed object is fully specified in the lowest level of decomposition. Transforms with multiple inputs and outputs should be identified as being insufficiently decomposed, even if fully specified. They are not complete. An unnormalized data structure or entity is not complete, and dataflows containing repeating groups should be decomposed. The completeness metric should approach unity.
- Defects — at a minimum, statistics on defects by type should be accumulated for each kind of model. If the source of defects is traced back to the phase in which the error was made, the analysis can be very informative. Any occurrence of an unusual number of defects, for a specific category, should be examined carefully. Determine how the errors might have been prevented, and then make recommendations as to how to prevent them in the future — with training, expertise, avoidance, guidelines, tools, measures, etc. Examples of types of requirements defects are shown in Table 14.1.

Error messages should refer to a unique object or relationship between objects. Otherwise, it will be impossible to interpret the message because of the complexity of the model. A CASE tool should provide the following information with every violation of a rule:

- Warning (if minor) or error (if major)
- A reference number in the manual for an expanded explanation
- ID of diagram on which the object appears

Table 14.1   Requirements defects

	Defect Type		Description
FUNCTION	COHESION	FC	Function does more than one thing
	CONGRUENCE	FG	Output cannot be derived from input
	DECOMPOSITION	FD	Too detailed or not detailed enough
	LOGIC	FL	Transformation rules are wrong
DATA	COUPLING	DC	Unnecessary data input or output
	DATAFLOW	DF	Dataflow unlabeled, undefined or duplicated
	DATASTORE	DS	Datastore unlabeled, undefined or duplicated
	DATA STRUCTURE	DD	Data structure incomplete or inconsistent
	DATA ELEMENT	DE	Data element undefined
INTERFACE	INTERFACE	IN	External interface wrong
	INPUT/OUTPUT	IO	Input or output wrong
ENVIRONMENT	HUMAN FACTOR	EH	Human Factor requirement wrong
	IMPLEMENTATION DEPENDENT	EI	Assumes a particular desing
	NON-FUNCTIONAL (PERFORMANCE)	EI	Non-functional requirement wrong
OTHER	ASSUMPTIONS	OA	Incorrect assumption
	NAME/TERMINOLOGY	ON	Undefined or inappropriate
	OTHER	OT	Unclassifiable defect
	REDUNDANT	OR	Unnecessary duplication
	STANDARDS	OS	Requirements do not meet published standards

- ID of objects affected
- A brief but specific description of the problem
- A classification of missing, wrong, or extra by type and phase, for capturing the defect metrics

It is possible to add many more features to the current set of CASE tools without leaving the realm of software engineering. For example, there is a need for graphic interactive models which would allow designers and users to see how menus, windows, and screens would be handled, and specify the interactive interfaces which are usually so poorly designed. CASE toolmakers should pay much more attention to the human factors requirements of their own tools. They should accept standards such as the Macintosh interface.

Determinacy diagrams, a very simple tool, would help us graphically depict functional dependency, which is critical to the process of normalizing data. When supporting prototyping, all CASE tools should capture valid and invalid data instances as entered during screen validation.

Any instance of an object should be specified once. All duplicate references to it must be derived from its relationship to other objects and its specification. This must be an absolute rule. It is essential that every instance of any object have a unique name and ID, and that they refer to one and only one instance of an object.

If a named object appears on more than one level, or more than one diagram on the same level, or in more than one type of model, it is the same object. Unless this is enforced, no consistency, completeness or tractability checking will be meaningful since any reference is potentially ambiguous. Also, linkage between models will be virtually impossible: CASE tools should enforce a unique rule for every object.

14.3 ATTEMPTS AT STANDARDS FOR CASE TOOLS

The ANSI X3/H4 Committee on data dictionary standards is also working on an EDIF/CASE set of standards. The vendors are ambiguous as to the need for a comprehensive set of standards or for a single body proposing a set of standards. Some vendors are proposing individual standards for their CASE tool.

The IBM Repository appears to be on the brink of being accepted as the standard for data dictionaries among the CASE industry.

Appendix A

LIST OF VENDORS AND ADDRESSES

Note: V=Vendor
           D=Developer

4-Front Strategy

Vendor/developer: Holland Systems Corporation (V)

Address: 3131 South State Street, Suite 303
                           Ann Arbor, MI 48108, USA

Telephone: 313-995-9595

Contact: Kerry B. Wozniak

Analyst/Core (Macintosh)

Vendor/developer: Systems Designers (SD) (V/D)

Address: Pembroke Broadway, Camberley
                           Surrey GU15 3XD, UK

Telephone: 0276-62244

Contact: Ken Whitehead

Analyst/Designer Toolkit

Vendor/developer: Yourdon International Ltd. (V)

Address: 15-17 Ridgemount Street
                           London, WC1E 7AH, UK

Telephone: 01-637-2182

Contact:	Alan Fitzpatrick
Vendor/developer:	Yourdon Incorporated (D)
Address:	1501 Broadway, Suite 601 New York, NY 10036, USA
Telephone:	212-391-2828

Anatool

Vendor/developer:	Arfang (D)
Address:	27 Rue Titon 75011 Paris, France
Telephone:	1-43-73-02-57
Vendor/developer:	Advanced Logical Software (V)
Address:	9903 Santa Monica Boulevard, Suite 2584 Beverly Hills, CA 90212, USA
Telephone:	213-659-5157
Contact:	Leslie Schneider
Vendor/developer:	Keith London Systems Limited (V)
Address:	2 Great North Road, Welwyn Herts AL6 OPL, UK
Telephone:	043871-8627
Contact:	Grahame Stehle

ASA Modelling Workbench

Vendor/developer:	Verilog SA (V/D)
Address:	150 Rue Nicolas Vauquelin Toulouse, 31081, France
Telephone:	01-61-40-38-88
Contact:	Dominique Vilbois
Vendor/developer:	Verilog UK Ltd.
Address:	Hammond House, 117 Piccadilly Mayfair, London W1V 9FJ
Telephone:	01-629-2484
Contact:	William Rigg (Product Support Manager)

Asset (Identical product to Must 3)

Vendor/developer:	Aims Systems
Address:	314-316 Harbour Yard, Chelsea Harbour London SW10 0XD, UK

Telephone:	01-823-3303
Contact:	Steve Dyson

Autocode

Vendor/developer:	Integrated Systems Inc. (V/D)
Address:	2500 Mission College Boulevard Santa Clara, CA 95054-1215, USA
Telephone:	408-980-1500
Contacts:	Jim Pollock Eleanor Vadeboncoeur
Vendor/developer:	Scientific Computers Ltd. (V)
Address:	Burgess Hill West Sussex, UK
Telephone:	044-46 5101
Contact:	Peter Humble

Auto-Mate Plus

Vendor/developer:	LBMS (V/D)
Address:	Evelyn House, 62 Oxford Street London W1N 9LF, UK
Telephone:	01-636-4213
Contacts:	Brendan Dunphy Gordon Biggar

Bachman

Vendor/developer:	Bachman Information Systems Ltd. (V)
Address:	Index House Royal Ascot, Berks
Telephone:	0990 23404
Contacts:	Philip Hill Paul Wiltshire Stuart Dunlop
Vendor/developer:	Bachman Information Systems Inc. (V/D)
Address:	Four Cambridge Center Cambridge, MA 02142-1401, USA
Telephone:	617-354-1414
Contacts:	Charles Bachman Alan Sarasohn

BIS/IPSE

Vendor/developer:	BIS Applied Systems
Address:	20 Upper Ground
	London SE1 9PN, UK
Telephone:	01-633-0866
Contact:	David Broughton

Blues

Vendor/developer:	Applecentre (West London) (V)
Address:	Springfield House, Hayes End Road
	Hayes, Middlesex UB4 8EH, UK
Telephone:	01-573-7797
Contact:	Patrick Ballin
Vendor/developer:	Interprogram BV (D/V)
Address:	Wildenborch 3
	1112 XB Diemen, Holland
Telephone:	20-99-61-21
Contact:	Mr. Velstra
Vendor/developer:	Interprogram BV (V)
Address:	Bezuiden Houtseweg 117
	2594 AD Den Haag, Holland
Telephone:	070-471-661

Cadware (previous name)
Sylva/System Developer (new name)

Vendor/developer:	DST Software Ltd. (V)
Address:	15 The Woolmarket
	Cirencester, Gloucestershire GL7 2PR
Telephone:	0285-69931
Fax:	0285-69926
Contact:	Mahboob Hussain
Vendor/developer:	Cadware Inc. (V/D)
Address:	869 Whalley Ave.
	New Haven, CT 06515
Telephone:	203-387-1853
Contact:	Frank Garvey (Executive Vice President)

Casepac

Vendor/developer:	Online Software International (V)
Address:	Tenterden House, 3 Tenterden Street Hanover Square, London W1R 9AH, UK
Telephone:	01-493-5102
Contact:	Derek Russell
Vendor/developer:	Online Software International (USA) (Joint D)
Address:	Two Executive Drive Fort Lee, NJ 07024, USA
Telephone:	201-592-0009
Vendor/developer:	Tata Research Design Development Centre (Joint D)
Address:	1 Mangeldas Road, Pune Maharashtra, 411 001, India
Telephone:	212-61608

Conceptor

Vendor/developer:	IBSI Software Technology SA
Address:	365 Rue de Vaugirard, F-75015 Paris, France

Consol (previous name)
Silverrun and Goldrun (new name)

Vendor/developer:	Peat Marwick Advanced Technology (V)
Address:	303 E. Walker Drive, Suite 2200 Chicago, IL 60601, USA
Telephone:	312-938-5002
Vendor/developer:	Systemoid Inc. (KPMM) (D)
Address:	1175 Avenue Lavigerie, Suite 90 Sainte-Foy, Quebec G1V 4P1, Canada
Telephone:	418-657-5582
Contact:	Lynne St. Maurice

Consultant Analyst

Vendor/developer:	Consensus (V)
Address:	Hawthorn House, 14 Manchester Road, Wilmslow, Cheshire SK9 1BG, UK

Telephone:	0625-537777
Contact:	Gerard Lennox
Vendor/developer:	Entellect (V/D)
Address:	2 Bedford Square, London WC1B 3RA, UK
Telephone:	01-580-4766
Contact:	Dr. J. Barat

Core Workstation (British Aerospace)

Vendor/developer:	British Aerospace Military Aircraft Ltd.
Address:	Warton Aerodrome, Preston PR4 1AX, Lancashire, UK
Telephone:	0772-633333 ext. 4966
Contact:	Peter Curwen

CorVision

Vendor/developer:	Cortex Ltd. (V)
Address:	1 Redcliff Road Bristol BS99 7JS, UK
Telephone:	0272-279180
Contact:	Caroline Charles
Vendor/developer:	Cortex Corporation
Address:	139 Technology Drive Waltham, MA 02154, USA
Telephone:	617-894-7000
Contact:	Craig Hill

Cradle

Vendor/developer:	3SL (Structured Software Systems Ltd.) (D)
Address:	74 Deep Street, Barrow-in-Furness Cumbria LA14 1RX, UK
Telephone:	0229-38867
Contact:	Mark Walker
Vendor/developer:	Yourdon International Ltd.
Address:	15-17 Ridgemount Street London WC1E 7AH, UK
Telephone:	01-637-2182
Contact:	Paul Clifford

Data Modeller

Vendor/developer:	Analyst Workbench Products Ltd.
Address:	85 Deepcut Bridge Road, Deepcut Camberley, Surrey GU16 6QP, UK
Telephone:	0252-836199
Contact:	David Gradwell

DEC*Case   Any DEC branch (V)

Deft

Vendor/developer:	Deft Inc. (V/D)
Address:	557 Dixon Road, Suite 110 Toronto (Rexdale), Ontario M9W 1H7, Canada
Telephone:	416-249-2246
Contact:	Robert Hill
Vendor/developer:	Kernel Technology (V)
Address:	Number Twenty-One, Queen Street Leeds LS1 2TW, UK
Telephone:	0532-465311
Contact:	Stuart Fuller

Depictor

Vendor/developer:	Computer Associates (UK)
Address:	Computer Associates House, 183-187 Bath Road, Slough Berks SL1 4AA, UK
Telephone:	0753-77733
Contact:	Kathryn Rand

Design-1

Vendor/developer:	Anderson Software (V)
Address:	2 Arundel Street London WC2R 3LT, UK
Telephone:	01-836-1200
Contact:	Nancy Mullen
Vendor/developer:	Arthur Andersen and Co. (D)

Address:	1 International Place, 100 Oliver Street Boston, MA 02110, USA
Telephone:	617-423-1400

Design Aid

Vendor/developer:	Nastec Corporation (V/D)
Address:	24681 Northwestern Highway Southfield, MI 48075, USA
Telephone:	313-353-3300
Contact:	Marty Sprusen
Vendor/developer:	Hoskyns Group Plc. (V)
Address:	Hoskyns House, 130 Shaftesbury Avenue London W1V 7DN, UK
Telephone:	01-434-2171
Contact:	Cally Ware

Design Machine

Vendor/developer:	Optima (formerly Ken Orr and Associates)
Address:	1725 Gage Boulevard Topeka, KS 66604, USA
Telephone:	913-273-0653
Contact:	Ken Orr

Developer

Vendor/developer:	Asyst Technologies Inc. (V/D)
Address:	1080 Beaver Hall, Suite 1400 Montreal, Quebec H2Z 1S8, Canada
Telephone:	514-871-0108
Contact:	Claude Morel

Epos

Vendor/developer:	Systematica (V)
Address:	Systematica House, 3-7 St. Stephen's Rd. Bournemouth, Dorset BH2 6JL, UK
Telephone:	0202-291180
Contact:	Michael Fish
Vendor/developer:	GPP (V/D)

Address:	Kolpingring 18a, D-8024 Oberhaching Munich, W. Germany
Telephone:	(0) 89-613-04-315
Contact:	M. Popall SPS (US) 3LP (V) France SPS (V) Canada

ER Modeler

Vendor/developer:	Chen and Associates Inc. (V/D)
Address:	4884 Constitution Avenue, Suite IE Baton Rouge, LA 70808, USA
Telephone:	504-928-5765
Contact:	Nicholas Prejean

Essay

Vendor/developer:	Tata Research and Development Centre (V/D)
Address:	1 Mangaldas Road, Pune Maharashtra 411 001, India
Telephone:	212-61608

Excelerator

Vendor/developer:	Index Technology Corporation (V/D)
Address:	One Main Street Cambridge, MA 02142, USA
Telephone:	617-494-8200
Contact:	Richard Carpenter
Vendor/developer:	Excelerator Software Products Ltd. (V)
Address:	Boundary Way, Hemel Hempstead Herts HP2 7SJ, UK
Telephone:	0442-232-345
Contact:	Simon Wright
Vendor/developer:	Value Added Consultancy (VAC) BV (V)
Address:	Europalaan 101 3526 KR Utrecht, Holland

Telephone: 030-888-042

Contact: Jenny Bruijn

Express

Vendor/developer: Scicon Ltd. (V/D)

Address: Wavendon Tower, Wavendon,
                            Milton Keynes MK17 8LX, UK

Telephone: 0908-585-858

Contact: G. Brennan

Exsys

Vendor/developer: Total Systems Ltd. (V)

Address: 394 City Road
                            London EC1V 2QA, UK

Telephone: 01-837-2844

Contact: Max Walker

Vendor/developer: Exsys Inc. (V/D)

Address: Chrysler Building, 39th floor
                            405 Lexington Avenue
                            New York, NY 10174, USA

Telephone: 212-983-4646

Contact: Rodger Nixon

Gambit

Vendor/developer: Institut fur Informatik (V/D)

Address: Eidgenossische Technische Hochschule
                            CH-8092, Zurich CH-8091, Switzerland

Telephone: 01-256-2243

Contact: Peter Leikauf

Idef-ine

Vendor/developer: MicroMatch Ltd. (V)

Address: 10 Salamanca, Wellington Park, Crowthorne
                            Berks RG11 6AP, UK

Telephone: 0344-772-794

Contact: Peter Yeomans

                                  Sophides (V/D)
                                  Netherlands

                                  Facilitech (V)
                                  Switzerland

                                  Wizdom Systems (V)
                                  USA

IDMS/Architect

Vendor/developer: Cullinet Software/Computer Associates

Address: Cullinet House, Elstree, Borehamwood
                                  Herts WD6 1LD, UK

Telephone: 01-207-2727

Contacts: Clive Vaus
                                  Clive Hollingshead

Vendor/developer: Computer Associates/Cullinet Software

Address: 400 Blue Hill Drive
                                  Westwood, MA 02090, USA

Telephone: 617-329-7700

Contact: Steve Scheidt

IEF

Vendor/developer: James Martin Associates (V/D)

Address: James Martin House, Littleton Road,
                                  Ashford
                                  Middlesex TW15 1TZ, UK

Telephone: 0784-245058

Contact: Fred Slack

Vendor/developer: Texas Instruments Inc. (V/D)

Address: Information Systems and Services
                                  6550 Chase Oaks Boulevard
                                  Plano, TX 75023, USA

Telephone: 512-250-7111

IEW

Vendor/developer:	KnowledgeWare Inc.
Address:	3340 Peach Tree Road NE, Suite 2900 Atlanta, GA 30026, USA
Contact:	Steve Kahan
Vendor/developer:	Arthur Yound (IES) Ltd.
Address:	7 Rolls Building, Fetter Lane London EC4A 1NH, UK
Telephone:	01-831-2191
Contact:	David Turner

Idef/Leverage

Vendor/developer:	Dacom (V/D part)
Address:	1334 Park View Avenue, Suite 220 Manhattan Beach, CA 90266, USA
Telephone:	213-546-7575

Irma

Vendor/developer:	Arthur D. Little Ltd. (V)
Address:	Berkeley Square House London W1X 6EY, UK
Telephone:	01-409-2277
Contacts:	Stephen Proud Hugh Small
Vendor/developer:	Arthur D. Little (US) (V/D)
Address:	Acorn Park Cambridge, MA 02100, USA
Telephone:	617-864-5770
Contact:	Robert Curtice

Kanga Tool/Sat

Vendor/developer:	Institute for Information Industry (V)
Address:	116 Nanking East Road, 6th Floor, Section 2 Taipei; Taiwan
Telephone:	02-542-2540
Contact:	Chung-Ming Li

Lyddia

Vendor/developer:	Cascade Software Systems Inc. (V/D)
Address:	Suite 12, 33 Bedford Street Lexington, MA 02173, USA
Telephone:	617-862-6246
Contact:	Kenneth Schoman

Mac-Cadd

Vendor/developer:	Logica Space and Defence Systems Ltd. (V/D)
Address:	64 Newman Street London W1A 4SE, UK
Telephone:	01-637-9111
Contact:	Bruce Collingwood

Maestro GWS

Vendor/developer:	Softlab GmbH (V/D)
Address:	Zamdorfer Strasse 120 D-8000 Munchen 80, W. Germany
Telephone:	089-9-30-010
Contact:	Bob Taylor
Vendor/developer:	Philip's Business Systems (V)
Address:	37 High Street, Marlow Bucks SL7 1AU, UK
Telephone:	06284-75881
Contacts:	John Williams Nick Wenman

Manager View

Vendor/developer:	Manager Software Products Ltd. (V)
Address:	4th Floor, Thames Tower, 99 Burleys Way Leicester LE1 3TT, UK
Telephone:	0533-537-999
Contacts:	David Blume Phil Redfearn

Vendor/developer:	Manager Software Products (US) (V/D)
Address:	131 Hartwell Avenue Lexington, MA 02173-3126, USA
Telephone:	617-863-5800

Master

Vendor/developer:	InfoDyne Inc. (V)
Address:	227 S. Main Street, Suite 200 South Bend, IN 46601, USA
Telephone:	219-233-3449
Contact:	Suzanne E. Wheeler
Vendor/developer:	GESI (Gestioni Sistemi per l'Informatica) (V/D)
Address:	Rome, Italy
Telephone:	396-359-5278

M-Case

Vendor/developer:	Mentor Graphics (UK) (V)
Address:	Mentor House, Western Centre, Western Road, Bracknell Berks RG12 1RW, UK
Telephone:	0344-482 828
Contacts:	Lynne Kimber Steve Elliott
Vendor/developer:	Mentor Graphics (USA) (V/D)
Address:	8500 SW Creekside Place Beaverton, OR 97005-7191, USA
Telephone:	503-626-1202

Must 3

Vendor/developer:	CCTA (Central Computer and Telecommunications Agency) (D)
Address:	H M Treasury, Gildengate House Upper Green Lanem Norwich NR3 1DWT, UK
Telephone:	0603-660181
Contact:	Keith Ireland
Vendor/developer:	National Computer Centre (V)

Address:	Oxford Road, Manchester
	M1 7ED, UK
Telephone:	061-228-6333

Multi-Cam

Vendor/developer:	AGS Management Systems Inc.
Address:	880 First Avenue
	King of Prussia, PA 19406, USA
Telephone:	215-265-1550
Contact:	Susie Stilson

Oracle * Case Designer

Vendor/developer:	Oracle Europe (D/N)
Address:	Oracle Park, Bittams Lane, Guildford Road,
	Chertsey
	Surrey KT16 9RG, UK
Telephone:	093287-2020
Contacts:	Richard Barker
	Ian Fisher

Natural Architect Workstation

Vendor/developer:	Software AG (V)
Address:	74-78 Victoria Street, St. Albans
	Herts AL1 3XH, UK
Telephone:	0727-44455
Contacts:	Fiona Crick
	Philip Joisce

Pacbase

Vendor/developer:	Compagnie Generale d'Informatique (V/D)
Address:	84 Rue de Grenelle
	Paris 75007, France
Telephone:	1-45-44-39-1
Contact:	Kathleen Peters
Vendor/developer:	CGI Systems plc
Address:	17a Cedar Road, Sutton
	Surrey SM2 5DA, UK

Telephone:	01-643-4443
Contact:	Robert Karssiens

Page (& Pagefit)

Vendor/developer:	Inforem (V/D)
Address:	Inforem House, Addlestone Road, Addlestone, Weybridge Surrey KT15 2UE, UK
Telephone:	0932-959011
Contacts:	Arthur Shareef Bob Carlsen

PA-Tetrarch

Vendor/developer:	PA Computers and Telecommunications (V/D)
Address:	Rochester House, 33 Greycoate Street, London SW1P 2QF, UK
Telephone:	01-828-7744

Pose

Vendor/developer:	Computer Systems Advisors Inc (V)
Address:	50 Tice Boulevard Woodcliff Lake, NJ 07675, USA
Telephone:	800-537-4262
Contacts:	Tom Haughey Sherman Drusin

	International Technology Institute (D) National Computer Board, Singapore
Vendor/developer:	Aims Systems
Address:	314-316 Harbour Yard, Chelsea Harbour London SW10 0XD, UK
Telephone:	01-823-3303

Powercase

Vendor/developer:	Cognos
Address:	Westerley Point, Market Street, Bracknell Berkshire RG12 1QB, UK

Telephone:	0344 486668
Contacts:	Mike Baggott (Technical Marketing)
	Colin Moden (Research and Development)
	Albert McMahon

Powertools

Vendor/developer:	Iconix Software Engineering Inc.
Address:	2800 28th Street, Suite 320
	Santa Monica, CA 90405, USA
Telephone:	0101-213-458-0092
Contact:	Neil E. McCoy

Precise * Tools

Vendor/developer:	Control Data Corporation (V/D)
Address:	83100 34th Avenue South
	Mailing Address/Box D
	Minneapolis, MN 55440, USA
Telephone:	800-828-8001
Contact:	R. W. Thyr
Vendor/developer:	Control Data Ltd. (V)
Address:	3 Roundwood Avenue, Stockley Park
	London WC2H 8AR, UK
Telephone:	01-848-1919
Contact:	Mike Stubber

Prokit * Workbench

Vendor/developer:	McDonnell Douglas Computer Systems
	Group (V)
Address:	66 Goldsworth Road, Woking
	Surrey GU21 1LQ, UK
Telephone:	04862-71311
Vendor/developer:	McDonnell Douglas Information Systems
	Group (V/D)
Address:	Box 516
	Saint Louis, MO 63166, USA
Telephone:	800-325-1087

Promod

Vendor/developer:	ProMod Inc.
Address:	23685 Birtcher Drive Lake Forest, CA 92630, USA
Telephone:	714-855-3046
Contact:	Thomas L. Scott
Vendor/developer:	GEI (Gessellschaft fur Elektronische Informationsverarbeitung)
Address:	Pascalstrasse 14, D-5100 Aachen, W. Germany
Telephone:	49-2408-130
Contacts:	R. Knippen Udo Kloeper

Prosa

Vendor/developer:	Cocad Ltd. (V)
Address:	Ashford House, Tufton Centre, Ashford Kent TN23 1YB, UK
Telephone:	0233-43445
Contact:	Jon Collins
Vendor/developer:	Insoft KY (V/D)
Address:	Kirkkokatu 5B SF-90100 Oulu, Finland
Telephone:	981-226-128
Contact:	Hanna Lehikoinen

Ptech

Vendor/developer:	Coopers and Lybrand (V)
Address:	Plumtree Court London EC4A 4HT, UK
Telephone:	01-583-5000
Contacts:	Jim Odell Mike Scott
Vendor/developer:	Associative Design Technology (V/D)
Address:	142 Brigham Hill Road, P.O. Box 518 North Grafton, MA 01536, USA
Telephone:	617-839-5416
Contact:	John Edwards

Quickbuild Workbench

Vendor/developer: ICL

Address: King's Road, Reading
Berks RG1 3PX, UK

Telephone: 0734-586211

Contact: Sue Schreiber Select

Select

Vendor/developer: ISS Ltd.

Address: Spa House, Oriel Terrace, Cheltenham
GL50 1XP, UK

Telephone: 0242-226553
Fax: 0242-577744

Contact: Stuart Frost

Softorg

Vendor/developer: Densitron Computers Ltd. (V)

Address: Unit 4, Airport Trading Estate, Biggin Hill
Kent TN16 3BW, UK

Telephone: 0959-76331 Fax:

Contact: Ivan Foldvari

Vendor/developer: Software Engineering Services GmbH

Address: Pappelstrasse 6
8014 Neubiberg, W. Germany

Contact: Harry Sneed

Software thru Pictures

Vendor/developer: Interactive Development Environments

Address: Surrey Technology Centre, 40 Occam Road,
Research Park, Guildford
Surrey GU2 5YH, UK

Telephone: 0483-502-003

Contacts: Ralph Hodgson
Howard Stone

Vendor/developer: Interactive Development Environments (US)

Address: 150 Fourth Street, Suite 210
San Francisco, CA 94103, USA

| Telephone: | 415-543-0900 |
| Contact: | Anthony Wasserman |

Specif-X

Vendor/developer:	IGL (Institute de Geric Logiciel)
Address:	41 Rue de la Chausser D'Antin Paris 75009, France
Telephone:	1-42-81-41-33
Contact:	Gilles Rigal

Speedbuilder

Vendor/developer:	Michael Jackson Systems Ltd.
Address:	22 Little Portland Street, London W1N 5AF, UK
Telephone:	01-499-6655
Contact:	Ron Mount

Stage 3

Vendor/developer:	Keith London Systems Ltd.
Address:	2 Great North Road, Welwyn Herts AL6 0PL, UK
Telephone:	043871-8627
Contact:	Geoff Waugh

Statemate

Vendor/developer:	i-Logix Inc.
Address:	22 Third Avenue Burlington, MA 01803, USA
Telephone:	617-272-8090
Contact:	Shmuel Halevi
Vendor/developer:	i-Logix (UK) Inc.
Address:	Shirley Lodge, 470 London Road, Slough SL3 8QY, UK
Telephone:	0753-580441
Contact:	Stanley Knight

Teamwork

Vendor/developer:	Hewlett-Packard (US) (V)
Address:	Logic Systems Division, 8245 N. Union Boulevard, P.O. Box 617 Colorado Springs, CO 80901-0617, USA
Telephone:	719-590-5621
Contact:	Jarl Aalbu
Vendor/developer:	Hewlett-Packard (UK) (V)
Address:	Heath Side Park Road, Cheadle Heath Stockport SK3 01B, UK
Telephone:	061-428-0828
Contact:	Alan Behrens
Vendor/developer:	Instrumatic Ltd. (V)
Address:	First Avenue, Globe Park, Marlow Bucks SL7 1YA, UK
Telephone:	06284-76741
Contact:	Richard J. Campbell
Vendor/developer:	Cadre Technologies (V/D)
Address:	222 Richmond Street Providence, RI 02903, USA
Telephone:	401-351-5950
Contact:	David Franks

TIP product set

Vendor/developer:	Technology Information Products (V/D)
Address:	Twelve New England Executive Park Burlington, MA 01803, USA
Telephone:	617-273-5818
Contacts:	Herb Jacobsohn Benny Popek

Toolcase

Vendor/developer:	Systems Advisers Ltd.
Address:	110 Strand London WC2R OAA
Telephone:	01-379-6351
Contact:	Bob Jarvis
Vendor/developer:	Systems Advisers Ltd.

Address:	P.O. Box 907
	Edinburgh EH16 5XF
Telephone:	031-662-4212

Virtual Software Factory

Vendor/developer:	Systematica (V/D)
Address:	Systematica House, 3-7 St. Stephen's Road
	Bournemouth; Dorset BH2 6JL, UK
Telephone:	0202-291180
Contact:	Michael Fish

Visible Analyst Workbench

Vendor/developer:	Semantics (V)
Address:	Wych Elm House, Wych Elm, Harlow
	Essex CN20 1QR, UK
Telephone:	0279-626111
Contact:	Mike Middleditch
Vendor/developer:	Visible Systems Corporation (V/D)
Address:	49 Lexington Street
	Newton, MA 02165, USA
Telephone:	617-369-1800
Contact:	Corrine L. Brandi

VS Designer

Vendor/developer:	Reflex Technology Ltd.
Address:	9 Buckingham Place, Bellfield Road, High
	Wycombe
	Bucks HP13 5HW, Uk
Telephone:	0494-465907
Contact:	Colin Downey
Vendor/developer:	Visual Software Inc.
Address:	3945 Freedom Circle, Suite 540
	Santa Clara, CA 95054, USA
Telephone:	408-988-7575
Contact:	Dave West

Appendix B

A GUIDE TO SELECTING CASE TOOLS: SAMPLE RESPONSES

LIFE-CYCLE PRODUCTIVITY SYSTEM

American Management Systems, Inc. (AMS) offers a practical solution to Computer-Aided Software Engineering: the Life-cycle Productivity System (LPS). LPS treats the productivity problem the way it should be treated: as a total life-cycle concern, rather than as the need simply to produce lines of code faster.

LPS is not just another paper methodology. Rather, it is a comprehensive set of computer software, user guides, and training designed to help you accomplish all life-cycle activities faster and better. It is compatible with all popular system development methodologies and can also be used with most in-house development standards.

LPS consists of the following five major components:

- Strategic Systems Planner
- Systems Designer
- System Implementer
- CORE Foundation Software
- Life-cycle Project Manager

Each of these major components has several modules corresponding to key life-cycle activities.

Because LPS is more than just a design aid, it would be possible to write a book and still not explore thoroughly each of the enclosed questions. However, the following adequately addresses the questions and coupled with our presentation should give you a more complete representation of LPS.

QUESTION 1: *Is the underlying structure of your CASE tool a DBMS or Data Dictionary?*

The Life-cycle Productivity System is composed of many modules encompassing the entire systems development and maintenance process. The Excelerator (by Index Technologies) portion of the LPS System Designer uses a data dictionary as the underlying structure, but also adds database capabilities for keeping track of other entities (like processes, data flows, and graphs). Other modules in LPS (Incident Tracking, Test Logging, Deliverables Tracking, etc.) are implemented with dBASE III+, utilizing that inherent database framework.

Although the Life-cycle Productivity System is composed of many modules from disparate sources, most modules can share data. Excelerator can feed data flow diagram information to the Matrix Organizer and Analyzer. Project Workbench data drives the Deliverables Tracking System. Screens and Reports designed in Excelerator are used to directly generate mainframe code. Records layouts and field lengths are converted to COBOL data divisions for use with the COBOL workbench.

By combining the best tools available for system design, planning, implementation, and management, LPS avoids being locked into one data structure or format. With bridges linking the parts together, LPS becomes far greater than just the sum of its parts.

QUESTION 2: *Does your CASE tool share or will it share, in the near future, file formats and specifications with other noncompeting CASE manufacturers? If yes, please explain.*

The microcomputer portion of LPS is built around Excelerator, Project Workbench, dBASE III+, Lotus 1-2-3, and the Micro Focus COBOL compiler. All share data among themselves, and all can share data with other programs. The following is a program-specific file-sharing overview:

Excelerator: Excelerator data file formats are published, and many interfaces to popular programs have been developed.

Project Workbench: Project Workbench exports most of its data to ASCII files for import into most popular programs.

dBASE: dBASE III can read and write ASCII data and comma delimited data. Most programs can write ASCII files easily read by dBASE.

Lotus 1-2-3: 1-2-3 can read and write ASCII data and comma delimited data. Most programs can write ASCII files easily read by 1-2-3. AMS supplies a direct interface to Excelerator export files.

Micro Focus COBOL compiler: Reads and writes ASCII text files.

QUESTION 3:   *Describe your CASE tools's ability to read procedure and source libraries and create CASE components specifications for existing systems.*

We are currently developing reverse engineering programs for inclusion into LPS. These programs will evaluate current systems and place specifications into the Excelerator dictionary.

QUESTION 4:   *Describe how your CASE tool interfaces with other CASE design tools.*

As described in question 2, LPS can communicate data to any program that reads ASCII data. In addition, Excelerator graph data can be converted into almost any format with C language programs.

QUESTION 5:   *Does the tool have graphical methodologies capable of exploding design diagrams and dictionary specifications to a reasonable depth?*

The Excelerator portion of Systems Designer allows for up to 9 levels of data flow diagram explosion, as well as 9 levels of structure chart and 9 levels of data modeling explosion.

QUESTION 6:   *Is your tool capable of executing with window capabilities?*

Because LPS is composed of system components built by other companies, we are dependent upon the windowing plans of other vendors. We intend on committing to a graphical interface, but must wait until implemented by our core products. Excelerator will offer windowing support in the future, as will 1-2-3 in version 3.0G. Ashton Tate and Project Workbench's windowing plans are presently unclear, but both can run as dominant tasks under Microsoft Windows.

QUESTION 7:   *Describe the tool's ability to do strategic planning on a corporate or functional unit basis.*

One portion of the Life-cycle Productivity System is the Strategic Systems Planner. In conjunction with the data modeling facility in Excelerator and the LPS Matrix Organizer/Analyzer, our system offers a complete implementation of IBM's Business Systems Planning methodology (BSP), as well as supporting the TIP variation. This methodology makes extensive use of matrices to describe organizational characteristics.

In addition to BSP strategic planning, Index Technology offers a program called PRISM, used primarily for strategic planning. PRISM works with Excelerator, and with all of the LPS modules.

QUESTION 8:   *Does your tool provide a thorough means of prototyping?*

The System Designer allows for screen and report creation, using data structures defined in the data dictionary. These screens can be linked together, as well as transferred to the System Implementer for conversion into program code.

Prototypes can be created with the System Implementer using the on-line screen generation capabilities of LPS's CORE Foundation Software.

QUESTION 9:   *Describe the tool's ability to provide physical design specifications from logical design specifications.*

System Implementer generates COBOL code for the data division of a program. A program is defined as a structure chart. In addition, the entire procedure division of COBOL programs can be generated, with each paragraph relating to function names on the lowest level structure chart, and the function description appearing as a comment below the procedure name. If the function description is entered as actual program code, then all the programmer needs to do is remove the comment character.

QUESTION 10:   *What design specification reports does your tool provide?*

The Excelerator portion of System Designer produces many specification reports. These reports include:

- Record Content Analysis
- Key Validation Analysis
- Data Model Validation
- Data Normalization Analysis
- Screen Report Data Usage
- Element Access and Derivation
- Graphical Analysis

In addition to predefined reports, the System Designer contains a report writer that allows the analyst to create and save his own reports.

QUESTION 11:   *Does your tool provide analytical support from design documentation? For example, does it indicate the completeness of relevant documentation?*

LPS provides several tools which generate portions of the design documents. A new mainframe-based capability of LPS will add "configuration management" of documentation in a future release.

QUESTION 12:   *Can your tool's design and development specification interface with particular DBMs and data dictionaries? For example, DATA MANAGER.*

LPS has been interfaced to several DBMs and data dictionaries. We have built an interface from the System Designer to DATA MANAGER for one of our clients. Using the Excelerator Programmers Interface, it is possible to build data links with most DBMs and data dictionaries, several of which currently exist in the public domain.

QUESTION 13:   *Can your tool be modified relative to an organization's existing design methodology? Please describe.*

LPS supports most design methodologies. DFDs can be either Yourdon or Gane and Sarson. Data modeling can utilize Chen or Merise. Both structure charts and structure diagrams can be used to model program logic. Most of the other modules are supplied with the program code, allowing them to be modified in any way required. LPS is compatible with most popular system development methodologies and can also be used with most in-house development standards.

QUESTION 14:   *Describe your tool's ability to generate design, operations, and end-user documentation.*

The LPS System Documentation tools extract information from the Excelerator System Dictionary for combination with other graphical and word processing files. These can be manipulated with a desktop publishing system for direct production of user and operations documentation.

QUESTION 15:   *Describe your tool's ability to maintain design and system changes.*

The new LPS mainframe-based repository will maintain all system documentation, from the planning and design to the implementation and testing. In addition, LPS allows system changes to be made at the PC level, tested, and then uploaded to the primary operating platform. Changes can also be made to the design documents by reverse engineering the changed program.

QUESTION 16:   *Describe your tool's ability to generate programs for a range of platforms from design specifications. For example, COBOL programs for PC and mainframe.*

LPS utilizes the Micro Focus COBOL Compiler for PC development of programs. System Designer interfaces with this compiler, automatically generating Data Divisions and Procedure Divisions. In addition, reports and screens created within System Designer are automatically generated to work with COBOL programs on our own CORE routines.

Our own CORE foundation software runs on the PC as well as on VAX machines and IBM mainframes. By allowing COBOL compilation, IMS and CICS development, and CORE to run on a PC, a system can be developed up to unit testing on an IBM PC running OS/2. In fact, an entire mainframe system can be developed and then maintained on a PC for testing and implementing changes. In the vast majority of cases, programs developed on the PC need only be uploaded and recompiled to work on the mainframe.

EXCELERATOR — INDEX TECHNOLOGY

QUESTION 1: *Is the underlying structure of your CASE tool a DBMS or data dictionary?*

Excelerator is built on an integrated and active dictionary: the XLDictionary. All of the facilities available in Excelerator are integrated with the XLDictionary. This integration provides the user with access to a comprehensive design database that collects information on over 50 unique entity types.

Unlike other CASE products, Excelerator's XLDictionary is both customizable and extensible. It is based on an open architecture that allows users to easily interface with other products. The XLDictionary is also highly differentiated. It is able to store, and report on, design information unique to each entity type defined to the system. In addition, it automatically collects detailed audit information for each entity, as well as information about the entity's relationship to other entities defined in the system. This information is extremely valuable in managing the overall design process.

QUESTION 2: *Does your CASE tool share or will it share in the near future file formats and specifications with other noncompeting CASE manufacturers? If yes, please explain.*

Index Technology's product line strategy emphasizes an open, customizable, and flexible approach to supporting the systems development life cycle (SDLC). Excelerator, the premier systems analysis and design product, functions as the core technology to which numerous other CASE tools are connected. Index Technology is committed to continuing to enhance Excelerator's base functionality in order to expand the depth of its support for systems analysis and design.

Future product and product line enhancements will include further integration with tools that support phases of the systems development life cycle not directly addressed by Index Technology's product line.

This integration includes additional connections to planning tools, code generators, databases, and other systems development processes, as well as specific project-related activities. Improved functionality in Excelerator and other Index Technology products will also include support for additional methodologies, operating systems, and software environments such as IBM's Systems Application Architecture (SAA).™

QUESTION 3: *Describe your CASE tool's ability to read procedure and source libraries and create CASE components specifications for existing systems.*

Excelerator currently addresses the maintenance phase of the systems development life cycle through interfaces to other tools that are designed to help the user work with existing system design components. These interfaces include programs available through our XL/Group User Exchange Library as well as products available from other companies such as AMS' RECGEN™ and RECBUILD.™

QUESTION 4:   *Describe how your CASE tool interfaces with other CASE design tools.*

A commitment to open architecture is a key element of our product strategy. Excelerator is built on an extensible architecture that allows users to add/change/delete virtually any aspect of the product.

Using standard features, users are able to exchange information between our products, as well as between other software tools they might be using. The data file formats used by our products are published in our user manuals. These specifications provide the information necessary for most needs.

Our XL/Programmer Interface™ supports the integration of user processes and other software products. It gives a "C" programmer direct access into the Excelerator dictionary for building a seamless interface to other software.

Index Technology's open architecture approach to product development, and our Customizer and XL/Programmer Interface products have resulted in a broad library of utilities that allow our users to successfully connect to a variety of software products. There are presently more than 20 interfaces to other CASE tools, 4GLs, database management systems, physical construction tools, and desktop publishing systems, such as:

- COBOL/2 Workbench™ − Micro Focus
- APS™ − Sage
- TELON™ − Pansophic
- PowerHouse™ − Cognos
- Personal Leverage™ − D. Appleton
- Ventura Publisher™ − Xerox
- Project Workbench − ABT

QUESTION 5:   *Does the tool have graphical methodologies capable of exploding design diagrams and dictionary specifications to a reasonable depth? Please describe.*

Yes. Objects in a diagram can be "exploded" or decomposed to either additional levels of graphical detail or to an Entity Definition Screen in the XLDictionary. Decomposition from one level to another can involve multiple diagram types. These explosion, or XLDictionary navigation, paths are customizable for each entity and type of graph. There is no limit to the number of "exploded" levels a diagram can contain.

QUESTION 6:   *Is your tool capable of executing with window capabilities?*

Index Technology is committed to using new and emerging technologies to continue to enhance Excelerator's functionality in response to our users' systems development needs. It is our intent to provide support for windowing environments such as the OS/2 Presentation Manager, XWindows, and its derivatives.

QUESTION 7: *Describe the tool's ability to do strategic planning on a corporate or functional unit basis.*

PC Prism, Index Technology's business and strategic planning product, is a flexible tool for modeling and evaluating an organization. PC Prism supports Information Systems Planning, Strategic Business Planning, Enterprise Modeling to name a few. It translates business goals into systems requirements by furnishing an automated environment for strategic planning, enterprise modeling, and priority setting. Information developed in PC Prism can be shared with Excelerator or other tools being used to design and develop systems.

The connection between Excelerator and PC Prism links the information developed in the planning phases of systems development with the analysis, design and other phases of the life cycle.

A copy of "A Guided Tour of PC Prism" is enclosed for your review.

QUESTION 8: *Does your tool provide a thorough means of prototyping? Please describe.*

Yes. Excelerator offers integrated screen and report design facilities. Each field in a screen and report mock-up can be tightly linked to elements, and their associated attributes stored in the XLDictionary. Screen Data Entry facilities allow users to easily prototype their designs, including the testing of edit criteria. The screens can also be used to create an actual database for testing or on-line usage (Index Technology uses these related screen data files on its own internal specification projects). In addition, the designs can be passed to many of the other tools that interface with Excelerator, eliminating the need to reenter design information.

QUESTION 9: *Describe the tool's ability to provide physical design specifications from logical design specifications.*

Index Technology will continue to offer tight connections between Excelerator and tools that generate either application code or Data Definition Language (DDL). For example, we currently generate SQL/DDL for tables and views with our DB2 interface. The company is also committed to providing its own "design-to-code" solution.

QUESTION 10: *What design specification reports does your tool provide?*

Excelerator offers many different reporting options. These include standard XL-Dictionary Reports that provide detailed information about an entity's dictionary definition, audit attributes, and relationships to other entities; Graph Analysis Reports that provide verification as to a graph's contents and correctness; Extended Analysis Reports (Standard and Matrixed) that provide Structured and Data Analysis information including affinity analysis, process analysis, and data normalization up to 3rd Normal Form; and an ad hoc dictionary Report Writer that allows the user to create reports about information currently stored in the XLDictionary.

QUESTION 11: *Does your tool provide analytical support from design documentation? For example, does it indicate the completeness of relevant documentation?*

Yes. While all analysis and design work can be done in Excelerator independent of a particular methodology, the product provides a comprehensive set of analysis tools that validate the design information according to widely accepted methodological practices. In addition to the standard XLDictionary Reports, and the product's ad hoc reporting capabilities, Excelerator includes seven major sets of reports: Graph Analysis, Record Content Analysis, Key Validation Analysis, Data Model Validation Analysis, Data Normalization Analysis, Screen/Report Data Usage Analysis, and Element Access and Derivation Analysis for a total of thirty-seven Standard Reports and twenty-five Matrix Reports.

In addition, the documentation facility provides a means to track and control the completeness of deliverable documentation.

QUESTION 12: *Can your tool's design and development specifications interface with particular DBMs and data dictionaries? For example, DATA MANAGER.*

Yes. Excelerator's Import/Export facility provides for a bi-directional transfer of any design data with any DBMS environment. The published specifications of the transfer file structure insure that any user can easily share data among tools and environments. Our present list of interfaces, which is available through our XL/User Group Library or Excelerator Services, includes links to:

- CCD/Plus™ from Digital Equipment Corporation
- Datamanager™ from Manager Software Products, Inc.
- DB2™ from IBM
- dBASE III™ from Ashton-Tate
- IDD™ from Cullinet Software
- IMS™ from IBM
- Oracle™ from Oracle Corporation

Index Technology is also developing products targeted at specific DBMS environments.

QUESTION 13: *Can your tool be modified relative to an organization's existing design methodology? Please describe.*

Yes. The ability to customize our products to meet an organization's needs is an important element of Index Technology's product strategy. Customizer and Programmer Interface products allow users to modify or extend Excelerator to meet their specific development needs. Customizer enables users to easily define their own graph types, add new entities to the XLDictionary, create new menu structures, as well as modify existing or develop new dictionary input forms. PR Define is the equivalent of Customizer for PC Prism.

Programmer Interface provides a set of "C" routines that enable developers to create seamless interfaces between existing products or specialized programs and Excelerator's XLDictionary. Together, these tools provide an organization with the means to develop an integrated workbench based on its own system design techniques.

QUESTION 14: *Describe your tool's ability to generate design, operations, and end-user documentation.*

Documentation is a by-product of the planning, analysis, and design efforts accomplished with Index Technology products. The information recorded in Excelerator's dictionary can be output on-screen, to a file, or to a printer, using one of Excelerator's extensive reporting capabilities. These include canned XLDictionary Reports, matrices and reports from Excelerator's structured and data analysis tools, user-defined reports from a flexible ad hoc report writing facility, or from the product's powerful Document Production Facility.

This last facility enables users to easily combine information from Excelerator's XLDictionary with information created/collected using other products, such as PC Prism, word processors or spreadsheets. All output can then be moved to either Ventura, PageMaker, or Interleaf desktop publishing environments for final packaging.

QUESTION 15: *Describe your tool's ability to maintain design and system changes.*

Excelerator's XLDictionary provides analytical capabilities unmatched by many other CASE products. The entity relationships and the implications of proposed changes can be ascertained and evaluated with standard "where-used" and related reports, as well as the full functionality ad hoc Report Writer. The audit attributes within the Excelerator XLDictionary track: modified by, added by, last project, date added, date modified, number of changes, locked by, date locked, and lock status.

QUESTION 16: *Describe your tool's ability to generate programs for a range of platforms from design specifications. For example, COBOL programs for PC and mainframe.*

The Excelerator interface to MicroFocus COBOL Workbench supports COBOL development in both PC and mainframe environments, as do a number of other interfaces.

Index Technology has sold over 12,000 copies of Excelerator at over 1,000 different customer sites. These sites span a variety of environments including many different types of information systems and real-time, or embedded systems including:

- A major information system for several AT&T groups
- The control system of the Bay Area Rapid Transit (BART)
- Digital flight systems at Honeywell

- A personnel staff system at a California public utility
- The development environment for space flight programs
- The ordering system for a major financial institution.

MSP — DICTIONARY MANAGER

QUESTION 1: *Is the underlying structure of your CASE tool a DBMS or data dictionary?*

Within the Proposed Environment, the structure of MSP's CASE tool is the Corporate Dictionary Repository. Although managerView operates on personal computer workstations, it is closely integrated with other MANAGER Products and their respective Corporate Dictionaries on the mainframe and is therefore considered dictionary driven. ManagerView also maintains its own local dictionary at the personal computer level representing work in progress.

QUESTION 2: *Does your CASE tool share or will it share, in the near future, file formats and specifications with other noncompeting CASE manufacturers? If yes, please explain.*

Within the Proposed Environment, the DICTIONARYMANAGER facility gives the user the ability to translate definitions from any MANAGER Products dictionary environment to the format of any chosen alien dictionary/directory. In a multi-dictionary environment, the strengths of each can be maximized for further control over automating the systems design process. Several vendors, competitive and otherwise, have written or plan to write interfaces to MSP's CASE environment. MSP feels it critically important to help ensure consistency of definitions across dictionaries/directories within a CASE environment.

QUESTION 3: *Describe your CASE tool's ability to read procedure and source libraries and create CASE components specifications for existing systems.*

Within the Proposed Environment, MSP does not provide a formal facility for what is commonly termed "reverse engineering," or the extraction of existing system components from source and procedural libraries for the purposes of reengineering the systems. However, SOURCEMANAGER does make extensive use of reusable data descriptions and procedural routines (collectively termed Reusable Code) already in use at a given organization. SOURCEMANAGER can, therefore, identify and map reusable routines to both existing systems and systems currently in development. If the components of an existing system have already been documented on the Corporate Dictionary/Repository (DATAMANAGER), then the constituent system components can be downloaded to managerVIEW and reengineered at the Intelligent Workstation. Upon completing the reengineering process, the proposed system design can be uploaded to the Corporate Dictionary/Repository and incorporated into the organization's Strategic Information Plan to identify missing components. After incorporation of the reengineered system into the Strategic Information Plan, the system is linked to a Tactical Implementation Plan for each of the application development areas. SOURCEMANAGER can then be used to repaint and prototype the user interface dialogs and upon approval regenerate the applications.

QUESTION 4: *Describe how your CASE tool interfaces with other CASE design tools.*

Within the proposed environment, while MSP's CASE tool does not overtly interface with other CASE design tools, the DICTIONARYMANAGER facility is a completely user-definable system that allows an organization to translate definitions from any MANAGER products dictionary to the format of any other chosen dictionary/directory. It helps keep definitions consistent, and it may also be used to generate database definition statements based on information contained in a MANAGER Products dictionary.

QUESTION 5: *Does the tool have graphical methodologies capable of exploding design diagrams and dictionary specifications to a reasonable depth? Please describe.*

Yes — In the proposed environment, managerVIEW provides a flexible and tailorable graphical engineering methodology that facilitates the explosion of diagram components to further levels of detail. Logical and physical attributes of diagram objects can be defined locally (and subsequently uploaded to the Mainframe Corporate Dictionary/Repository (DATAMANAGER)) or automatically downloaded from the Corporate Dictionary/Repository. Diagram objects can be exploded to either like diagram types (for example, an object in a Presentation diagram could be exploded to another Presentation diagram) to show an additional level of detail, or, to a different diagram type (for example, an object on an Entity-Relationship Diagram could be exploded to a Dataflow Diagram) to provide additional semantic information. There is no limitation for leveling "depth." Supplied diagram types can be easily modified or new diagram types introduced with managerVIEW's Diagram Schema Editor.

QUESTION 6: *Is your tool capable of executing with window capabilities?*

Yes — managerVIEW operates in the Microsoft Windows (Presentation Manager) environment. The ergonomics of managerVIEW's Human/Computer Interface are directly derived from this environment. managerVIEW uses extensive multiwindow and "pop-up"/"pull-down" menu capabilities.

QUESTION 7: *Describe the tool's ability to do strategic planning on a corporate or functional unit basis.*

In the Proposed Environment, METHODMANAGER's Strategic Information Planning (SIP) component enables the creation of a prioritized master plan for analyzing and satisfying an organization's information needs. The Strategic Information Plan takes a wide view of an organization, to ensure that the plan produced is comprehensive and does not omit significant interaction between different parts of the organization. METHODMANAGER is driven by a comprehensive and automated methodology — The Manager Method. The MANAGER Method divides Strategic Information Planning into the following phases:

- Preparation
- Management Overview Study
- Full Strategic Information Plan

These phases identify and refine the organizational structure, the business processes and functions, and the data usage and dependencies. Automated checkpoints are positioned throughout the development process to ensure the completion of each phase before work can begin on the next. METHODMANAGER automatically utilizes Function Point and Affinity (cluster) analysis techniques to provide the planner with decision confirmation or mathematical backup for intuitive "hunches" about the overall Information Plan and the identification of potential subject databases. METHODMANAGER also automatically generates Matrix Diagrams showing relationships between many objects in terms of either the existence of a relationship or, if a relationship exists, the properties of it (for example, Inputs, Outputs, Assumed). Through the generation of Matrices, the analysis and Corporate Rating of Objectives, Goals, Requirements and Critical Success Factors, and the utilization of System Priority Tables, the Information Planner is able to produce accurate reports regarding the progress and completeness of the Strategic Information Plan. Finally, the Strategic Information Plan is linked to a Tactical Implementation Plan for each Application Development project.

QUESTION 8:   *Does your tool provide a thorough means of prototyping? Please describe.*

Within the proposed environment, SOURCEMANAGER's Prototype Facility allows a proposed application(s) to be viewed as a cohesive unit before (or after) the generation of code or requirement specifications. Screens can be painted in either Live or Prototype mode; the former requires the input of requirement specifications for literal and variable fields. SOURCEMANAGER's Prototype Facility enables the developer to view these screens (live or Prototype) either individually or as complete dialogs by gathering previously painted screens into Prototype Lists. In this way, the developer can ensure the satisfaction of end-user requirements before the generation of code and/or the implementation of the application. Also, by presenting proposed applications to the end-user community as prototypes, end users have an opportunity to become involved in the development of applications that they will be using on a day-to-day basis. Finally, upon verification and approval of a proposed application, the application prototype can be easily reconciled with managerVIEW Dialog-Flow Diagrams to ensure accurate and consistent documentation on the Intelligent Workstation.

QUESTION 9: *Describe the tool's ability to provide physical design specifications from logical design specifications.*

Within the Proposed Environment, for each application development project the relevant parts may be iteratively refined using the techniques of Functional Analysis/Design and Entity Analysis. This process would take place within the first three phases of Application Development of METHODMANAGER; Feasibility study, Business System Design, and User Interface Design. (For a full explanation of the phases, please refer to the enclosed METHODMANAGER literature.) The result of this process is a functional model which consists of elementary functions with a corresponding entity model. Data accessed by elementary functions is represented in a Userview. The Userviews for a particular application are merged and input to a Conceptual Design Process which results in a Conceptual Schema. This schema (bottom-up) is then reconciled with the entity model (top-down) and after any discrepancies have been resolved, a first-cut Physical Data Design is produced.

QUESTION 10: *What design specification reports does your tool provide?*

Within the proposed environment, Entity and Userview models stored as Entity Association Diagrams can be uploaded to a DESIGNMANAGER Workbench Design Area (WBDA). Models stored in the WBDA can then be normalized to First, Second, or Third Normal Forms. A variety of design specification reports can be generated from models having undergone the rigor of normalization.

Some of the more common reports include Dependency, Relation and Record lists, Logical Schema and Network Reports and Cluster Plots, IMS and DL/1 physical design specification reports, DB2 and SQL/DS CREATE TABLE statement specifications and Intersecting Data-element reports (for the identification of potential Homonym/Synonym situations). Workbench Design Areas can be easily stored on the MANAGER Products Administrative Information Dataset (MPAID) for later retrieval. All design specification reports are available from the Intelligent Workstation (managerVIEW). Normalized models can be subsequently downloaded to the Intelligent Workstation to ensure accurate and consistent documentation of proposed database designs.

QUESTION 11: *Does your tool provide analytical support from design documentation? For example, does it indicate the completeness of relevant documentation?*

Within the proposed environment, the METHODMANAGER facility automatically guides you through all phases of systems analysis, design and development. METHODMANAGER employs a set of methods (The MANAGER Method) which consists of four components: The Functional Model, Knowledge Base Structure, Role Model, and A Set of Methods. The MANAGER Method will not only remind you of information you need to gather, but also verifies the completeness and consistency of data at every stage. It also generates reports and diagrams which can be easily reviewed by IS Professionals and End Users. For example, within the Functional Model, there are relationships between functions. These are the tangible results of one function which feed into other functions. These results may be represented in the form of a CID

(Component Interface Diagram). The increasing degree of detail and the increasing rigor of the automated consistency and completeness checks ensure that the eventual design is correct, and that the implementation phases may be reliably carried through. For more information about Component Interface Diagrams, please refer to the enclosed METHODMANAGER documentation: Why Component Interface Diagrams?

QUESTION 12: *Can your tool's design and development specifications interface with particular DBMs and data dictionaries? For example, DATA MANAGER.*

Within the proposed environment, managerVIEW, the intelligent workstation product, is architected to be DATAMANAGER dictionary driven. It is close-host connected to the mainframe Corporate Dictionary/Repository and, therefore, a user need never be concerned whether a command is for local (personal computer) or mainframe processing. ManagerVIEW routes all commands automatically within a design/development session. In addition, the DATAMANAGER facility directly interfaces with a number of DBMSs, including; IMS/DLI, TOTAL, ADABAS, and System 2000/80. The DATAMANAGER facility in conjunction with Dictionarymanager offers support for interfacing with DB2 and SQL/DS. SQL CREATE statements can be generated for processing by the DBMS. The DICTIONARYMANAGER facility also provides support for IDMS/IDD and will allow users to define their own translation rules for converting MANAGER Products definitions to the syntax and format of any chosen dictionary/directory.

QUESTION 13: *Can your tool be modified relative to an organization's existing design methodology? Please describe.*

Yes — User definability is seen by MSP as key to the successful implementation of effective Information Resource Management (IRM) in the CASE environment. Within the proposed environment, MANAGER Products provide a comprehensive and flexible approach to the tailoring of diagram types and constituent objects and connectors on the Intelligent Workstation and member-type hierarchies and logical/physical attribute specifications on the Corporate Dictionary/Repository. MANAGER Products facilities such as User Defined Syntax, User Defined Commands, User Defined Output, User Defined InfoSystem (on-line documentation), and the Diagram Schema Editor enable an organization to easily tailor the CASE environment to incorporate its terminology and Systems Development Methodology requirements. In an environment where Intelligent Workstations are closely connected to a Mainframe resident Corporate Dictionary/Repository, it is of paramount importance that these two components are compatible and synchronous (it is the only way that Close Host Connectivity is possible). Within the proposed environment Corporate Dictionary/Repository based member-type hierarchies, attributes, and connection rules can be automatically downloaded to the Intelligent Workstation tool (managerVIEW) in the form of a Host Dictionary Schema that becomes the governing rules table for managerVIEW. In this way, the Mainframe and Workstation environments are rendered consistent and compatible.

QUESTION 14:   *Describe your tool's ability to generate design, operations, and end-user documentation.*

Within the proposed environment, the CONTROLMANAGER facility allows an organization to use the Basic Dictionary Management software not only to model a complete system, but also to generate the appropriate descriptive documentation from it. There are multiple reporting functions within each MANAGER Products facility.

The DESIGNMANAGER facility, for example, provides an overall perspective of a logical design which is generated from its workbench, as well as a graphical overview of associations between records. There are multiple reporting functions within each MANAGER Product facility. Commands such as REPORT, LIST, PRINT, GLOSSARY are part of the Basic Dictionary Management Software and are not only tailorable, but flexible and powerful enough to provide instant where-used and impact-analysis reporting.

Complete on-line MANAGER Products documentation is provided via MSP's INFOBANK facility. Since every organization is unique, the user also has the ability to tailor MSP's documentation and/or append it with its own installation standard material. This documentation may be tailorable as appropriate for technical, operational or end-user staff as necessary. In addition, the SOURCEMANAGER application generation facility provides extensive documentation both embedded in the source code and printed separately. This will show both the program's function as well as provide a graphic illustration of its structure.

QUESTION 15:   *Describe your tool's ability to maintain design and system changes.*

Within the proposed environment, design and system elements may be maintained either at the local personal computer level, as in specific diagrams, and/or held as members in various logical views on the Corporate Dictionary/Repository. System and design elements may then be tracked in various ways, for example, either by project or on a historical basis.

QUESTION 16:   *Describe your tool's ability to generate programs for a range of platforms from design specifications. For example, COBOL programs for PC and mainframe.*

MSP has not yet investigated the compatibility of SOURCEMANAGER-generated COBOL code on platforms other than the IBM System 370 Architecture. While OS/VS COBOL and COBOL II are fully supported, MSP cannot in good conscience state that other hardware platforms are supported at this time.

DESIGNAID — ANSWERS TO QUESTIONNAIRE

1.   The underlying structure of DesignAid includes a DBMS for storing "design dictionary" data and DOS files containing the text and graphic documentation.

2. Dictionary data from DesignAid is accessible in a flat file format. It can produce and accept through the load/unload facility its contents for use by other software products. There is also an Application Programmer Interface (API) that allows external software to access DesignAid's dictionary data through a set of common calls.

3. There is a COBOL Scanner in the DesignAid product that will scan code and populate the design dictionary with the referenced data elements.

4. DesignAid interfaces to other products as outlined in item two above for dictionary data. An example would be DesignAid's API interface to SAGE's APS (COBOL generator). In addition, there are utilities to allow DesignAid's files to be transported to such products as the Ventura Publishing System.

5. DesignAid has a feature referred to as file nesting that allows diagrams to be interconnected for decomposition purposes. There is no prescribed limit to the number of levels.

6. DesignAid has a split screen capability that allows the analyst to view two workspaces simultaneously.

7. DesignAid supports the graphical syntax for construction and maintenance of strategic models. If full methodology and analysis support of the methodology is required, we recommend the TIP Plan and/or TIP Define products marketed exclusively by Nastec.

8. DesignAid is used for screen and report mockups or user view prototyping. This allows screens and reports to be easily created and changes to be easily made. The tool has facilities for linking screens so screen sequence and interrelation can be demonstrated to the user.

9. The dictionary captures and reports considerable data that can assist in going from logical to physical design. In addition, if E-R modeling is done at the logical level, DesignAid can normalize the logical model, redraw the model, and create the input data needed for schema generation.

10. There are a variety of reports and outputs that represent and support the design specification.

11. The tool has complete analysis support for data modeling, process modeling, and real-time systems modeling.

12. The tool can interface with DBMs and DDs through the API or load/unload facility.

13. The tool can be modified and tailored in many areas to assist in deployment of an organization's standards.

14. DesignAid's unique integrated text and graphics editor allows for the creation and easy maintenance for *any* graphic and textual documentation.

15. There are extensive features in DesignAid to facilitate the changes to the systems documentation.

16. COBOL program generation is done by interfacing to TELON or APS. In addition, other code generators can be interfaced to, quickly and easily, due to Nastec's Application Programmer's Interface.

OPTIMA, INC.

Response to Questionnaire
Selection Criteria for CASE Tools

General Notes   The questions supplied to vendors are meant to address the capabilities of a single CASE tool. Optima, Inc., in fact, supplies three separate tools which provide modular support of the development process, and in combination cover the complete systems development life cycle. The tools, which run on standard PCs, are:

- DesignVision, a methodology-neutral interactive diagramming and documentation facility running under Microsoft Windows.
- DesignMachine, which provides comprehensive support for the Data Structured Systems Development (DSSD) methodology, from Requirements Definition through Logical Database Design phases.
- Brackets, an interactive Warnier-Orr diagramming tool for building program structures, which includes COBOL code generation facilities.

Answers to the questionnaire will address Optima's complete product line. Where a special feature exists for a particular product within our offering, the product will be identified.

Additionally, all features described are as available in the current product releases (version 1.1 for DesignVision, 2.0 for DesignMachine and Brackets). Any items which are under development or in design stages will be clearly identified as such.

QUESTION 1:   *Is the underlying structure of your CASE tool a DBMS or data dictionary?*

Optima's philosophy is to segregate development efforts from production and operations. Therefore, one or more Design Dictionaries capture the status of development efforts, and can be exported to the corporate Data Dictionary of choice upon completion. PC DBMS technology is used to manage the information contained in the Design Dictionary, and to facilitate querying and reporting.

QUESTION 2:   *Does your CASE tool share or will it share, in the near future, file formats and specifications with other noncompeting CASE manufacturers? If yes, please explain.*

Optima not only provides this type of information to all registered customers, but also supplies query and reporting tools with DesignVision and DesignMachine to facilitate such access to design dictionaries. Additionally, Optima's experienced field consultants have provided direct support to clients wishing to develop product interfaces to support in-house development tools.

QUESTION 3:   *Describe your CASE tool's ability to read procedure and source libraries, and create CASE components specifications for existing systems.*

While reverse engineering features are not currently available in Optima's products, two approaches were under development for release in 1990. The process-oriented approach will employ a code-structuring tool which will read in existing code and analyze its inherent structure. It will then reduce the structure to Warnier-Orr diagrams for subsequent modification and regeneration of source code.

A second, data-oriented approach will utilize the output specifications of an existing system (e.g., screens, reports, and files). After importing this information to a tool which will permit redesign of the output, the modified requirements can be distilled into the requisite database and process designs, and the code for the modified system can be regenerated.

QUESTION 4:   *Describe how your CASE tool interfaces with other CASE design tools.*

DesignVision is supplied with an interface which permits exportation of data to DesignMachine. DesignMachine creates various Warnier-Orr diagrams, which can be stored or exported to Brackets for further development. Brackets can then import the diagrams as developed by DesignMachine.

Custom interfaces can be developed, as discussed in the reply to question 2. For example, one client uses Brackets to generate ADABAS database queries in the Natural2 fourth-generation language, and utilizes Brackets' export facilities to transfer the completed query to the mainframe for execution.

QUESTION 5:   *Does the tool have graphical methodologies capable of exploding design diagrams and dictionary specifications to a reasonable depth? Please describe.*

All three products support this requirement. DesignVision permits the graphical decomposition of design diagrams, to a maximum depth of 1023 levels. Each step is automatically checked for balanced levels of inputs and outputs. Release 2.0, which was due for release in early 1989, will allow unlimited levels.

DesignMachine allows recursive definition of application designs through the establishment of subsystems. This means the depth of decomposition is theoretically unlimited.

Brackets allows the chaining of branches of a Warnier-Orr diagram to continue in separate files. Again, this approach permits unlimited number of levels of decomposition.

QUESTION 6:   *Is your tool capable of executing with window capabilities?*

DesignVision was the first CASE tool available which provided full support for Microsoft's Windows environment. Windows has since evolved to become the industry standard, and has been endorsed by IBM for use as the OS/2 Presentation Manager. It provides comprehensive hardware device support independent of application software packages, as well as the ability to share data between such applications and execute them simultaneously to maximize productivity.

Support of Presentation Manager is a key facet of Optima's strategic direction to be a full service CASE vendor supporting IBM's Systems Application Architecture (SAA); DesignVision is the first step in the process. DesignMachine and Brackets currently can run as Windows Standard applications, and was to be released with full Windows/Presentation Manager support during 1989.

QUESTION 7:   *Describe the tool's ability to do strategic planning on a corporate or functional unit basis.*

DesignVision would be the tool of choice for strategic planning. Its methodology-neutral approach can allow planners to choose from a variety of established techniques (e.g., entity-relationship modeling), or through the extensive customization capabilities, planners can create their own diagram types, determine design dictionary attributes, and design reports and documentation for presentation.

QUESTION 8:   *Does your tool provide a thorough means of prototyping? Please describe.*

Prototyping is not currently an integral part of Optima's tool set. To date, the approach has been to allow the developer to use one of many tools commonly available on site, and once the prototype is finalized, it is brought into the DesignMachine to serve as the base for database design. As discussed in the reply to the third question, a prototyping tool is under development, which will permit not only the specification of new output designs, but the revision of existing system deliverables.

QUESTION 9:   *Describe the tool's ability to provide physical design specifications from logical design specifications.*

The primary orientation of the current tool set is toward logical design, followed by code generation. A future release of DesignMachine will generate SQL DDL statements from its fifth normal logical database designs.

QUESTION 10:   *What design specification reports does your tool provide?*

DesignVision provides a standard set of report templates for the methodology models delivered with the product. As these models are changed by the user, or additional models are defined, the user has complete control over the appearance of the associated reports, through template control. These templates exist on up to three levels, so that alternative output definitions can be defined for the organization, specific methodologies, and/or individual projects. The interactive SQL query facility can also be used to generate custom reports from the design dictionary beyond those production reports defined with the product.

DesignMachine supplies the complete set of reports defined by the DSSD methodology, from the data accumulated in the design dictionary. Examples are the output requirements form, output definition form, data requirements form, data definition form, logical output structures, and fully normalized database design.

QUESTION 11:   *Does your tool provide analytical support from design documentation? For example, does it indicate the completeness of relevant documentation?*

DesignVision's interactive SQL query facility permits project leaders to design their own queries to determine task completion. Frequently executed queries can be defined as one-word macros, which can further be augmented with SQL clauses at execution.

DesignMachine provides the most comprehensive support of completeness, predicated upon the DSSD methodology. It maintains application facts in its design dictionary, and guides analysts through the steps of DSSD, actually generating much of the work for the analyst from its inferential base at each step of the process. Completeness is documented by checklists, and reinforced as each task is recommended for completion. Subsequent changes to earlier phases of the design will produce a ripple effect, identifying which areas of the project need to be reexamined in light of the changes. This ensures the referential integrity of the final design.

QUESTION 12:   *Can your tool's design and development specifications interface with particular DBMs and data dictionaries? For example, DATA MANAGER.*

Optima supports interfaces through both product features and the philosophy of an open data architecture. See answers to Questions 2 and 9.

QUESTION 13:   *Can your tool be modified relative to an organization's existing design methodology? Please describe.*

DesignVision is *extremely* flexible in this respect. Through the use of pull-down menus and dialog boxes, users can create their own diagram symbols or choose from the library provided, and combine symbols into a diagram model for use with a specific methodology. For each graphical item, the client may specify what information is to be captured in the design dictionary, and how such information should be formatted on production reports. The ability to specify interactive syntactic and semantic validation rules (beyond the currently available edge balancing and SQL query features) is planned for a future release.

In DesignMachine, the rigorous support of the DSSD methodology allows for a lesser degree of flexibility. The tradeoff is superior support and maintenance of design integrity, as well as the ability to predict and execute much of the work routinely performed by the analyst. The next release of the product will introduce "expert" modes of operation, which relax the application of methodology rules and afford greater flexibility in operation.

QUESTION 14:   *Describe your tool's ability to generate design, operations, and end-user documentation.*

In addition to its flexible design dictionary specification and output formats, DesignVision is the perfect documentation tool by virtue of its support for the Windows environment. Using any Windows-compatible word processing package, or even desktop publishing software such as Aldus Pagemaker, it is possible to cut and paste information between these packages. This allows clients to choose the Windows product set they are most comfortable with, rather than requiring CASE vendors such as Optima to attempt to double as a word processing software supplier.

QUESTION 15: *Describe your tool's ability to maintain design and system changes.*

DesignMachine's abilities in this respect have already been discussed, in reply to Question 11. By describing the changes in the requirements definition of an application, the areas where design modifications are necessary are automatically highlighted by the product. Such comprehensive support at a design level (as opposed to code level modification) not only improves the quality of the finished product, but also results in accurate, updated documentation of the changes.

QUESTION 16: *Describe your tool's ability to generate programs for a range of platforms from design specifications. For example, COBOL programs for PC and mainframe.*

The DSSD development methodology applies equally well to all projects, regardless of their size. The effort required is proportional to the size of the task; there is no prohibitive overhead incurred up front for small systems, and the largest systems can utilize the same techniques without a geometric increase in complexity. Optima's tools work in concert with the methodology to provide support for a wide variety of environments.

Rather than using application generation techniques, which employ special development meta-languages to generate perhaps 80% of the boilerplate code for a system, Brackets works at a code generation level. This means the leverage factor in terms of inputs is not as high as an application generator, but the result is 100% of the application source code. Brackets is also not sensitive to particular physical implementation environments, as application generators typically are, which allows it to generate COBOL code for PCs and mainframes. Pascal and C language generation capabilities will be added in the next major release.

AMERICAN MANAGEMENT SYSTEMS

Questionnaire Selection Criteria for CASE Tools

QUESTION 1: *Is the underlying structure of your CASE tool a DBMS or Data Dictionary?*

The underlying structure of the APS Development Center is a "process"-level dictionary. It contains information on each component of an application system (i.e., screens, report layouts, programs, data structures, etc.) and its relationship to any other component. It also stores process logic specifications, screen and report layouts, and database structure information. All of these database specifications are used to generate one hundred percent (100%) of the code necessary to run a program.

QUESTION 2:   *Does your CASE tool share or will it share, in the near future, file formats and specifications with other noncompeting CASE manufacturers? If yes, please explain.*

Yes. The APS Development Center offers an optional Excelerator Integrator. This component links the Excelerator project dictionary with the APS/PC sub-dictionary. It allows you to transfer screen and report layout as well as data structure specifications transparently from Excelerator to the APS/PC Workstation. Parameters are entered in a menu mode and the link is initiated by a mouse/window selection.

Sage is currently developing an interface to DesignAid and is a leading contributor in the EDIF CASE effort (see Appendix A, Nastech, and EDIF). The Electronic Data Interchange Format (EDIF) effort is attempting to define a standard interface to integrate any front-end tool with any back-end tool. Sage, and others, feel that this approach allows the customer to choose the best product in each class.

QUESTION 3:   *Describe your CASE tools's ability to read procedure and source libraries and create CASE components specifications for existing systems.*

At this time, the APS Development Center can import existing BMS maps into its dictionary. That map can then be edited and modified using the APS Screen Painter. This is Sage's first released product in the area of reverse engineering (see Appendix A, Research Highlights).

QUESTION 4:   *Describe how your CASE tool interfaces with other CASE design tools.*

See Question 2.

QUESTION 5:   *Does the tool have graphical methodologies capable of exploding design diagrams and dictionary specifications to a reasonable depth?*

No. Not applicable to code generators and the APS Development Center.

QUESTION 6:   *Is your tool capable of executing with window capabilities?*

The only APS component that uses window technology is the APS/PC Link, Sage's micro-mainframe link. The APS Development Center can be used in a windowed environment, but the product itself (other than APS/PC Link) does not have windowing capabilities.

QUESTION 7:   *Describe the tool's ability to do strategic planning on a corporate or functional unit basis.*

Not applicable to the APS Development Center and code generator.

QUESTION 8:   *Does your tool provide a thorough means of prototyping?*

The APS Scenario Prototype facility allows the user to display application screens in any desired sequence, enter data in those screens and save that data for future sessions, create or change the screens, and pass data values to identically named fields or other screens. All of this can be done without generating COBOL code.

The conversation flow is determined by placing screen names in order in an ISPF environment. The list of screen names and their associated titles and descriptions can then be modified using ISPF editing commands.

QUESTION 9: *Describe the tool's ability to provide physical design specifications from logical design specifications.*

The APS Development Center does not translate diagrams into physical design specifications. However, the APS Logical View DB/DC commands do provide a logical design approach to entering specifications.

QUESTION 10: *What design specification reports does your tool provide?*

The APS Development Center reports on entities in an application (programs, screens, reports, etc.) and their format/layout. Cross-reference reports are also available. Program reports show the scope of logical DB/DC commands used.

QUESTION 11: *Does your tool provide analytical support from design documentation? For example, does it indicate the completeness of relevant documentation?*

No. No.

QUESTION 12: *Can your tool's design and development specification interface with particular DBMs and data dictionaries? For example, DATA MANAGER.*

Yes, the APS application dictionary can interface with most popular data dictionaries. Some customers have created links to Data Manager.

QUESTION 13: *Can your tool be modified relative to an organization's existing design methodology? Please describe.*

There is no need to modify the APS Development Center to fit an organization's development methodology. There is no enforced methodology inherent in the APS technology (see Product Overview).

To tailor the technology to a specific DP shop, Sage offers an optional Customization Facility (see Unique Qualities). This component allows you to create site-specific verb sets and routines. This magnifies your productivity gains by custom coding macro-type facilities unique to your installation.

QUESTION 14: *Describe your tool's ability to generate design, operations, and end-user documentation.*

The APS Development Center can generate Application definition, Scenario definition, Data Structure definition, Program definition, Report Mock-Up and Screen Hardcopy/Field attribute reports can be produced.

For more information, see Question 10.

QUESTION 15:   *Describe your tool's ability to maintain design and system changes.*

Maintenance and enhancement changes are made at the specification level, not in native COBOL. This provides productivity gains to maintenance programmers as well as developers.

QUESTION 16:   *Describe your tool's ability to generate programs for a range of platforms from design specifications. For example, COBOL programs for PC and mainframe.*

The APS Development Center is the only code generator available for OS/2 as well as MVS environments (see Product Overview). The APS Development Center is also unique in its capability to generate to MVS or PC file structures. PC targets include Micro-Focus CICS, IMS DB/DC, V-ISAM and XDB (PC based SQL DBMS). For mainframe targets, see Product Overview.

An application development can now reside entirely on a workstation (analysis through unit test). With front-end design tool, APS/PC, and Micro-Focus emulation environments developers can perform analysis, design, prototype, main build and unit test functions without leaving the workstation. A developer would then regenerate for a mainframe target and upload compiler-ready source code.

MAESTRO RESPONSE

1. MAESTRO resides upon a DBMS.
2. MAESTRO's open architecture allows interfacing to most any other product on the market.
3. Using MAESTRO's procedural language, existing documents/programs can be scanned and data extracted into the various MAESTRO tools.
4. Data can be exported as a flat file from the other products, and then read into MAESTRO.
5. Yes. There are no limits on the number of refinements within a graphic.
6. Yes — 12 maximum.
7. MAESTRO allows planning across an entire project, or local areas of a project. Planning information includes time estimated, elapsed time, resources, responsibilities, and task assignment.
8. Two types or prototyping are supported within MAESTRO: The first uses some procedural code and allows the user to toggle between screens developed in the analysis phase. The second method allows the user to input data into the above-mentioned screens. This data is stored and can be replayed later within MAESTRO or to the target machine for testing purposes.
9. Information can be extracted from graphics (for example, a Data Flow Diagram) and passed to a data dictionary.

    For procedural design, a logical top-down process can be followed to produce the logical flow of an application. MAESTRO can take this pseudo-code and generate a skeleton program in the target language which can then be further refined.

10. The type of reports are methodology dependent. Reports such as list attributes, relations, and "where used" are possible reports. The Project Management System supports up to 2000 report output formats.

11. Time accounting for any document can be collected and reported against. It is up to the developer of that document to "flag" it as completed. MAESTRO's Project Management can monitor the status of all documents and tasks in the project.

12. MAESTRO can interface to all data dictionaries to a degree. In the case of Data Manager, extra routines have been built to ease queries, adds, updates, etc.

13. MAESTRO is not tied to any one methodology. The procedural language is supplemented by a powerful procedural/rule language on the PC that can enforce any standard. Currently, Yourdon and LSDM have been created and are supported as "shelf" products.

14. MAESTRO is a complete environment as well as a CASE tool. Documentation can be handled in a team approach through MAESTRO's extensive word processing capabilities. The documentation can be logically attached to a project and be stored on-line. Also, the design specs, graphics, etc., can be routed to a laser printer for hard copy.

15. MAESTRO can handle many versions of an application. With this version control, it is possible to list or back out any changes made to the system.

    MAESTRO also has a variety of tools to work on code not developed in MAESTRO. While this code cannot yet be returned to a graphic, tools for understanding and editing the logic exist today. All existing code can also be stored under the above-mentioned version control.

16. MAESTRO is compiler independent. Any language can be used in all of MAESTRO's functions.

    Generation of codes is table driven and can be completely modified for richness or even a new language.

    MAESTRO will use any platform as a target machine. Multiple interactive and batch links to minis, mainframes, or PCs are supported.

THE INFORMATION ENGINEERING FACILITY™ (IEF)™

Questionnaire Selection Criteria for CASE Tools

QUESTION 1: *Is the underlying structure of your CASE tool a DBMS or Data Dictionary?*

Yes, the Central Encyclopedia of the Information Engineering Facility is the cornerstone of the product. It is a DB 2 application, which stores all the information relevant to the business enterprise and its information systems. The Central Encyclopedia stores this information as a model and manages the relationships between the model data for each stage in the system life cycle.

The Local Encyclopedia is a logical duplicate of the Central Encyclopedia and stores the information relating to a model or model subset which has been downloaded to a professional workstation.

Model management activities occur on the Central Encyclopedia, and include defining user access to models, copying, deleting, and renaming models. Model history tracking provides a record of activities that change model contents.

The model merge feature allows multiple models to be merged into one model for further data sharing and control. The reverse capability is provided also on the Central Encyclopedia through model subsetting. The model subsetting feature allows multiple developers to work on the same analysis and design project simultaneously to facilitate large projects. Subsets are defined on the Central Encyclopedia and can then be downloaded to multiple workstations for parallel development. As each segment of the development process is finished, developers upload the subsets into the original model.

QUESTION 2: *Does your CASE tool share or will it share, in the near future, file formats and specifications with other noncompeting CASE manufacturers? If yes, please explain.*

Yes, file formats and specifications are currently shared via the IEF Public Interface. The bidirectional Public Interface allows import and export of information to and from the Central Encyclopedia. The Import facility creates an IEF model from files created outside the IEF, typically from data contained in some other data management product.

The Export facility provides a series of DB2 views and tables from the Central Encyclopedia from which information can be extracted. This information can be queried using any ad hoc reporting facility that supports DB2 databases, including IBM's QMF product, or formatted for transmission to another software tool (e.g., a data dictionary).

QUESTION 3: *Describe your CASE tools's ability to read procedure and source libraries and create CASE components specifications for existing systems.*

Reengineering is a strategic direction for the IEF product and is being investigated in detail within the research and development efforts established to support TI's CASE product. However, we are unable today to read existing source code or procedure languages and reengineer it into Process and Procedure Action Diagrams for use with the IEF.

We have, however, written programs to read existing data sources (i.e., Data Manager, DL1 Databases, and DB2 Databases), format it into the IEF Public Interface Format, and load it to the Central Encyclopedia. The IEF then produces an Entity-Relationship Diagram and Entity-Hierarchy Diagram (if appropriate) for analysis and design activities.

We have also imported data, process, and function information from the IEW product to the IEF Central Encyclopedia and thereby generated an Entity-Relationship Diagram and a Process-Hierarchy Diagram for further analysis.

QUESTION 4: *Describe how your CASE tool interfaces with other CASE design tools.*

The IEF will interface with other CASE design tools through the Public Interface. For further details, please see answers to Questions 2 and 3 above.

QUESTION 5: *Does the tool have graphical methodologies capable of exploding design diagrams and dictionary specifications to a reasonable depth?*

Yes, we support the Information Engineering Methodology. One of the benefits of this methodology is that there are deliverables from each stage, which feed the next development stage. For example, the Entity-Relationship Diagram can be developed in the Information Strategic Planning stage and will then be utilized and further developed in the Business Area Analysis, the Business System Design, and the Technical Design stages. It will then be implemented physically through the Database Generation Toolset. The Entity-Relationship Diagram could also be developed in the Business Area Analysis stage if no Strategic Plan is required. The same is true of business function/process information.

Within a given diagram there are many hierarchical levels which can be diagrammed as well. For example, the Entity-Relationship Diagram and Entity Type can be broken down into subtypes. Those subtypes (Entity-Hierarchy Diagram) can then be further decomposed to as many levels as necessary to define the business requirements. The business functions can also be decomposed into multiple levels until an elementary process level is reached. There are no restrictions within the IEF toolsets on the number of levels within a given hierarchy.

QUESTION 6: *Is your tool capable of executing with window capabilities?*

Because Texas Instruments did not want to exceed a 640K memory requirement or significantly degrade the PC response time when using the IEF software, the IEF does not use windowing software in its execution. It does, however, provide similar functionality through the use of pop-up menus. At any point in the toolsets, if you need information that is provided within another diagram, it can be selected from a submenu and the information will be provided in textual format. With the advent of the Presentation Graphics in OS2, windowing will be provided.

QUESTION 7: *Describe the tool's ability to do strategic planning on a corporate or functional unit basis.*

The Information Engineering Methodology suggests beginning with an Information Strategic Plan when developing requirements for business automation. The IEF provides a Planning Toolset on the PC to automate portions of that stage. This toolset contains a Matrix Processor, an Indented List Editor, and Global Entity-Relationship and Function Hierarchy diagrams.

The Matrix Processor provides a set of predefined matrices used to analyze business needs and information requirements. It utilizes cluster analysis and affinity analysis techniques to identify the logical Business Areas, Natural Data Stores, and Natural Business Systems within the enterprise. The Indented List Editor provides a means to represent and manipulate organizational units and business functions. The Global Entity Relationship Diagram is used to define the highest-level business entities and the relationships between the entities. The Function Hierarchy Diagram is used to define the major business functions.

The outcome of this strategic plan is an Information Architecture, a Business System Architecture, and a Technical Architecture on which the automation of that business can be supported.

QUESTION 8:   *Does your tool provide a thorough means of prototyping?*

Yes, once Business Area Analysis is complete and the Business System defined, the application can be generated to run under TSO for prototyping purposes. There is a TSO debugging facility for use which traces the business system activities back to the Action Diagram statements causing that action. In the event that processing changes need to be made, it is apparent to the Analyst/Designer what portion of the Action Diagram should be modified to trigger that change. Once the prototype is approved by the customer base, it is a short project to regenerate for an IMS-DC or CICS environment.

QUESTION 9:   *Describe the tool's ability to provide physical design specifications from logical design specifications.*

The fourth stage of the methodology, Technical Design, addresses physical implementation of the data. At that time an automated transformation can be invoked to transform the Entity-Relationship Diagram to a Data-Structure Diagram. The presence of this transformation means that an analyst does not have to be trained as a DBA in order to move from analysis to code generation. The DSD does allow those persons trained as DBAs to review and edit the "first-cut" design provided by the IEF.

The IEF will implement each entity type as a DB2 table, the relationships and partitionings as linkages, the identifiers as entry points, and the attributes as fields. The DBA can then specify additional indices to improve performance. Within the DSD additional specification takes place, such as the definition of the properties of the DB2 databases, tablespaces, indexspaces, and datasets.

QUESTION 10:   *What design specification reports does your tool provide?*

All the graphic diagrams can be printed or plotted. Textual reports are also provided by the IEF.

The following reports are provided within Information Strategic Planning:

Business Function Indented List, Organizational Unit Indented List, Entity Type Object List, Business Function Object List, Business Area Object List, Current Business System Object List, Natural Business System Object List, Current Data

Store Object List, Natural Data Store Object List, Information Need Object List, Organizational Unit Object List, Performance Measurements Object List.

The following reports are provided within Business Area Analysis:

Entity Hierarchy, Entity Definition, Process Hierarchy, Process Definition, Attribute Cross Reference, Attribute Definition.

The following reports are provided within Business System Design:

Procedure Definition, Procedure Step Definition, Commands List, Exit State List.

The following reports are provided within Technical Design:

Field Definition, Implementation List, Data Definition Language.

The following reports are provided within the Central Encyclopedia:

User Access, Model Access, Duplicate Object Name, Model Contents, Model Index, Entity Definition, Attribute Definition, Function Hierarchy, Function Definition, Elementary Process Information View Definition, Model Merge Conflict, Subset Expansion Conflict, Public Interface Import, Scoping Object Where Used, Function Point Calculation, Action Diagram, IEF KWIC Index.

QUESTION 11:   *Does your tool provide analytical support from design documentation? For example, does it indicate the completeness of relevant documentation?*

Yes, the IEF does provide analytical support within all stages of development. Since the model you build is the system documentation, it is important to check that model as it is being completed. There is an embedded consistency check which implements the Information Engineering Methodology rule base. Models can be checked in full or part while working within a methodology stage. Furthermore, the portion of a model that has been scoped for use in the next methodology stage is automatically verified for consistency and completeness by the IEF.

QUESTION 12:   *Can your tool's design and development specification interface with particular DBMs and data dictionaries? For example, DATA MANAGER.*

Yes, the IEF information captured during planning, analysis and design can be exported from the Central Encyclopedia to products such as Data Manager. This has been done by an existing customer, as well as the information imported to the Central Encyclopedia from Data Manager. See Questions 2 and 4.

QUESTION 13:   *Can your tool be modified relative to an organization's existing design methodology? Please describe.*

The IEF implements the Information Engineering Methodology. In order to provide the rigor and consistency required to generate error-free code and 100% application generation from diagrams, a methodology must be enforced. The Information Engineering Methodology is a proven methodology. It's a top-down, data-driven approach using both data and process modeling techniques. The IEM provides a framework of clearly defined stages, each with specific output deliverables. Within each stage, techniques are employed which lead to the development of high-quality, integrated information systems.

QUESTION 14:   *Describe your tool's ability to generate design, operations, and end-user documentation.*

The models you generate using the IEF become the system and business documentation. All diagrams can be plotted or printed, with additional reports provided, as referenced earlier (see Question 10). Much of what is generated can be used in User Documentation as well. There is an interface in the Ventura Desktop Publishing System, which can be used in conjunction with the IEF, for publishing User Documentation.

QUESTION 15:   *Describe your tool's ability to maintain design and system changes.*

Traditionally design and system changes are made at the source code level, and then sometimes reflected in the system documentation. Within the IEF the changes are made with the graphic tools on the PC, so the model analysis and/or system design is changed there. Then the portion of the system affected is regenerated, compiled, linked, and placed in test/production. This ensures your documentation is always equal to the system in production, and it also ensures the changes are properly defined prior to implementation. This technique will save your corporation time and money in the maintenance cycle, as well as produce higher-quality systems.

QUESTION 16:   *Describe your tool's ability to generate programs for a range of platforms from design specifications. For example, COBOL programs for PC and mainframe.*

Currently the IEF will generate applications to run in an MVS, IMS-DC or CICS, DB2, VS Cobol-II environment. Work is underway to expand this environment further to include C-language for PC and mainframe applications, and to move to a Unix-based platform with additional SQL-compatible DBMS. Since the business area and system design are done independently of physical implementation considerations, they will remain valid for any platform we support in the future. Only the Technical Design and some Construction parameters will differ by environment.

BIBLIOGRAPHY

Atre, S., *Data Base: Structured Techniques for Design, Performance and Management*, J. Wiley & Sons, 1988.

Brathwaite, K. S., *Analysis Design, and Implementation of Data Dictionaries*, McGraw-Hill, 1988.

Brathwaite, K. S., *Data Administration*, J. Wiley & Sons, 1985.

Brathwaite, K. S., "Management Involvement in Data Security, Integrity, and Privacy," AGT Tech. Memo, No. 15, 1980.

Brathwaite, K. S., "A Study of Data Base Security, Integrity and Privacy in a Large Public Utility," AGT Tech. Memo, No. 20, 1980.

Brown, D., "RACF — A Program to Enhance Security and Control," EDPACS, Vol. 6, No. 12, Institute of Internal Auditors, June 1979.

Brown, P. S., "Computer Security — A Survey," NCC, 1976, AFIPS Press.

Brown, P. S., Security: Checklist for Computer Center Self-Audits, AFIPS Press, 1979.

Chen, P. P., Ed., Proceedings of the International Conference on Entity-Relationship Approach to Systems Analysis and Design, North-Holland Publishing, New York, 1979.

Chen, P. P., Ed., Proceedings of the International Conference on Entity-Relationship Approach to Information Modeling and Analysis, North-Holland Publishing, New York, 1981.

Courtney, R. H., "Security Risk Assessment in Electronic Data Processing Systems," AFIPS Conf. Proc. 46, 1979, NCC 97–104, AFIPS Press, 1977.

Davenport, R. A., "Data Analysis for Database Design," The Australian Computer Journal, Vol. 10, No. 4, 1979, pp. 122–137.

Dinardo, C. T., *Computers and Security*, AFIPS Press, 1978.

Durrell, W. R., *Data Administration*, McGraw-Hill, 1985.

Engelman, C., "Audit and Surveillance of Multi-level Computing Systems," MTR-3207, The Mitre Corporation, June 1975.

Fernandez, E. B., *Database Security and Integrity*, Addison-Wesley, 1981.

Fisher, A. S., *CASE Using Software Development Tools*, J. Wiley, 1988.

Fosdick, H., *Using IBM's ISPF Dialog Manager*, Van Nostrand Reinhold, 1987.

Gillenson, M., *Database: Step-by-Step*, J. Wiley & Sons, 1985.

Gillenson, M., and Goldberg, R., *Strategic Planning Systems Analysis and Data Base Design*, J. Wiley & Sons, 1984.

Grady, R., *Software Matrics*, Prentice-Hall, 1987.

Hoffman, L. J., *The Formulary Model for Access Control and Privacy in Computer Systems*, SCAC Report No. 119, May 1970.

Hsiao, D. K., *Computer Security*, Academic Press, Inc., 1979.

Hubbard, G., *Computer-Assisted Data Base Design*, Van Nostrand Reinhold, 1981.

Kahn, B. K., *A Method for Describing the Information Required by the Data Base Design Process*, Proc. Int. ACM/Sigmod Conf. Management of Data, 1976.

Katzan, H., *Computer Data Security*, Van Nostrand Reinhold, 1973.

Korth, H. F., and Silbersehatz, R., *Database System Concepts*, McGraw-Hill, 1986.

Larson, B., *The Database Expert's Guide to DB2*, McGraw-Hill, 1988.

Lusardi, F., *The Database Expert's Guide to SQL*, McGraw-Hill, 1988.

Lusk, E. L., *A Practical Design Methodology for the Implementation of IMS Databases Using the E-R Model*, ACM Vol. 4, 1980, pp. 9–21.

Martin, J., *Information Engineering*, Prentice-Hall, 1989.

Martin, J., and McClure, C., *Structured Techniques: The Basis for CASE*, Prentice-Hall, 1988.

McClure, C., *CASE Is Software Automation*, Prentice-Hall, 1989.

Novak, D., and Fry, J., "The State of the Art of Logical Database Design," Proc. 5th Texax Conf. Computing Systems (IEEE), Long Beach, CA, 1976.

Statland, N., *Data Security and its Impact on EDP Auditing*, EDPACS, Vol. 3, No. 4, Institute of Internal Auditors, Oct. 1979.

Weldon, J. L., *Database Administration*, Plenum Press, 1981.

Whitmore, J. C., "Design for Multics Security Enhancements," ESD-TR-74-176, Honeywell Info. Systems, 1974.

Whitten, N., *Managing Software Projects*, J. Wiley & Sons, 1980.

Yao, S. B., "An Integrated Approach to Logical Database Design," NYU Symposium on Database Design, May 18–19, 1978.

GLOSSARY

Configuration management — The ability to specify a set of objects, each at a specified version level, that makes up a "baseline;" that is, a particular project state.

Control integration — The close coordination of a collection of CASE tools to support the software development process.

Data integration — The sharing of design information among tools, developers, and projects.

Enterprise model — A description, in abstract terms, of the enterprise for which applications will be developed. It contains information related to the organizational structure, business goals and strategies, business rules and constraints, business processes, and data required by those processes.

Framework — A CASE framework is an architecture for the integration of a collection of CASE tools.

Impact analysis — The ability to use the information contained in a dictionary to assess the impact of proposed changes on existing systems or programmers.

Information engineering — An interlocking set of automated techniques in which enterprise models, data models, and process models are built up in a comprehensive knowledge base and are used to create and maintain data processing systems.

Link management — The ability to keep track of the relationships among entities and objects as the information model changes. This facility is critical for change management, configuration management, and requirements tracing.

Meta model — The model used to define and store information required to document the enterprise, develop applications, and manage the development process.

Platform — The required hardware and operating system environment.

Presentation integration — Providing a consistent access mechanism and look-and-feel across all the tools in a CASE environment.

Referential integrity — Predefined or user-definable rules that guarantee referential integrity of stored contents. For example, a mandatory relationship between two entities will guarantee that both entities must be defined upon creation, and that both entities will be deleted together.

Repository — The database management facility of the CASE environment which provides data integration services among all the tools in the environment. The repository saves design information in an abstract form like a dictionary, but also captures project and enterprise information so that it can act as the focal point for both tactical and strategic decisions involving software development.

Software process model — A description of the software development process, its techniques, phases, milestones, and deliverables.

Standards compliance — An indication of the official or de facto standards that vendors comply with. Some of the most significant standards are IRDS, PCTE, EDIF, and SAA.

INDEX